Action Figures

Men, Action Films, and Contemporary Adventure Narratives

by

Mark Gallagher

ACTION FIGURES
© Mark Gallagher, 2006.

First published in 2006 by
PALGRAVE MACMILLAN™
175 Fifth Avenue, New York, N.Y. 10010 and
Houndmills, Basingstoke, Hampshire, England RG21 6XS
Companies and representatives throughout the world.

PALGRAVE MACMILLAN is the global academic imprint of the Palgrave Macmillan division of St. Martin's Press, LLC and of Palgrave Macmillan Ltd. Macmillan® is a registered trademark in the United States, United Kingdom and other countries. Palgrave is a registered trademark in the European Union and other countries.

ISBN 1–4039–7012–2

Library of Congress Cataloging-in-Publication Data

Gallagher, Mark, 1968–
    Action figures: men, action films, and contemporary adventure
    narratives / by Mark Gallagher.
        p. cm.
    Includes bibliographical references and index.
    ISBN 1–4039–7012–2 (hard: alk. paper)
        1. Adventure films—United States—History and criticism. 2. Men in
    motion pictures. 3. Masculinity in motion pictures. 4. Heroes in motion
    pictures. I. Title.
PN1995.9.A3G35 2006
791.43'655—dc22   2005049189

A catalogue record for this book is available from the British Library.

Design by Newgen Imaging Systems (P) Ltd., Chennai, India.

First edition: January 2006

10 9 8 7 6 5 4 3 2 1

Printed in the United States of America.

Transferred to digital printing in 2007.

For Elaine Roth

Contents

Acknowledgments

I am fortunate and grateful to have had many scholars, friends, and family to help me refine my understanding of late-twentieth-century active masculinity. Kathleen Karlyn consistently challenged me to perform the most rigorous, professional scholarship, and her extensive commentary on my work has left a permanent, positive imprint on my writing and thinking. I am particularly indebted as well to the following scholars, all of whom offered extensive support and criticism: at the University of Oregon, Julia Lesage and Janet Wasko; at the University of California-Berkeley, Ian Duncan; at Oklahoma State University, Leonard and Linda Leff, Edward Jones, and Jeff Walker; at Georgia State University, Jack Boozer and Niklas Vollmer; and at the University of Missouri, Bill Kerwin, Andy Hoberek, and Brad Prager. Thanks also to all those who read and provided valuable feedback on manuscript chapters, including Jean Amato, Susannah Beck, Tom Billings, Andy Deck, Kevin Gallagher, Anne Gallagher Billings, Michael Pebworth, Erich Reed, and Michele Ricci. I owe thanks also to Tom Atkins, Karen Eng, Aron Golden, Todd Henry, Adam Kitzes, Mark Meritt, Nate and Mark Nichols, Meredith Webb, Lea Williams, Peter Witkow, and Dan Wojcik for their roles in my professional and personal development.

Portions of some chapters were previously published in different forms. An earlier version of chapter 2 appeared as " 'I Married Rambo': Spectacle and Melodrama in the Hollywood Action Film" in *Mythologies of Violence in Postmodern Media*, ed. Christopher Sharrett (Detroit: Wayne State University Press, 1999). Earlier versions of chapter 5 appeared as "Masculinity in Translation: Jackie Chan's Transcultural Star Text," in *Velvet Light Trap* 39 (Spring 1997); and also as "Rumble in the USA: Jackie Chan in Translation," in *Film Stars: Hollywood and Beyond*, ed. Andy Willis (Manchester, UK: Manchester University Press, 2004). Thanks to the editors for their permission to include this material. Thanks also to the anonymous reviewers who provided valuable comments on this manuscript.

Most of all, thanks to Elaine Roth, who has spent years cultivating and critiquing my own somewhat active masculinity and without whose love and patience this work would not have been possible. I dedicate this book to her.

Introduction: Popular Representations of Active Masculinity since the Late 1960s

Consider these contemporaneous developments in popular U.S. culture in the late 1990s: Pfizer in 1998 introduced the male potency drug Viagra, which stimulates erectile function in middle-aged men, to great public demand and media attention. Wealthy, white, middle-aged President Bill Clinton's extramarital sexual affair with Monica Lewinsky, a privileged young office worker, overwhelmed national news coverage and spawned an abundance of books, films, and other commentary. The Promise Keepers conservative Christian men's movement filled stadiums with adult men who professed to resolve their family crises by playing a more dominant paternal role. Nation of Islam leader Louis Farrakhan organized a Million Man March in New York City in 1996, using an exclusionary strategy to promote black male solidarity. Jon Krakauer's 1997 *Into Thin Air*, a nonfiction account of a disastrous Mount Everest ascent that results in the deaths of eight men and one woman, became a national bestseller and reignited public interest in the previously moribund "adventure nonfiction" category of book publishing. Susan Faludi's 1999 book *Stiffed: The Betrayal of the American Man* argued that U.S. men have become victimized—and in effect, feminized—by an "ornamental culture" that robs them of their self-worth. Just weeks after the release of Faludi's book, the film *Fight Club*, based on Chuck Palahniuk's 1996 novel, appeared in theaters, presenting viewers with a dark fantasy of male empowerment through bare-knuckle brawling, combating the consumption-based lifestyles that Faludi posits as one source of male anxiety.

These incidents, movements, and texts all indicate the culturally visible conflict surrounding contemporary masculinity. What roles do (or should) men play in contemporary U.S. public and private life, and how do a range of behaviors and attributes contribute to the social constructions of gender identity, to masculinity in particular? Intersecting with issues of class, race, politics, and industry, the signs of U.S. men's behaviors and predilections provide fertile ground for cultural analysis. The incidents noted above, though in many ways linked to disparate historical forces and circumstances, all point to conflicts underlying preferred models of male comportment at the end of the twentieth century. With the exception of *Fight Club*, these cultural phenomena operate in the realm of historical reality: though subject to exaggeration and misapprehension, and though often filtered through other media texts (e.g., print and television news coverage of Viagra, the Clinton/Lewinsky scandal, and the Million Man March), they represent real actions and their consequences. Yet each is informed by a range of prominent cultural mythologies. The Clinton sex scandal, as portrayed in tabloid journalism as well as in voluminous government documents, acquired the aspect of an unimaginative pornographic novel. Viagra commodified the social fantasies and expectations of male sexual prowess, literalizing the popular myth that money can produce sexual stimulation. The Promise Keepers movement transformed a locker-room mentality of male kinship into a compelling rhetoric of empowerment through contrition and domination. The Million Man March, in its audacious name as well as the spectacle it presumed to offer—albeit a spectacle relayed only sparingly by major news outlets—represented a preconceived attempt to lend broad cultural significance to a single, isolated event. *Into Thin Air*'s popularity attested to a public fascination with putatively authentic experiences of danger and survival, a riposte to a capitalist, consumerist society that avowedly strips men's everyday lives of variety and excitement (and by extension, of virility). Similarly, Faludi's book and the film *Fight Club* tried to explain and respond to male disaffection, the former through an overarching argument about the dilution of male self-worth, the latter through a sensational parable of misdirected male aggression.

Locating numerous high-profile narratives of masculinity in a given historical period requires little effort. A survey of any other cultural-historical epoch—for example, the late 1890s in the United States, or the late 1790s in France, or the late 1490s in Spain—would likely produce a long list of events or issues bearing on men's lives or on constructions of male identity: the physical and political battlefields of the Spanish–American War, the political and cultural repercussions of the French Revolution, and the imperial seafaring of Columbus. Men's activities, and perceived obstacles to those activities, have always figured prominently in historical events and in the construction of a society's public face. Similarly, contemporaneous texts, whether historical records, scholarly accounts, works of art, or popular fictions, represent men's behaviors and perspectives in many ways. Fiction and nonfiction texts in different genres record men's activities, lend them dramatic or aesthetic weight, or fix or challenge understood beliefs about the motivation for those activities and the character of the men behind them. The sheer multitude of possible representational modes and strategies means that perspectives on men's activities, men's expected roles, and men's actual relation to some culturally determined notion of masculinity are always contested or in flux.

This work seeks to demonstrate the ways an array of popular texts, produced or received in the United States since the 1960s, contributes to the fluctuating constructions of normative masculinity. Popular film and literature employ numerous strategies to define particular spaces and environments as settings for action and male agency, to reestablish men's privileged position in active space, and to code a range of activities as inherently masculine, even in the relatively rare cases in which women undertake those activities. I argue that cinematic and literary representations of male action compensate for threats to stable, traditional masculinity, threats posed by economic and cultural changes affecting men's roles in the workplace and in the domestic space. In addition, figurations of action offer both male and female viewers and readers utopian solutions to social problems, privileging the transformative effects of physical agency in a world increasingly organized around sedentary pursuits. While my argument foregrounds cinematic representation, the diffusion of cultural preferences into multiple media demands a comprehensive outlook. With some exceptions, film and media scholars have insufficiently incorporated literary texts into their areas of study, yet print fiction and nonfiction remain a primary source of film narratives. One goal of this book is to stress the complementarity of cinematic and literary representations.

Men, Feminism, and Popular Texts

At the outset of the twenty-first century, cultural critics and social historians continue to evaluate gender-based definitions of male and female social roles, both to understand the gender constructions of previous eras and to speculate about ongoing or future developments in social roles. Several generations of feminist scholars and commentators have shed light on women's social roles, prompting subsequent backlashes and rebuttals from social conservatives. As feminist scholarship in the humanities has expanded its scope to encompass psychology, sociology, history, textual and cultural studies, and other disciplines, studies of gender construction have grown to include assessments of men's social roles and their supporting institutions as well. Progressive studies of masculinity aim to understand male psychology, group behavior, and cultural attitudes; to grasp the complexity of male and female interactions within the world's predominantly patriarchal societies; and to recognize the forces contributing to those interactions—in short, to understand and destabilize male power in nuanced ways. As part of the evolving discipline of feminist criticism, masculinity studies can redress sometimes reductive conceptions of men and masculinity. Not simply a monolithic embodiment of patriarchy, masculinity is—like femininity—a fluid and complex category of social codes and behaviors. Like other works of progressive masculinity studies, this book strives to understand how social forces, institutions, and texts define masculinity, exercise male power, and conceal the prejudicial effects of that power.

Monolithic prescriptions for ideal masculinity may no longer exist, having been replaced by a range of templates through which men define themselves apart from and in relation to women and the social world: romantic partner, husband, father, caregiver, warrior, patriot, crusader, hardbody, stud, playboy, artist, businessman, and so forth, to name only a few of the preferred adult male roles. Where some see diversity and productive difference, others see disunity and incoherence. After her far-reaching feminist analysis *Backlash* (1991), the journalist Susan Faludi may have seemed unlikely to champion the cause of disenfranchised men. Nevertheless, Faludi's case studies in *Stiffed* point to men's increasing lack of job security, low self-esteem, and alienation from the people and institutions that surround them. She argues that these problems result from a broad condition of cultural abandonment, a betrayal of the optimistic social compacts of the New Deal and World War II. Adopting a self-help vocabulary, Faludi suggests that present-day commentators inadequately account for men's changing cultural situation: "What gets discussed is how men are exercising or abusing their control and power, not whether a lack of mooring, a lack of context, is causing their anguish."[1] While Faludi argues that men since the late 1940s have become increasingly enthralled by a celebrity-driven consumer culture, she only passingly acknowledges that men—at all levels of government, business, education, journalism, the arts, and entertainment—still exercise disproportionate control over the diffuse culture she describes. The idea that a limited number of powerful men may act against the best interests of the majority of men is certainly not a new perspective, as such conditions long pre-date capitalism and democracy. Yet Faludi, in search of a cause for the problems she finds men facing, ultimately attributes blame to manipulative media texts. She argues that popular media, in showcasing hollow fantasies of masculinity, undermine an earlier social system that provided men a sense of belonging and self-worth. (Gesturing back at the apparent golden age of the pre–World War II years, Faludi ignores racial segregation, 1920s and 1930s labor agitation and corporations' violent reprisals, the hardships of the Great Depression, and other cases of male disenfranchisement.)

Despite her attention to the plight of contemporary working-class men, Faludi's argument affirms the suspicion of the popular that characterizes much critical discourse from both the Left and the Right. In this book, I address the ways popular texts—specifically, male action films since the late 1960s, popular-fiction thrillers of the 1980s and 1990s, and late-1990s adventure nonfiction—construct active masculinity. I hope to demonstrate how popular cinematic and literary texts both respond to and elide contemporary crises of gender identity. Because of their cultural visibility and resilience, male action narratives offer exceptional opportunities to understand the contradictory pleasures that popular texts offer.

Popular film and literature shape and reflect preoccupations of the popular imagination, and thus constitute a dominant feature of contemporary cultural ideology, both in the United States and in other regions of the world that receive U.S. popular media. I approach popular texts with close attention to historical and cultural contexts; contexts essential to understanding the global nature of gender relations and sex-role definitions, as well as the effects of social and economic conditions, in shaping human behavior. Only with recognition of a broad cultural context can the social forces and institutions that bear on men and women be substantively critiqued and their imbalances addressed or ameliorated. U.S. culture, entertainment media, and consumer products have penetrated, or cannibalized elements of, the majority of global cultures. Thus, while I emphasize U.S. cultural conditions and products, I draw connections across historical periods, between U.S. and East Asian cultures, and among different forms of popular representation.

At many levels of textuality and reception, the contemporary Hollywood action film and its related cultural texts offer a useful platform for the analysis of active masculinity. Social taboos still inhibit the reasoned, public discussion of many issues surrounding male identity, issues such as sexual behavior, workplace- and community-based social roles, men's positions as husbands and fathers, and interactions between the sexes in general. Popular film and literature, however, generate much unabashed commentary from cultural consumers across categories of age, education, and income. Popular cinematic representation, particularly, offers few barriers to comprehension, and most viewers, whether neophytes or connoisseurs, swiftly apprehend genre conventions. For viewers, such ease of access leads in turn to immediate gratification: film studios make available the pleasures of narrative and spectacle for a minimal investment of time and money. Within this putatively pleasurable viewing space, issues surrounding masculinity are raised and resolved in exaggerated, fantasy settings. In action films, the spectacular, fantastic realm—that is, the genre's deliberately unrealistic narratives, its functionally superhuman protagonists, and its excesses of violent, kinetic spectacle—intersects with the real or putatively real social world, which involves family and personal conflicts, racial and ethnic differences, and political intrigue, espionage, and global or regional warfare. Conventional narrative structures partly contain the disparities between the action milieu and viewers' real lives. Action films and popular novels can offer scenarios of empowerment in which viewers' actual physical and social limitations become irrelevant.

Despite their apparent transparency, action films and their related cultural forms contribute, through their occupation of the popular imagination and their saturation of entertainment media, to conceptions of political ideology and national identity as well as gender. My aim here is to view the action film and its parallel literary texts in terms of specific formal and narrative conventions as they develop over time, with an emphasis on the interplay among culture, genre, and representation. I focus on the period from the late 1960s to the present for many reasons, including what I believe is a scholarly duty to the world we now inhabit. Major corporations began acquisitions of U.S. film studios in the mid-1960s, giving film producers access to global distribution networks and to multinational capital investment. The globalization of popular publishing industries occurs in tandem with this development, and media conglomerates' film-production and publishing holdings begin to intersect. To come to terms with such developments, I draw from feminist and Marxist analyses of popular film and literary genres, analyses sensitive to articulations of gender, politics, class, race, and other ideological categories. Feminist reconsiderations of popular genres such as comedy and melodrama inform my understanding of action narratives, also long categorized as too juvenile, too escapist, or simply too conservative to be the subject of a serious analysis. Constructions of masculinity carry intertextual meanings linked to genre, as viewers evaluate male heroes in relation to previous cinematic representations rather than in terms of heroes' resolution of real-world social dilemmas. At the same time, generic transformation always parallels cultural shifts. Rather than ceaselessly reiterating the same conservative clichés, popular texts adopt new strategies over time to engage readers and viewers. Even when writers and filmmakers employ retrograded plots and forms of address, such frameworks acquire different significance in different hands and for different audiences.

Popular genres may traffic in fantasy, but they are nevertheless often received with suspicion. Faludi's appraisal of contemporary manhood regards media texts as corrosive to civic good, promoting fantasies of individualism rather than democratic virtues. *Stiffed* attributes the problems faced by men in the contemporary United States not to the inherent contradictions of patriarchal society but to films, television, and magazines that represent men as part of what she calls an "ornamental culture" (35). This culture, increasingly prevalent since the 1950s, redefines men as empty vessels for display and consumption while stripping them of any meaningful social purpose. One facet of this corrosive culture, which Faludi finds in 1950s television cowboy shows, generally occurs in the contemporary action cinema as well: "The essential question to be resolved, in episode after episode, sequel after sequel, was not whether our hero had been socially engaged and useful, but whether he had maintained control and survived" (12). Faludi's critique of such texts, though, largely misinterprets the goals of popular media: while representations of social utility may provide laudable civic lessons, they do not necessarily give pleasure to readers or film- or television-viewers nor make profits for media industries. Action cinema in particular engages viewers by dispensing with questions of social utility. Popular films frequently present a world, as in *Point Blank* (1967) or *The Killer* (1989), in which attention to immediate, personal goals such as revenge, maintenance of honor, or romantic fulfillment takes precedence over questions of social good. In other cases, as in films ranging from *Dirty Harry* (1971) to *Face/Off* (1997), institutionally sanctioned heroes indulge their antisocial, personal desires while ultimately contributing to prosocial causes, eliminating violent threats to the films' public worlds.

Active Masculinity in Postwar U.S. Film

World War II initiated sweeping social and economic changes worldwide, the impact of which continued to be felt decades later. The material and psychological devastation wrought by the huge number of combat deaths, coupled with the civilian deaths of the Holocaust, the atomic bombings of Japan, and the Allied and Axis bomb campaigns in Western Europe and Japan, made the consequences of international violence omnipresent in virtually all industrialized societies. At the same time, women's entry into the workforce, as replacements for men at war and as necessary for expanded wartime industrial production, undermined long-honored separations of male/working and female/domestic spheres. After the war, in the wake of European and Asian economic recessions brought on by wartime infrastructure damage, the U.S. film industry expanded production to take advantage of expanded worldwide audiences. Hollywood benefited in particular from exports to nations such as France, Italy, and Germany, whose domestic film industries had been decimated economically or materially by the war.

In the United States, cinematic and literary texts have responded in varied and often contradictory ways to social and economic changes surrounding gender relations after World War II. In mainstream U.S. cinema, prescriptions of film genre and style have shaped and codified textual responses: the postwar film noir movement, for example, represents the anxiety provoked by cultural changes as a general suspicion of authority; a broad critique of social, corporate, and government institutions; and a wariness of female sexuality. Postwar domestic melodramas consider the local consequences of broad social trends, focusing on interpersonal relations in the home and workplace. With film noir and domestic melodrama emphasizing damaged or compromised masculinity, and with westerns and war films appearing less frequently after the end of the studio era in the mid-1950s, heroic, physically active (if not invulnerable) males take center stage in other genres: in historical epics such as *Ben-Hur* (1959) and *The Vikings* (1958), and in Cold War thrillers such as *The Manchurian Candidate* (1962). These films either project heroic masculinity backward in time (to periods in history perceived as more accommodating to male physical strength) or reimagine the psychological conflicts germane to noir and melodrama as heroic struggles that define masculinity through mental exertion and thus create a new space of cerebral heroism. Psychological conflict often assumes a physical aspect, represented through facial expressions and body language; films help code mental effort as active rather than passive. In addition, film genres of the 1960s often map out particular arenas for male activity: the gladiatorial coliseum of *Spartacus* (1960), the political briefing-rooms of *Fail-Safe* (1964) and *Seven Days in May* (1964), or the city of *Bullitt* (1968). Popular cinema foregrounds these male arenas as women increasingly occupy other material and psychological spaces. Women's growing political presence—for example, within the civil rights movement, and later in the 1960s, in the women's movement and in opposition to the war in Vietnam—and their increasing visibility in the workplace and in the capitalist economy challenge male dominion over public spaces and institutions. Facing these challenges, cultural texts and discourses preserve existing social and cultural hierarchies, or less frequently, acknowledge social transformations and provide a sheltered space in which to come to terms with changing social conditions.

By the 1960s, constructions of heroic masculinity linked physical and mental ideals from opposite ends of the class spectrum. This marriage of working-class and upper-class styles helped defend masculinity as the province of men. The James Bond films of the 1960s, for example, while assuring audiences of their hero's physical dexterity and endurance, foreground the character's psychological fortitude, his canniness, resourcefulness, and mental toughness. The Bond films connect physical and mental

qualities as interdependent facets of male style, a style that appears cultivated and yet often effortless. (Such a style embodies a contradiction: it
appears both refined and inborn; it is a posture of both calculated ease and
naturalness.) This apparently unforced style, visible in figures such as Sean
Connery's Bond and in other rugged stars popular in the 1960s such as
Burt Lancaster, connotes a claim to a universal masculine aura available
to those who resist the era's ongoing social transformations largely by
ignoring them. Such representations of stable masculinity offer men an
implicit promise: that through willful blindness, one may endure the challenges and conflicts of an evolving capitalist system that increasingly values women's abilities outside the domestic sphere. As a part of this textual
reconstruction of masculinity, the Bond films also define masculinity in
terms of style. In Ian Fleming's novels and in the Connery Bond films,
released between 1962 and 1971, patrician breeding, unflappability, and
rakishness appear as components of active, heroic masculinity. Bond's
concern with personal grooming and luxuries recuperates fashion and
consumerism from the realm of the feminine, promoting the ideology of
male style that undergirds men's magazines such as *GQ* and *Esquire*. This
development merges with the ornamental culture identified by Faludi,
muddying the waters of normative masculinity. Like other popular masculinities, the Bond films simultaneously advocate the working-class ideal
of physical strength and the upper-class values of good breeding and
luxury accessories. These dueling emphases create untenable prescriptions
for male behavior, but also widen the range of acceptable male types.

Men's lifestyle magazines such as *GQ* and *Esquire* profitably circulate
the recognition that male style exists. They simultaneously acknowledge
that masculinity is a floating signifier, something that can (and must) be
performed rather than something that men, and only men, innately possess. In *Masked Men*, Steven Cohan persuasively traces the dynamics of
performativity in 1950s Hollywood film, noting not only the performative
masculinity of the closeted Rock Hudson but also that of heterosexual
stars such as William Holden and Humphrey Bogart.[2] Cohan studies
celebrity magazines and publicity photos as well as films, thus giving
prominence to texts that withhold male activity. Many locate their male
subjects in static positions (e.g., the photographs) or in narratives of
romance or the workplace, such as *The Seven Year Itch* (1955) and *The Man
in the Grey Flannel Suit* (1956). Even without physical activity, regimes of
masculinity depend upon performance, upon display and comportment.
The innovation of the 1960s Bond films lies in their marriage of workplace
concerns, romance, and spectacular action. Like many other scenes in the
films, the requisite office meeting that initiates each film's central narrative
condenses these elements: Bond visits the office for a meeting with his

superior, M; exchanges mild sexual and romantic innuendo with the perennially unattached receptionist, Miss Moneypenny; then meets with another manager, Q, for a demonstration of the customized vehicles and weapons that will accompany him in later action. In each phase of the office visit, Bond demonstrates a different facet of his comprehensive male style: encyclopedic knowledge of esoteric subjects (such as diamond mining in *Diamonds are Forever* [1971]), smooth talk with women, or easy aptitude with deadly weapons and high technology.

Changes in Hollywood filmmaking practice in the late 1960s and early 1970s sharply modified the Connery/Bond model of cool, refined masculinity. Studios paid attention to collegiate and countercultural audiences, and the industry correspondingly made intermittent concessions to young filmmakers who used film to transmit their personal visions of conflicted, damaged male identity. The Vietnam-era films of male stars such as Steve McQueen, Charlton Heston, and Lee Marvin showed the labor and rigor necessary to maintain a functional male identity in a time of social unrest. During this period, the three stars portrayed male heroes who were jaded, toughened, or scarred by experiences. Such qualities could appeal to younger viewers disenchanted with earlier models of straitlaced, prosocial masculinity. Figurations of mature masculinity could also appeal to older viewers who saw their own physical maturation reflected in the actors' faces and bodies. Both cases involve interplay between normative and rebellious behavior. In *Stars*, Richard Dyer provides a model of the rebel hero's production and function in cinematic texts.[3] Rebel figures permit viewers to entertain fantasies of antisocial or autonomous behavior while reaffirming viewers' own (unrebellious) social positions. Dyer asks "whether these represent real challenges to the status quo and the dominant ideology or [. . .] simply 'holidays' from it," a question partly answered by "the degree to which the image points to the legitimacy of rebellion or its inadequacy" (59). Many male star images in the late 1960s and early 1970s oscillate between rebellion against and support for established authority. Interestingly, the rebel roles that Lee Marvin and other gray or graying stars assumed in the 1960s counters the prevailing associations of rebellion with youth. Dyer argues that the young-rebel figure allows viewers to regard rebellion as a passing stage in the maturation process.[4] Images of mature rebels upset this ideological project. The popularity during the Vietnam War years of alternately countercultural and prosocial stars indicates how demographically and ideologically distinct audiences interpret this era's constructions of masculinity. To young or countercultural audiences, male heroes such as McQueen, Heston, and Marvin may appear socially rebellious but still in possession of key aspects of ideal masculinity, and thus worthy of emulation or idolization.

For older viewers, the intensity of the stars' personas situates each star's masculinity at a remove from normative, prosocial categories: the three signify tough, uncompromising masculinity despite their characters' recurrent associations with mainstream values and institutions. The embodiment of traditional male identity, with its attendant rigors, is thus offered as a means to achieve social autonomy. The stars' films thus create a space in which rebellion appears as a facet of ideal masculinity, or idealized masculinity appears inherently rebellious.

By the mid-1970s, male stars such as Clint Eastwood and Charles Bronson had risen to prominence, particularly in their roles as urban vigilantes. Meanwhile, Marvin, Heston, and McQueen increasingly appeared in roles as conventional, mature authority figures.[5] Eastwood's westerns and cop films such as *Dirty Harry*, and Bronson's vigilante films such as *Death Wish* (1974) offer complex figurations of embattled masculinity. *Death Wish* narrates the transition of the male protagonist from victim by association (through violence against his female family members) to vigilante hero. Similarly, *Dirty Harry* represents the authoritarian male as an individual hero at odds with institutional authority, demonstrating a form of rebellion that can be interpreted as either countercultural or reactionary (principally the latter, as despite his long, unkempt hair and sideburns, Harry articulates a decidedly conservative critique of police and government, lambasting bleeding hearts and civil libertarians). Joan Mellen argues that Eastwood's films of the 1960s and 1970s "are a response to the growing loss of confidence on the part of American males in the old systems of virility, which itself results from the political failure to demand a decent society amenable to human need."[6] Paul Smith also locates Eastwood's films amid U.S. social and political conflicts, discussing the ideologies the films advance and audiences' mobilizations of those texts.[7] Eastwood's films, as Mellen and Smith suggest, privilege an alternately authoritarian and vulnerable masculinity, and this dual persona supplies resilient models for subsequent cultural discourses and texts.

The figure of Eastwood offers a useful marker of changes in cultural models of masculinity from the 1970s to the 1980s. Just as Eastwood's successive films increasingly construct the hero's physical body as the site of suffering and resistance (as Smith cogently observes), action films in the 1980s generally foreground elements of visual spectacle, particularly the spectacle of the male body in action or in pain. Simultaneous with this formal development, cinematic constructions of active masculinity began to address a predominantly teenage and young-adult audience. During the Reagan era, Hollywood studios refined action-film narrative conventions to a marked degree of similarity, producing a large body of films— including the *Rambo*, *Die Hard*, and *Lethal Weapon* series—devoted to individualistic, ostensibly anti-authoritarian or anti-government heroes. Meanwhile, popular novels, directed largely at an adult readership, increasingly articulated versions of masculinity informed by their cinematic counterparts. Not coincidentally, a literary subgenre that might be termed the neo-espionage thriller also grew to prominence in the 1980s, particularly through the novels of Tom Clancy.[8] Most of Clancy's novels feature a white, married, middle-aged protagonist, Jack Ryan, who becomes involved in plots involving international terrorism or the late–Cold War threats of the Soviet Union. Drawing on the model of earlier spy novelists such as Frederick Forsyth and Robert Ludlum, Clancy's novels represent an updated version of the 1950s "organization man" as the ideal representative of aging, white masculinity.[9] Buoyed by his managerial expertise and problem-solving abilities, Clancy's protagonist (like that of fellow thriller writer Clive Cussler) negotiates the changing dynamics of contemporary social relations by transforming the personal world into a world of work. In this world, rational—and implicitly masculine—decision-making skills take precedence over psychological depth or complex emotions. The privileging of these heroes' cerebral capacities also mitigates older men's corresponding anxieties about declining physical strength, validating mental toughness rather than sheer physical power.

Similarities between the vigilante cop Harry Callahan of *Dirty Harry* and the CIA functionary Jack Ryan of Clancy's novels might not be immediately apparent. Still, the rebel tough guys of Vietnam-era films substantially inform the managerial male heroism evident in 1980s popular fiction. In popular film and fiction, the youthful, radical male heroes of the 1970s give way to the mature centrist or conservative heroes of the 1980s, echoing the political transformation of the influential Baby Boom generation. Numerous Vietnam-era films offer images of rebellion and present male heroes at odds with traditional authority. However, these rebellious heroes themselves tend to act in conventional, ritualized ways. (Witness the cop-film cliché of the protagonist who angrily casts off his badge, or has it stripped from him by a superior, only to retrieve it later.) The recurrence of particular gestures of rebellion largely neutralizes these figures' critical stances. Particularly from the mid-1970s onward, popular discourses reshape figures such as Steve McQueen and Lee Marvin into icons of prosocial, hegemonic masculinity. Similarly, popular novels of the 1980s, such as those of Clancy, replace models of solitary masculinity with fantasies of autonomous but socially responsible men. In the 1980s mass-market fiction, team values and U.S. corporate ideology become materials for a male heroism defined principally through cerebral rather than physical qualities. These developments in film and fiction contribute substantially to the production and reception of subsequent popular texts.

Building Masculine Men: Action Narratives and the Construction of Masculinity

Masculinity is a product of culture; the attributes and behaviors that signify it shift over time and are constantly under negotiation. While the cultural category of masculinity bears only an abstract relation to the biological category of maleness, popular understandings of masculinity determine responses to men's varied behaviors. In this book, I refer frequently to the conventional definitions and signifiers of heroic masculinity at different points in U.S. history and in film history. I reproduce these conventional definitions not to reinforce cultural prejudices, but to establish a position from which to recognize the contradictions and consequences of artificially established prescriptions for male behavior.

As Judith Butler and many others have observed, gender categories depend on performance, on ascription to or deviance from culturally designated attributes and behaviors. No culture designates a single model for a given gender; cultural ideology is sufficiently flexible to admit a range of templates. Thus, athletes, intellectuals, artists, and laborers may each satisfy accepted definitions of normative or exceptional masculinity. Models of exceptional gender performance, notably, contain within them the prescriptions for normative gender attributes. For example, while popular discourse typically situates world-class athletes at a remove from gender norms, their personas and experiences often overlap with normative categories. Cyclist Lance Armstrong won fanfare for his exceptional string of Tour de France victories from 1999 to 2005, but in the United States, his status as a strong-willed cancer survivor located him powerfully within a normative category of perseverant but ordinary men. This book considers ways that exceptional performances of masculinity, performances of physical and mental agency, contribute to discourses surrounding normative, everyday masculinity. Action narratives offer a powerful site for the performance of active masculinity. Their idealized, heroic protagonists model exceptional masculine behavior that crosses into normative terrain: areas of heterosexual romance, family relationships, problem-solving operations, and elsewhere.

Popular narratives of male heroism often demarcate the boundaries of active masculinity. Because agents of profit-seeking multinational corporations produce many popular texts, these texts often proceed cautiously, aligning themselves closely with perceived gender norms and ideals. Popular texts are subject to negotiation by their readers and viewers, and none are reducible to single, culturally preferred meanings. Still, popular texts periodically assure their audiences that existing social formations can accommodate changing paradigms of masculinity and femininity, even as those changes expose the arbitrariness and inefficacy of the categories themselves. (For example, James Heartfield shrewdly observes that threats to male power largely imperil women as well, yet it is women who typically shoulder the blame for conditions attributable to capitalism.[10]) In the United States, normative masculinity has historically been linked to physical capabilities, yet late-capitalist society utilizes male physical and intellectual labor differently than the societies of the previous eras. White-collar and service-industry occupations now far outnumber trade and industrial jobs that rely on physical labor. Nevertheless, patriarchal capitalism continues to privilege men's political, economic, artistic, and ideological power over women's. However, given the predominance of sedentary labor in late-capitalist society, as well as women's growing presence in the administrative and managerial workforce, patriarchal biases built on assumptions about male aggressiveness and rationality have become increasingly difficult to justify. Such widespread societal shifts have eroded fiction texts' ability to construct spaces of autonomous male power within the corresponding historical reality.

Many popular writers and filmmakers insist on the integrity of conventionally male terrain, from the battlefield to the boardroom. The borders of these spaces are maintained as a defense against perceived encroachments of women and the feminine. This patrolling of gender-role boundaries itself signifies anxiety and contradiction. If men and women were physically incapable of acting outside their gender norms, such vigilance would be unnecessary (and as a corollary, definitions of masculinity and femininity would never fluctuate). Nevertheless, popular texts do patrol the boundaries of gender, often successfully. Throughout the 1980s, action films systematically exclude or marginalize women's perspectives, as do other film and literary genres that feature ritualized male interactions. To legitimate such exclusions, male-centered thrillers such as *Lethal Weapon* (1987) and *Die Hard* (1988) promote the universality of male experience, implying that conflicts among men provide the raw materials for narratives engaging to both sexes. With women absent or incapacitated, heroism—and effectively, the dispensation of social justice of any sort— becomes the *de facto* province of men. Not surprisingly, the absence of women produces a different crisis of masculinity, the inability to demonstrate heterosexuality. In a reading of two Sylvester Stallone films, Chris Holmlund argues that the films' homophobic paranoia and their maintenance of male heroes' rigorous facade of masculinity highlight the anxiety that these facades may crumble at any moment. As Holmlund observes, "the insistence in both films on the inviolability of masculinity has a hysterical ring to it."[11] The notion of hysteria—or the attribution of a putatively feminine condition to a discourse of masculinity—suggests the contradictions inherent in texts invested in a cultural category that can never be verified, only performed or demonstrated to the point of exhaustion. The term hysteria connotes both a problem surrounding gender and one located outside the body (the Greek *hystera* designating the womb, and the related *hysteros* designating latter or later, a physical effect on a body traveling behind its cause). Male-centered action films rely on this out-of-body construction of masculinity as well. In contemporary films, bluescreened, greenscreened, and digitally simulated action sequences literally separate their male stars from their surrounding environments. The masculinities on display represent a composite of physical bodies and separately orchestrated spaces.

However tenuous their foundations or hysterical their representations, film and popular literature's active male heroes continue to enjoy widespread international appeal. Few viewers of action films are sutured unproblematically into the films' manifest ideological positions. Action heroes tend to exhibit personalities so streamlined, or find themselves in situations so removed from viewers' experiences, that identification with the heroes' crises or endorsement of their behaviors becomes a fantastic proposition. To respond to the films' situations, viewers must immerse themselves in the generic world of the action hero and divest themselves of an often conflicting real-world logic. Readers and viewers can savor the unreality of these scenarios while also using them as projections of their own ideal activities. At the same time, progressive readers and viewers cognizant of their ideological opposition to the premises and institutions that many action films and literary thrillers celebrate—police violence, vigilantism, military and espionage activity, subordination of women, and punishment of nonwhite or gay characters—can find pleasure, diversion, and cultural critique in the exaggerated and conflicted nature of such texts, not to mention their sometimes comic level of transparency. Action films' glorification of violent spectacle or popular novels' overemphasis on patriotic, prosocial values, for instance, can offer solace to viewers or readers who recognize the somewhat desperate quality of such formal or narrative strategies. Action films that explicitly promote conservative ideologies can provide disturbing spectacles, but their *reductio ad absurdum* of historically rooted social and political conflicts may demobilize those conservative positions, to the relief of progressive viewers.

Significantly, conservative viewers too may find rewards in action cinema beyond the explicit celebrations of military power, government competence, and esteem of family. As suggested above, action narratives engage taboo subjects—for example, the fundamentals of race, gender, and social class—in relatively safe spaces of representation. In these spaces, readers and viewers may confront and modify their own beliefs without fear of reprisal. Action films and popular literature act in dialogue with historical reality. They simulate scenarios of psychological, interpersonal, political, and military conflict in accessible ways. Moreover, they validate highly dangerous, mentally demanding, usually low-paid occupations (e.g., soldier or police officer) largely excised from high-culture discourses. Popular action and adventure narratives help their audiences negotiate their own positions within systems of power. While fantasy empowerment may take the place of tangible social power, the texts' rhetorics of validation carry marked cultural weight nonetheless. Action narratives' populist appeals are crucial to their global resonance.

Action films manifestly appeal to viewers through their huge production budgets, dynamic editing, and sophisticated special effects. They also intersect crucially with material concerns such as gender and race relations, violence, and global politics. To interrogate them in original ways, this work combines textual analysis with consideration of popular texts' historical, cultural, and industrial situations. Through this book, I hope to contribute to the productive analysis of cinematic masculinity and the action genre now flourishing in film studies. I am heavily indebted to early-1990s works such as Susan Jeffords's *Hard Bodies* and Yvonne Tasker's *Spectacular Bodies*, both of which compellingly analyze action films and their cultural situation. Jeffords's 1994 book locates developments in film masculinity alongside the political and cultural environment of the Reagan-dominated 1980s. She surveys models of masculinity in the action genre as well as in successful comedies and dramas of the same period, and identifies in early-1990s films a tendency to define heroic masculinity through fathering. I trace related lineages of heroic masculinity through the late 1990s, interrogating not only the increasing prevalence of paternal heroes across the decade but also the genre's correspondingly melodramatic situation. Similarly, I draw upon Tasker's 1993 book, which examines dynamics of gender, race, and class in the action films of the 1980s and early 1990s, and situates these categories in relation to patterns of genre evolution and hybridity. With Tasker's volume as a point of reference, I consider how transformations in film genre, and surrounding cultural discourses in the United States and abroad, have produced the contemporary male action hero. Jeffords's and Tasker's works provide the critical foundation for the study of masculinity in the contemporary Hollywood action film. This book, in comparison, links the contemporary action genre to a number of earlier U.S. films, to popular literature of the 1980s and 1990s, and to popular Hong Kong films of the same era. I examine popular literature and non-U.S. films' engagement with Hollywood's models of active masculinity, an interplay that lends the U.S. action genre continued legitimacy.

This book's organization is partly chronological and partly dialectical. I first assess the cultural situation in which the contemporary U.S. action hero is located, then examine that figure's many compelling facets. Following that I turn to the contemporary action hero's origins, then to his corollaries in print fiction. I look finally at an alternative to the U.S. action hero, a figure who provides quite literal comic relief from his Hollywood counterparts. Though I engage with a range of texts produced since the 1960s, I begin with contemporary nonfiction texts to demonstrate the ways discourses of action and adventure shape our understanding of specific events in historical reality. Chapter 1, "Armchair Thrills and the New Adventurer," deals with a recent popular manifestation of the continued cultural appetite for action narratives. In this chapter, I examine the outpouring in the late 1990s of nonfiction-adventure literature, looking at a number of texts that became best-sellers not only because of their chilling narratives of real-life tragedy, but also because of their fealty to conventions of popular fiction and film. Books such as *The Perfect Storm* and *Black Hawk Down* have not only sold well but also been recast (and in the process, fictionalized) as big-budget Hollywood productions. The imprimatur of authenticity, I argue, enables writers and filmmakers to reinvigorate tired conceptions of male solidarity and fortitude.

Contemporary U.S. action films constitute the *lingua franca* of global film audiences. Whatever their opinions of particular films or of the genre as a whole, most moviegoers worldwide have at least a passing familiarity with male-dominated action spectaculars. The structure of this work proceeds from this basic understanding. In chapter 2, " 'I Married Rambo': Action, Spectacle, and Melodrama," a case study of *True Lies* (1994) exemplifies the genre's redefinition of masculinity according to social pressures related to gender in the late twentieth century. To demonstrate the importance of genre with regard to the cinematic representation of masculinity, I examine the increasing presence of melodrama—a genre or mode associated with women and femininity—in the male-oriented action film. Through melodrama, action films offer both male and female viewers access to a rigidly codified narrative world. The action genre's slowly growing interest in female representation suggests that only conditions of ritualized behavior and personal style exclude women from the connotatively masculine world of action—the world of military and government installations, high technology, lethal weaponry, and pyrotechnic spectacle. To inhabit this world requires a demeanor of aggressive professionalism, which contemporary Hollywood films have rarely assigned positively to female characters. Despite still-prevalent social obstructions to female power, developments in the generic world of the action film (such as the shift toward melodramatic settings and themes) mark a subtle but significant evolution in gender representation and address.

Chapter 3, "Omega Men: Late 1960s and Early 1970s Action Heroes," moves back historically to a period crucial to an understanding of the contemporary action hero and his milieu because the films of this period develop models for that hero. Vietnam-era films recurrently depict conflicted but conventionally "tough" male heroes during a period of severe challenges to many pillars of traditional Western masculinity. The U.S. military's problematic experience in Vietnam raised questions about the utility of prevailing notions of military engagement, home-front opposition to the war resulted in unprecedented acts of political dissent aimed at the male-dominated government and institutions, and the feminist movement called attention to grave gender imbalances in the workplace and in the domestic sphere. In their showdowns with onscreen foes, the period's action-film protagonists wrestled with these larger developments as well.

Significantly, Vietnam-era action heroes' generic descendants in film—the proficient, muscular heroes of the 1980s and 1990s—bear few of their predecessors' scars. However, the legacies of feminism and the Vietnam War are apparent in the literary blockbusters of the same period, albeit through exaggeration and omission. Chapter 4, "Airport Fiction: The Men of Mass-Market Literature," follows the audiences of the earlier films into midlife and to a different venue—that of the popular novels of Tom Clancy and Clive Cussler—through which aging men's attitudes are represented and validated. Despite the well-reported consolidation among the film and publishing industries since the 1980s, contemporary critical work on popular film has only sparingly addressed its literary offshoots. A thorough cultural analysis of contemporary masculinity requires attention to literary as well as cinematic texts, particularly given filmmakers' reliance on name recognition of popular novels to lure audiences into theaters. Clancy's and Cussler's novels replicate, transform, or respond to the contemporary action film's models of masculinity and narrative action. Both writers make emphatic appeals to readers' work situations and domestic roles. At the same time, their novels recuperate the sterile world of white-collar male professionals as a sphere of intrigue, adventure, and national service.

Chapter 5, "Restaging Heroic Masculinity: Jackie Chan and the Hong Kong Action Film" returns to films but looks to an alternative to Hollywood's generic and industrial frameworks. In the early 1990s, Hollywood studios began borrowing narratives of Hong Kong action films, their visual styles, and performers and directors such as Chan, Jet Li, and John Woo. Chan's Hong Kong–produced films, popular throughout Asia, made him the world's most popular action star long before his late-1990s Hollywood successes. Chan's persona suggests ways active male identity can be formed through a combination of physical dexterity, comic self-effacement, and a perceptible "naturalness" or ordinariness. In addition, the racial dynamics of Chan's Hong Kong films—particularly the enactment of both comedy and masochism on the nonwhite male body—provide a telling counterpoint to the economy of race representation in U.S. action films. I approach Chan and his films through analysis of film comedy, masochistic subversion, and carnivalesque pleasure. With their mixtures of comedy and masochistic spectacle, Chan's films unsettle paradigms of active male identity. These films raise questions about bodily spectacle, kinesthetic pleasures, and generic blends of action and comedy in both U.S. and Asian cinemas.

Following the 9/11 terrorist attacks on the United States, media commentators anticipated a return to earnest dramatic fare within the action cinema. No such shift really occurred: solemn narratives of male heroism such as *Tears of the Sun* (2003) and *Ladder 49* (2004) performed poorly in their U.S. releases. Instead, the disturbances of 9/11 were mapped intriguingly onto fantastic fare such as *Spider-Man 2* (2004), which included a sequence in which New Yorkers in a crowded train-car join in solidarity to support the wounded teenaged superhero. The film's overall comedic tone creates a space for this and other dramatic moments, making them emotionally resonant but not so heavy-handed as to disrupt viewers' immersion in the comic-book inspired fiction. Throughout the last few decades, U.S. culture has produced a rich body of film and literature venerating, lampooning, and interrogating active manhood, invigorating the category of masculinity for readers, viewers, and scholars.

1

Armchair Thrills and the New Adventurer

The representation of male activity enjoys countless permutations. Fiction and nonfiction accounts of male activity and heroism appear throughout the history of recorded narrative itself, from *The Epic of Gilgamesh* to NFL post-game summaries, from *The Iliad* to *Soldier of Fortune*, and from *Beowulf* to video games such as *Halo* or *Doom*. Representations of male agency signify differently according to the writers' or characters' proximity to the situations depicted and the historical circumstances in which those representations appear. Immediacy aids in engagement, as do particular ideological affiliations. Nationalist sentiment, religious or philosophical beliefs surrounding death and warfare, and attitudes toward real, social violence all help dictate responses to narratives of violent action. In whatever form, and however received, narratives of dangerous male activity carry indelible popular appeal.

This chapter analyzes a constellation of popular nonfiction texts of the late 1990s: Sebastian Junger's *The Perfect Storm*, Jon Krakauer's *Into Thin Air*, and Mark Bowden's *Black Hawk Down*. The first deals with a fatal commercial-fishing voyage, the second with a fatal mountain-climbing expedition, the third with a fatal U.S. military battle. I find Bowden's book the most compelling in its thriller-narrative form, and Krakauer's most absorbing in its appeals to readers. Junger's book represents part of the same phenomenon of massively popular nonfiction adventure texts, though the book itself diverges from its cohorts because its most gripping events lack eyewitnesses. Each of these texts merges popular-narrative form with conspicuous realist appeals. This combination lends renewed credence to the texts' constructions of active masculinity, revitalizing venerable popular-fiction models with claims to authenticity. At the same time, the texts explicitly recount catastrophic male ventures, favorably complicating narratives of male heroism as they search for meaning amid fatality.

The 2001 film adaptation of *Black Hawk Down* robustly manages the terrain between realism and artifice. Visually, it adopts the long-familiar shorthand for cinematic realism: location shooting, a handheld and highly mobile camera, natural lighting, obstructed views, and limited establishing shots. (Later non–reality-based thrillers such as *Behind Enemy Lines* [2001] and *The Bourne Supremacy* [2004] use a similar visual vocabulary.) *Black Hawk Down* also relies on mediated perceptions of the real. The film's cinematographer, Slawomir Idziak, understands realism as an effect achieved through aesthetic manipulation. Remarking on the film's color palette, Idziak observes, "The colors also lent authenticity to the visuals. On the night scenes, for example, the decision to use green tones was made because [. . .] 'TV nights,' like those presented on CNN, are almost always greenish, so we automatically associate that color with authentic events."[1] The film's visible distortions of color thus approximate the highly mediated look of cable-news programming. A recognizable lens-filter effect signals the real. Perhaps unsurprisingly, the familiar connotations of "TV reality" resonate more strongly than unmediated historical reality, which lacks a distinctive visual signature. In its reenactment of a 1993 military operation, the film prefers the visual language of another medium as a yardstick for realism. Similarly, Bowden's book owes more to the structures of popular fiction than to works of military history. Such mediated views reshape popular definitions of heroic masculinity: constructions of male agency once relegated to fantasy spaces find acceptance in nonfiction realms.

The texts analyzed in this and later chapters emerge from a global culture of postindustrial capitalism. This system does not require men to perform spectacular feats of heroic activity on a regular basis, if ever. Within this culture, accounts of survival amid extreme danger affirm the possibility of unmediated experiences of physical punishment and triumph. This affirmation may contribute more to armchair daydreams than to active, physical pursuits, though. The deployment of popular fiction's generic conventions in 1990s works of popular nonfiction affirms these armchair daydreams as a legitimate substitute for real experience. The reconfiguration of venerable constructions of active masculinity also impedes a complex view of historical reality. As in many other popular discourses, individual men's exploits overshadow geopolitics and history.

Many of the world's cultures define masculinity principally through agency and activity in the public world, through the physical trials of sports and labor as well as through participation and financial risk-taking in arenas such as business and government. When rising standards of living permit large numbers of people to enjoy leisure time or freedom from regular manual labor, imperatives arise to encourage activity away from population centers. Historically, such activities—including military ventures, natural-resource exploitation, or simply exploration to satisfy scientific or aesthetic curiosity—have been undertaken principally by men. This activity, necessitating travel to unfamiliar, avowedly unpopulated regions of the planet, can inspire a fanatical excitement, as occurred, for example, in England in the late nineteenth century. Martin Green argues that it was during this period, "the age of conscious imperialism," that "the cult of adventure was most developed."[2] In the literature of this period, Green locates adventure as the "sponsor" of two stages of male experience: on the one hand, boyhood and play; and on the other, manhood, citizenship, and violence (31). The fundamental incompatibility of these categories—particularly the disparities among citizenship, play, and violence—suggests that adventure offers a highly unstable foundation for male identity. Green acknowledges this instability, and notes as well the global impact of European and American zeal for adventure: "Historically, adventure has been a white idea as well as a male idea; it has been the means by which the people of one particular culture have taken possession of most of the globe" (226). In this chapter, I call attention to more localized frameworks for adventure, works of popular U.S. nonfiction that construct a conventional space for male fantasies of autonomous activity. Published more than a century after the official closing of the American frontier—a concept that Green notes is, like empire, closely associated with adventure—these works champion anew the risks and rewards of male activity outside the civilized world.

A case from England in the twilight of the age of empire will help illustrate the preoccupations of adventure literature, preoccupations that inform the texts I refer to in this chapter. Britain's imperial expansion in the late 1800s provided the content for countless books of male adventures in faraway locales, from Robert Louis Stevenson's *Treasure Island* (1881) and H. Rider Haggard's *King Solomon's Mines* (1885) to Rudyard Kipling's *Kim* (1901). By the turn of the century, conventions of imperial-adventure literature had become sufficiently ingrained that they could be penetratingly critiqued, as in Joseph Conrad's *Heart of Darkness* (1899), or cleverly parodied, as in Arthur Conan Doyle's *The Lost World* (1912). I invoke Conan Doyle's novel because it clearly articulates a number of the genre's key themes and appeals, specifically those surrounding gender construction and male aspirational fantasies. These appeals also emerge in a range of adventure texts that became bestsellers in the United States in the late 1990s.

Like the U.S. texts that appear more than eighty years after it, *The Lost World* represents remote adventure as a means to negotiate the social pressures of twentieth-century Western civilization. The novel invokes anxieties about relationships with women, acknowledging potential threats to patriarchal privilege from women. It also articulates fears of purposelessness and softness in the capitalist world. Making an appeal particularly to men of letters, Conan Doyle's novel also reconciles the sedentary, writing life with the desire for experience and adventure. *The Lost World* is narrated by an initially timid journalist, Ned Malone, a man motivated to join a presumably hopeless expedition to South America because of his sweetheart's desire for "a man who could do, who could act, who would look Death in the face and have no fear of him—a man of great deeds and strange experiences" (6). Made aware of his own directionlessness, his virtual impotence, Ned implores his editor for a new assignment:

> "What sort of a meesion (*sic*) had you in mind, Mr. Malone?"
> "Well, sir, anything that had adventure and danger in it. I would really do my very best. The more difficult it was the better it would suit me."
> "You seem very anxious to lose your life."
> "To justify my life, sir." (9)

Ned thus implies that adventure, with its inherent dangers, guarantees self-renewal and stabilizes an unmoored male identity. (As in most adventure texts, women are virtually absent from the work, so the problem of aimlessness, and the corresponding need for self-justification, becomes entirely a male pathology.) One of Ned's companions on the expedition, the aristocratic hunter Lord Roxton, identifies the attendant comforts of civilized society as a related source of Ned's malaise: " 'a sportin' risk, young fellah, that's the salt of existence. Then it's worth livin' again. We're all gettin' a deal too soft and dull and comfy' " (53). Roxton, Ned's idol, staves off this softness not only through big-game hunting, but by keeping exclusively male company. At the novel's end, upon the completion of many dangerous adventures and after the surprise dissolution of Ned's marriage prospects, he and Roxton set off for another adventure as a duo. In the novel's somewhat parodic logic, exemplary masculinity is forged in the company of men, and its enemies are women and civilization (or women as the embodiment of civilization). Wealth and high social standing do not diminish this masculinity, but instead, for Lord Roxton, make possible the pursuit of virile adventure.

Conan Doyle's narrator combines intellectual exercise with physical danger. His adventure-nonfiction descendants rely on similar appeals, implicitly venerating their own acts of bearing witness to or transcribing other men's endangerment. In *The Lost World*, Ned relays his journal entries from the field back to his London newspaper. As he and his fellow adventurers become embroiled in a war between two remote tribes, he realizes a recurring dream. "Often in my dreams have I thought I might live to be a war correspondent," he muses just before introducing "my first dispatch from the field of battle" (158). The transformation of a journalistic assignment into a heroic enterprise animates many current writers of adventure nonfiction. When such a transformation is not possible, writers often substitute speculation about late men's perceptions of danger to construct a surrogate and posthumous heroism. (*The Perfect Storm*, the extreme-weather account of a fishing-boat crew's drowning deaths investigated and written long after its fatal events occur, uses this second strategy.)

The Men of Adventure Nonfiction

Many contemporary nonfiction accounts of heroic adventure represent male activity in ways parallel to the popular fiction and film that are this work's larger focus. Both groups of texts offer physical activity as the chief determinant of male identity, with men's psychological efforts principally mobilizing that physical activity. The textual forms differ principally in their claims to realism. Popular nonfiction narratives construct the real in ways indebted both to realist literature and to documentary media. Bill Nichols notes two ways of understanding documentary cinema: as "*evidence from* the world," and as "*discourse about* the world."[3] Nonfiction adventure texts shape historical events into coherent, linear narratives. They legitimate their discourse with evidence, just as they transmit their evidence as discourse. Their authors necessarily intervene into the historical world, through interviews with people involved in the events the books recount and, sometimes, through participation in the events themselves. (Although the first-person account usually occupies a separate space of testimonial literature, *Into Thin Air* features the author's efforts simultaneous with those of other mountain climbers.) Like American literary realism of the late nineteenth and early twentieth centuries, these texts rely on observational detail to fortify their claims to objectivity and the production of comprehensive knowledge. In addition, realist texts tend to define the real according to an inverted class hierarchy. The working class, transparent and unself-conscious in its behaviors, always proximal to physical labor and suffering, rests atop this hierarchy. The middle and upper classes, in comparison, softened by consumerism and schooled in artifice, claim only contingent and mediated access to the real. Looking beyond these problematic templates, critical discourse understands realism in shifting political terms, as, in Amy Kaplan's words, "progressive force exposing social conditions" or "conservative force complicit with capitalist relations."⁴ Nonfiction adventure texts encompass these conflicting categories. Simply by foregrounding adventure itself—trials of the body and mind in nature or in hostile human environments—the genre privileges a physicality linked to the working class. Class boundaries are patrolled as well. *The Perfect Storm* and *Black Hawk Down*, for example, recount catastrophes that beset small groups of men in dangerous, working-class occupations (commercial fishing and soldiering, respectively). *Into Thin Air*, meanwhile, emphasizes the lethal bad judgment of prosperous travelers who take on the physical challenge of an Everest climb with insufficient training. In varying ways too, these texts expose the life-threatening dangers faced by men of the working class, while also presenting realms of adventure as locations for (unremunerative) male accomplishment. Consistent rhetorical and evidentiary engagement with historical reality contributes to the multiple claims of these texts.

By adopting the style and structure of popular fiction, works of print nonfiction invoke historical reality differently than many previous journalistic accounts. The new model arranges real events according to an overriding narrative logic, with abbreviated chronologies and conventional character typage. Authors such as Krakauer and Bowden move popular nonfiction, a *de facto* realist mode, toward the category of adventure literature once regarded as the antithesis of serious, realist genres. As Green discusses at length in *The Adventurous Male*, English literature through the early twentieth century sought to distance itself from the apparent sensationalism and frivolity of adventure as a subject. The realist English novel, argues Green, emphasized moral responsibility and the truth of adult relations, constraints of emphasis that adventure-minded writers such as Stevenson and Kipling could not abide.⁵ (In the United States, novelists from James Fenimore Cooper to Jack London to Ernest Hemingway unashamedly foregrounded adventure, contributing to their critical subordination well into the second half of the twentieth century.) In terms of realism, contemporary adventure nonfiction shows allegiance to a relatively narrow set of facts: verifiable locations, acts of nature, and people's visible responses to life-threatening situations. Writers in the genre tend to offer only tentative moral or political hypotheses. Books such as *Into Thin Air* and *The Perfect Storm*, despite their often harrowing subject matter, partly liberate readers from rigorous moral investigation, reclaiming nonfiction for popular rather than elite readerships.

The 1990s rise of nonfiction-adventure literature also corresponds to a resurgence of realist appeals in popular film in the broader U.S. culture. Particularly in the wake of blockbusters such as *Titanic* (1997)—based on a real event, let us not forget—Hollywood studios have clung to the rhetoric of realism to promote each new spectacular event film, however laden with computer-generated effects.[6] In the current privileging of realism, textual producers and consumers bring renewed expectations of emotional, psychological, or social resonance to popular texts. Realist appeals are appeals for engagement, not promises of escape. Meanwhile, popular texts repeatedly eschew visual signifiers of reality. Nonfiction adventure texts define the real more often through historical or technical passages than through imagery, which they use instead for creative effect. In popular film, the reduced presence of human actors, real locations, and actual sets makes realism a weak evaluative criterion. Nevertheless, fidelity to or successful manipulation of the world we inhabit guides readers' and viewers' reception of popular texts.

Realist texts have long served men's interests rather than women's. Presently, because most work and leisure arenas for activity and violence in the United States are open to women as well as men, these forums or pursuits can no longer be defined as the exclusive provenance of men or as the constituents of masculinity alone. Masculinity is a historically and culturally shifting category, comprising a set of behaviors, attitudes, and forms of bodily display deemed as desirable, acceptable, or at least expected in men. It is also a category in service to a vanished but somehow recognizable ideal. "Masculinity is a nostalgic formation," argues Judith Kegan Gardiner, "always missing, lost, or about to be lost, its ideal form located in a past that advances with each generation in order to recede just beyond its grasp."[7] Adventure-nonfiction texts tend to frame their subjects in terms of men and masculinity, and relatedly, to link contemporary men's exploits to venerable historical accounts. The Perfect Storm, Into Thin Air, and Black Hawk Down all recount events principally involving men, and they all locate their subjects within historical pantheons of notable male enterprises. The books thus participate in the privileging of male experience, though they also raise questions about the practicality of that experience.

Nonfiction narratives of male adventure act as a key site for the circulation of models of exceptional or heroic masculinity. Historical narratives of explorers and adventurers—Columbus, Magellan, Lewis and Clark, Robert Falcon Scott, Sir Edmund Hillary—delineate an overwhelming male realm of experience, socially and geographically removed from female lovers, spouses, children, and patrons. Such narratives depend on activity at a spatial remove from domesticated social groups. In popular narratives, folk belief, and countless cultural rituals worldwide, manhood's parameters are tested and extended in the wilderness. Crucibles staged outside civilized society typically distinguish the men involved as more fit to reintegrate into society. The men forged by such experiences are then esteemed as models for the other members of that society. The strategic exclusion of women leaves intact the belief that only men are physically capable of certain activities, and also preserves the experience of adventure as a shared, homosocial endeavor. Women's centrality or equality in adventure nonfiction would both diminish readers' perception of the risk and endurance involved, and would compromise the solidity of the male relationships depicted.

Adventure narratives themselves contribute to civilizing and gendering processes. Books represent adventurers' exploits in cohesive, compact form. Moreover, the act of reading restages far-flung events in expressly civilized spaces. However rugged the content of a popular history, more readers encounter Scott's Antarctic expedition from the comfort of the home than from the frigid deck of an icebreaker. Despite such conditions, consumption of adventure narratives itself plays a role in male identity formation, with male readers gaining knowledge of active pursuits through the act of reading. Such textual consumption can fulfill an aspirational function, stirring readers' desires to enact similar exploits (as is the case for Conan Doyle's Ned Malone). However, most people who read adventure narratives do not become explorers, big-game hunters, or combat journalists. For most readers, such texts are surrogates for real experience, supplying models of both idealized and normative masculinity for readers.

In other forms, the actual, physical experience of adventure can provide a surrogate for different experiences. Engaging in outdoor recreation activities, the more rarified the better, can not only elevate participants' self-worth but also rehabilitate flagging public images, particularly when those activities are reconstructed as narratives. Men's outdoor pursuits can resuscitate a putatively authentic (but temporarily inactive) masculinity, stripping away the accoutrements of a sedentary corporate and consumer culture. Corporate executives periodically engage in adventure-based retreats, often modeled on armed forces basic-training regimens, to hone vaguely defined leadership skills. Individual physical achievement can attest to a fitness of character transportable to other arenas. For example, during Al Gore's 2000 presidential campaign, one television commercial highlighted the vice president's character through images of his 1999 ascent of Washington State's Mount Rainier. The advertisement's voice-over included this assertion: "Strength of character, perseverance, grace under pressure—these are qualities you look for in a mountaineer; they're even better in a president."[8] Here, success in solitary or small-group endeavors removed from civic life signifies an ability to rise to challenges, face adversity, and achieve goals, however disparate such acts might be from the specific technical and physical feat of mountain climbing. The visual image of success in Gore's commercial stood in for any substantive legislative accomplishments. Instead, the commercial asked voters to transport Gore's accomplishment from one arena of male endeavor to another: from the great outdoors to the far more exclusive sphere of the U.S. presidency.

Into Thin Air's Crucibles of Manhood

Outdoor activity's efficacy as a public relations tool depends upon the reception of images or narratives of such activity. The most successful result is the production of a satisfying, vicarious experience for readers or viewers. As with the Gore campaign commercial, numerous contemporary nonfiction texts use events occurring in remote locations as signifiers of bravery and determination. Simply by offering their exceptional images and events to the public, these texts grant conditional but still vivid access to situations far removed from everyday experiences. Thus, the texts fulfill not only their explicit function—to mobilize support for a politician, or to maintain reader interest—but also substitute for or supplement the physical and psychological experience of remote adventure. Representatives of the texts go where most men (and women) lack the resources to tread.

Fiction can just as easily deliver remote destinations and dangerous activity, but what distinguishes nonfiction is its realist dimension. Jon Krakauer's *Into Thin Air* retraces a set of spring 1996 climbing expeditions on Mount Everest, including the author's own, all undone by an ill-timed blizzard. Peril ensues for all the mountaineers, and the storm leaves nine people dead. *Into Thin Air* engages readers not merely because of its exotic setting and descriptions of physical hardship, but also because of its explicit claims to realism in a publishing market cluttered with multitudinous fictional representations of action and adventure. In much of its narrative structure, *Into Thin Air* is indistinguishable from a popular novel. Krakauer's book lacks the nefarious characters, cloak-and-dagger plots, or gunplay of a Tom Clancy or Ken Follett novel. However, it shares with such works a breathless narrative pace, international intrigue and conflict among a relatively wide cast of characters, and a high body count, which is by turns horrifying and mesmerizing. Genre fiction provides conventional settings and events that recur from narrative to narrative, offering pleasure through familiarity and repetition with slight variations. Adventure nonfiction, in addition to satisfying generic expectations, delivers the vicarious experience of lived suffering and exertion. Krakauer recognizes that signifiers of authenticity and immediacy contribute to this experience. He literally anchors readers in the text's present, for example: each of the book's chapters begins by noting the location, date, and altitude of the events to follow.

The explicit location of events prevents Krakauer's narrative from being dismissed as simply another contribution to the enormous body of literature of risky male adventure. Krakauer reconstructs a principally male experience, and he imprints his book's besieged masculinities with a stamp of authenticity. The ascription of realness to perils faced by men makes abstract anxieties tangible. This sense of omnipresent peril creates another paradox: if male fulfillment depends upon the risk of death, then why does Krakauer emerge from his experiences so shaken, so unself-assured? In some respects, such psychological scars are a component of a complete, active masculinity. *Into Thin Air* is, after all, largely a memoir of the author's "return from the edge," and his scars grant him the authority to deliver his own account without impeachment. (This kind of scarring also structures the well-received 2004 documentary *Touching the Void*, which reenacts a grim two-man expedition in which one climber, in a desperate act of self-preservation, leaves his partner for dead, though both ultimately survive after stunningly difficult descents. Their improbable travails, and the fallout of their literally imperiled male friendship, lend their testimony immeasurable gravity.)

Masculinity in crisis is masculinity recognized. In part, this is the project of Faludi's *Stiffed* as well—to call attention to deep-seated pain or anxiety among American men. Public discourse (and legislation) often stands mute regarding women's subordination in work relations, access to childcare and abortion, susceptibility to domestic violence, and other demonstrable inequities. Conversely, many public forums exist to redress any lack of recognition of male achievement or pain. While I support Faludi's position regarding the difficulties faced by men since World War II, it seems clear too that these difficulties have been long publicized. They appear in film noir and the 1950s boardroom dramas that Steven Cohan scrutinizes in *Masked Men*, in the Kinsey Report's disclosures about sexual behavior (which Cohan also studies), in the stroking of the male ego performed by publications such as *Playboy* since the 1950s, and in many other texts, discourses, and laws up to the present. White, heterosexual men are in little danger of being forgotten or shortchanged. Still, claims of realism carry much argumentative force and are repeatedly invoked to privilege already dominant male perspectives. In another late 1990s example, nonfiction works such as Tom Brokaw's *Greatest Generation* histories of World War II veterans appeared at a time when many of them were near the end of their life expectancy, and when most readers were still further removed from the experiences of the War. Dozens of polar histories recounting the exploits of early 1900s military explorers such as Scott and Ernest Shackleton (the latter of whom also became the centerpiece of a historical cottage industry including major museum exhibitions, television documentaries, and feature films) were also published in the late 1990s. These popular texts issue compensatory appeals to rehabilitate already dominant masculinities.

Like other nonfiction adventure narratives, *Into Thin Air* uses a range of strategies to stake its claim to authenticity. Unlike many journalists and historians, Krakauer participates in the ill-fated expedition he chronicles, allowing him to incorporate his own struggle for survival into the larger narrative of misfortune and loss of life. Because of this, the book alternates between the modes of investigative journalism and memoir, exhibiting the sort of deliberate subjectivity popularized in 1960s New Journalism. In addition to detailing the author's personal experiences, the work records interviews with other people involved in or related to the event. In the text, Krakauer presents the interview material somewhat casually, a conventional presentation mode in mass-market nonfiction. He supplies direct quotes even for conversations during which tape recording or note-taking would have been impossible (e.g., during a blizzard while climbing Mount Everest), and as with many popular histories, the book includes no footnotes. Consequently, his work only intermittently meets the evidentiary burden associated with historical research. To bolster its realist claims, though, the book routinely departs from its chronological narrative to present technical information and figures, principally involving weather patterns. The deployment of an assortment of meteorological statistics may be insufficient to ground the work in empirical reality, but this appeal echoes the strategies of popular-fiction genres such as legal and medical thrillers and war fiction. In each of these genres, digressions into technical details—about jurisprudence, medical procedures, or military tactics and weaponry, for example—identify the authors and their works as dependable sources of information on particular subjects. Krakauer's book, in comparison, asserts its realism through an emphasis on location, noting the specific positions and actions of real people at the onset of a snowstorm. Krakauer's spatial emphasis literally situates his subjects, most still living at the time of the book's publication. The technique balances the author's broader psychological speculations about people's thoughts and motives.

Journalism has historically been coded as male discourse. It relies on empirical evidence and scientific objectivity, not overt empathy and emotion. Still, a dimension of sensational appeal, linked to growth in women readerships, has infused journalism since at least the late nineteenth century in the United States and England.[9] So-called yellow journalism is distinguished by excited, adjective-laden prose, privileging writers' subjectivity over impersonal accuracy. Nonetheless, the profession of journalism historically has been practiced disproportionately by men. While women account for just over forty percent of journalists in all media (newspapers, magazines, broadcasting, and other media) in the Americas, they represent only about four percent of newspaper journalists in the United States.[10]

Even the flaunted subjectivity of New Journalism came from a cadre of almost exclusively male writers who plunged into predominantly male worlds, including sports, politics, and the acid-test counterculture.[11]

Into Thin Air similarly depicts a gendered milieu. Men appear as climbers, guides, equipment bearers, and pilots, while women play marginal roles as base-camp nurses and other support staff. While the dozens of climbers on the mountain include a handful of women, Krakauer interacts, by coincidence or design, principally with other men. These men enjoy a range of characterizations—from humble Sherpas to eccentric loners to altruistic group members to risk-loving egomaniacs—denied to women in the account. The woman climber to whom the book devotes the most attention is Sandy Hill Pittman, who Krakauer characterizes as an excessively wealthy, pampered prima donna, a "shameless" publicity seeker (156), and a "grandstanding dilettante" (155).[12] In addition, Krakauer reports her decision to travel with an espresso maker and gourmet beans, as well as her receipt of express-mailed copies of fashion and celebrity magazines. It is scarcely coincidental that this massively popular adventure-nonfiction book depicts its principal female presence as an unwelcome interloper who possesses negative traits linked to both masculinity (imperiousness and egotism) and femininity (vanity and attention to domestic comfort and material luxury, particularly in an incongruously rugged setting). A few of the book's male characters receive similar treatment, but the book's large cast of men includes many more esteemed figures. Krakauer's unflattering depiction of Pittman demonstrates that women do not belong in the mountaineering world, an implicit argument borne out when Pittman later becomes incapacitated and must be carried by other, male climbers.

Paradoxically, Pittman's travails allow Krakauer to adhere to a primary convention of adventure-nonfiction texts: conveying viscerally the events and physical hardships that their subjects face. In addition to pure physical description of human and environmental conditions—such as extremes of temperature, fatigue, and illness—real-adventure narratives typically invoke philosophical issues that arise from such undertakings. Weather conditions and physical and mental pain set up commentaries on the human condition or on individual psychology. As Krakauer recounts his participation in the Everest expedition, he observes, "I quickly came to understand that climbing Everest was primarily about enduring pain. And in subjecting ourselves to week after week of toil, tedium, and suffering, it struck me that most of us were probably seeking, above all else, something like a state of grace" (174). Krakauer's statement attests to a desire to regain access to a more primal, unmediated physical state. This desire is in part a fantasy of class slumming, as Krakauer implicitly laments the fact that not all citizens of developed societies can experience ceaseless toil and suffering. Grace is apparently inaccessible to the comfortable. With his predominantly male cast, and with himself as a further example, Krakauer also locates the achievement of grace particularly in the male body. In invoking grace, he also gestures toward a secular version of the desire for spiritual transcendence (the sublime, really), otherwise attained through religious practices or folk rituals. In a contemporary world that calls attention to physical traits through health care, fitness subcultures, spectator sports, and media representations but makes few demands for physical endurance, *Into Thin Air*'s chronicle of physical punishments supplies a bridge between sedentary readers and active, risky endeavors. Readers, then, can use the book as a call to action: as an inspirational tome, it might spark their own outdoor activities. However, as suggested earlier with regard to adventure literature generally, the book alternately provides readers with a surrogate trial that poses no risk of death or discomfort. In either case, the book's popularity suggests ways contemporary masculinity is constituted through a combination of reality and fantasy.

Whatever use readers make of the text, the goals and perspectives of *Into Thin Air*'s cast of characters build up an emphatically male subjectivity. Krakauer's thematic emphases and reportage consistently rearticulate conventional tenets of male mythology: stoic endurance of physical and mental adversity, the transformative power of pain caused by the elements, struggles for leadership, and acts of individual heroism. In addition, as an Australian doctor in Krakauer's party comments, the controlled, collective hardships of climbing replicate the disciplined, masculine environment of the military. The doctor, Vietnam veteran John Taske, admits that after leaving the military, he "lost his way" and "couldn't really speak to civilians" (176). Next he describes his reclamation of self-confidence: "All I could see was this long, dark tunnel closing in, ending in infirmity, old age, and death. Then I started to climb, and the sport provided most of what had been missing for me in civvy street—the challenge, the camaraderie, the sense of mission." For Taske, the civilian world generates anxieties because of its incompatibility with the masculinist mindset of his military training, and the physically demanding, male-dominated pastime of climbing effectively alleviates these anxieties. (Though he does not explicitly mention his attitude toward women, his fear of a "long, dark tunnel" is rather telling.) Taske's brief account reads like one of the case studies in *Stiffed*, a chronicle of male frustration and lack of fulfillment. Taske, who indicates that he has previously defined his identity through a homosocial world of shared ordeals, requires such trials to retain his connection to notions of male power and purpose. Faludi's case studies include men engaged in assembly-line labor and working-class sports fandom, among others. For these men, the narrowing or elimination of traditional arenas of gender-identity formation produces anxiety and frustration. Just as Taske's earlier military training furnishes a male identity within a group, arduous adventure pursuits supply a concrete, individual goal. The achievement of this goal contributes significantly to a public and private index of male achievement.

As *Into Thin Air* demonstrates, even intangible achievements such as the experience of danger can burnish masculinity. In Krakauer's and other works, danger proves a crucial component in the formation of exceptional masculinity or the reaffirmation of a masculinity made lax by a comfortable, middle-class lifestyle. Undertakings such as those Krakauer describes carry the inherent, substantial risk of a torturous or spectacular death. While most people's lives end unceremoniously, adventure fatalities consistently arouse public interest due to their apparent novelty and infrequency. As Krakauer observes in his attempt to come to terms with the multiple deaths he has witnessed:

> I'd always known that climbing mountains was a high-risk pursuit. I accepted that danger was an essential component of the game—without it, climbing would be little different from a hundred other trifling diversions. [. . .] Climbing was a magnificent activity, I firmly believed, not in spite of the inherent perils, but precisely because of them. (352)

Krakauer's firsthand experience with tragedy, he implies, changes his perspective, but he does not fully articulate a revised philosophy. Despite the book's accounts of fatal mishaps and gruesome deaths, Krakauer venerates a model of identity in which exposure to risk leads to self-fulfillment. The author's own pain and guilt at having survived when hardier climbers died presents a curious paradox with regard to masculinity: Krakauer's survival attests to his weakness, to his selfish instinct for self-preservation, while he portrays many of those who died as heroes who perished in the service of the group. By this logic, the strong do not survive. Even without John Taske's accompanying analogy between climbing and the military, Krakauer's definition of the experience parallels a wartime combat situation, with casualties becoming heroes by default.

By chronicling a number of solitary, unspectacular deaths instead of a range of brawny, eventful lives, Krakauer's book departs from hoary accounts of male heroism. Rather than engaging in a courtship of danger that elevates those involved to some higher plane of endurance and self-knowledge, the book's principals either die or emerge from the experience with substantial physical and psychological scars. Although Krakauer indicts male hubris and folly, his book ultimately foregrounds the men's scars as marks of distinction. We see then a further attraction for readers: we not only register the experience of physical danger, but also gain apparent insight into the process of coping with the aftermath of that experience. In this respect, nonfiction adventure books function like self-help books for men, with the addition of a gripping, high-risk narrative. By reflecting on disastrous events some years after they have occurred, *Into Thin Air* offers a case study that can be used for therapeutic applications. In comparison, Krakauer's previous book, *Into the Wild* (1996), about the disappearance of a young outdoorsman, can only speculate about the mindset of its vanished protagonist. *The Perfect Storm* similarly tries to maintain interest in a narrative enigma: what were men thinking and doing in the hours preceding their deaths? Because Krakauer and many others do live through the Everest crisis, though, *Into Thin Air* can devote much time to the exploration of posttraumatic psychology. In the logic of Krakauer's work, the trauma contributes to a fully realized male identity rather than to its breakdown.

The transformative experience of remote adventure, and the narrative conventions surrounding it, has become sufficiently popular to merit cliché status. The theme of remote adventure as crucible of male identity stretches from Homer's *Iliad* and *Odyssey* to Defoe's *Robinson Crusoe* to contemporary action films such as *Rambo: First Blood Part II* (1985). In these and other male crucible narratives, the willingness and ability to endure extreme physical hardships, often in solitude, grants men entry into a privileged space of achievement. In works such as *Into Thin Air* and *Robinson Crusoe*, male achievement is measured through sheer fortitude. Unlike the wartime scenarios of *Rambo* or *The Iliad*, in which characters defend home or country and contribute to some social good, *Into Thin Air* narrates physical trials that serve no practical purpose. In a *New York Times Book Review* parody, Margalit Fox calls attention to the frivolousness of real-adventure literature's subject matter and its characters' deliberate flirtations with disaster. Fox imagines a book cowritten by Krakauer and Junger entitled *The Perfect Mess*, in which "the authors set sail for Everest in a small flammable boat stocked with a ton of nitroglycerine and a single M&M."[13] Fox's parody indicates the degree to which narratives of outdoor misfortune depend not only on their participants' zeal for such endeavors and their willful pursuit of danger, but also their incompetence, lack of foresight, or sheer bad luck. In subject matter, Fox's imagined bestseller is nearly indistinguishable from some actual publications. Works such as Martin Dugard's *Knockdown: The Harrowing True Account of a Yacht Race Turned Deadly* (1999) similarly offer stories of well-to-do men who blunder into danger during costly recreational activities.[14] Meanwhile, the protagonist of *Into the Wild* sets off into the wilderness carrying little more than a large bag of rice. Still, for the most part, readers do not consume such narratives to marvel at their subjects' foolhardiness but to share the exceptionality of the risk-taking recounted. As an index of masculine will and striving, adventure narratives validate the desire to depart from the comforts and routines of the developed, capitalist world.

Adventure nonfiction typically represents disparate and complex events in an easily apprehended form. Krakauer's book raises both global and local questions, invoking international border disputes, national and commercial interests in global tourism, the author's own social relationships and marital discord, and an abundance of complicated personal rivalries. The book's narrative priority, though, is to recount the disastrous climbing expedition. This priority allows the author to withhold judgment about many of the issues his work introduces. Krakauer's occasional digressions into vague, philosophical speculation about fate and the vicissitudes of nature close off discussion of subjects that go beyond his work's immediate focus. In addition, Krakauer periodically interrupts the chronological account of actions and relationships with his own meditations or with esoteric renderings of Nepalese beliefs. These interruptions grant readers a reprieve from the unrelenting discomfort and malaise of the central events, and successfully delay the narrative's resolution. Much of the event narrative is authentically and unavoidably distressing to readers, as we learn of the characters' physical pain and their inabilities to control or make sense of their situations. Amid this central series of events, the book interjects local superstitions and religious lore about the supposed curse of Mount Everest, as well as musings of previous writers about the mountain's beauty and the dangers it presents to climbers. The combination of mountain-literature excerpts, Sherpa lore, and physical description contributes to the theme of adventure as determinant of male identity. References to earlier explorers and chroniclers link Krakauer's book to the substantial corpus of male exploration literature. Allusions to Nepalese spirituality and folklore lend cultural-historical weight and purpose to the climbers' efforts. The varied associations partly protect the expeditions from the charge of leisure-class frivolity. In addition, geographic descriptions literally ground the narrative and its subjects, locating them in a rugged landscape wholly separate from the comparatively homogenous spaces of the urban, capitalist world. Overall, geographic and spiritual elements bolster the implicit claim that adventurers can attain a transcendent experience of selfhood and thus reclaim their position in a natural order removed from capitalism, social class, and (with few exceptions) the company of women.

Virtually all late-1990s accounts of extreme adventure attest to similarly life-changing experiences regardless of geographic situation, historical period, or surrounding circumstances. Given this similarity, these experiences may not be so unique or rarefied as correspondents maintain. Such manufactured "peak experiences," to use the terminology of early-1990s motivational literature, attest to a continuum of experience in the contemporary developed world: for financially stable Westerners, climbing Everest offers parallel satisfactions to rafting on the Amazon, hiking across Antarctica, or orienteering in the Gobi Desert. Ultimately, engagement in each of these pursuits reaffirms one's status less as an adventurer than as a person of privilege. The mass-market popularity of narratives of individual or small-group hardships implies that the subjects of capitalism seek ways to induct themselves willfully into an imagined fraternity of armchair adventure-seekers. Shared participation in the reading and transmission of such mass-market narratives substitutes for the scarcer, authentic experience. Just as fictional thrillers, mysteries, and romances promise pleasures and dangers outside readers' everyday experience, so do real-adventure texts offer a bulwark against the perceived demasculinization or underphysicality of postindustrial capitalist society. Even if readers are not engaged in high-risk adventure, the texts offer assurance that at least someone is, and stories of fatal mishaps can allow readers to rationalize their own relative inactivity. Acceptance of one's mortality typically justifies, in a culturally acceptable way, the lack of engagement in potentially life-threatening pursuits.

The Perfect Storm's Male Enigmas

Not all adventure narratives involve men who court danger; some men, at least, are motivated by financial necessity. Sebastian Junger's *The Perfect Storm* traces the disappearance of a New England swordfishing boat and its crew during a severe storm in the fall of 1991. Junger opens the book with an admission of his basically impossible task as a journalist: "Recreating the last days of six men who disappeared at sea presented some obvious problems for me" (xi). No visible, written, or oral evidence exists to flesh out the men's final hours. Such is not a recipe for compelling narrative, but Junger pushes ahead, privileging the account's "unknowable element" (xii). His rhetorical sleight-of-hand extends to his use of evidence: "I wound up sticking strictly to the facts, but in as wide-ranging a way as possible" (xi). While he professes to eschew conjecture, he asks readers to accept other seafarers' accounts in place of his central subjects': "I would interview people who had been through similar situations, and survived. Their experiences, I felt, would provide a fairly good descriptions of what the six men on the *Andrea Gail* had gone through, and said, and perhaps event felt" (xi, Junger's italics). Most of his book avoids this tentative and conditional voice, though. Instead, he rounds out a present-tense narrative of the crew's preparations for the voyage with a discussion of New England's maritime history, an overview of the economics and perils of swordfishing, and much meteorological and oceanographic information. The extensive scientific and historical sections transitively assure readers of the overall objectivity of Junger's book, even as it serves up cryptic speculation as fact. (Based on interviews conducted years after the storm, for example, Junger quotes a premonition of impending disaster from a crewmember's girlfriend as the men prepare to depart.)

The Perfect Storm is nothing if not a narrative of masculinity in crisis. The first page of the narrative proper introduces crewmember Bobby Shatford, asleep in a shabby motel. He has a black eye, administered by his girlfriend, who sleeps next to him (5–6). Junger thus locates readers in the realm of kitchen-sink realism, where men are physically besieged even in bed. In this world, workplace dangers complement physical threats at home. As Junger later asserts, "[m]ore people are killed on fishing boats, per capita, than in any other job in the United States" (70). He also comments on the economics of commercial fishing, noting a downturn in the industry after the 1980s that results in more frequent, always risky trips for wage-earning fishermen. Junger adds to these conditions the figure of the driven-to-near-recklessness fishing captain Billy Tyne, who "has a particular reputation for pushing things to the limit" (72). Thus all the pieces are arranged for a male contest of gender, economics, and work hierarchy. These various struggles merely serve as backdrop for a grander elemental conflict, as the book's subtitle, "A True Story of Men Against the Sea," reminds us.

By necessity, Junger sets up these numerous contests but cannot really stage them. His male protagonists are principally enigmas, defined by those they leave behind and by men and women with similar experiences. At a climactic point, Junger incorporates testimony from another New England fisherman who survived a similar experience in 1982, then segues into a mostly third-person scientific account of the experience of death by drowning. When the *Andrea Gail* disappears from narrative view, Junger shifts the book's attention to another boat, the *Satori*, whose crew is rescued, and to a helicopter rescue crew's own crash and subsequent rescue. For much of the book, Junger thematically constructs his male protagonists as ghostly and irrecoverable:

> If the men on the *Andrea Gail* had simply died, and their bodies were lying in state somewhere, their loved ones could make their goodbyes and get on with their lives. But they didn't die, they disappeared off the face of the earth

and, strictly speaking, it's just a matter of faith that these men will never return. Such faith takes work, it takes effort. The people of Gloucester must willfully extract these men from their lives and banish them to another world. (213, Junger's italics)

Junger here calls on tropes of the uncanny: the men "didn't die" but later had to be "banished" by others. The absence of bodies contributes to this view of men as enigmas. The book begins with the slightly wounded male body of Bobby Shatford and finally emphasizes the absence of all the crew's bodies. Masculinity's defining feature of the physical body disappears, and Junger relates the struggle to account for this absence.

The Perfect Storm's real achievement, perhaps, is its reversal of the terms of masculinity itself. Steve Neale argues that "[m]asculinity as an ideal, at least, is implicitly known. Femininity is, by contrast, a mystery."[15] Yet here men are the mystery, and women are known. Women appear as characters before and after the disastrous storm, and at the end of the book where Junger acknowledges seven interview subjects, all women. In addition, the two storm survivors whose accounts he cites in the most detail are women: Judith Reeves and Karen Stimson. To counterbalance these women's voices, Junger repeatedly reasserts the subject of men and his own work as a male journalist, watching storms himself and drinking beers at the Gloucester inn where his subjects congregate. He begins his acknowledgments with the statement that "[o]ne of the most difficult tasks in writing this book was to get to know—to whatever extent this is possible—the men who died at sea in the Halloween Gale" (226). Like Krakauer, he asserts his own mental anguish as a badge of honor. Similarly, in the book's foreword, he locates himself at the scene of the event, a man on the border between land and sea, where the urge to investigate strikes: "My own experience in the storm was limited to standing on Gloucester's Back Shore watching thirty-foot swells advance on Cape Ann, but that was all it took" (xii). Physically situating himself in the dead men's environs—on the shore just after their deaths, and in their favorite bar later—Junger makes a rhetorical claim for his own worth as an investigative journalist. He leaves present the enigma of the dead men's experiences, but with a counterimage of himself as an indefatigable, truth-seeking investigator.

Black Hawk Down's Men at War

In their search for compelling stories of true-life male activity, writers and publishers can scour the historical record of the early twentieth century, turn to narratives such as Into Thin Air or The Perfect Storm that participate in an existing nonfiction genre (e.g., mountain or maritime literature), or look to other present-day arenas where men's actions take center stage. Mark Bowden's 1999 bestseller *Black Hawk Down* finds such an arena in contemporary military activity. Bowden's book chronicles U.S. military action in Somalia in 1993, which culminated in a failed counterinsurgency mission and the capture of a U.S. helicopter pilot by Somali soldiers. Like Krakauer's book, *Black Hawk Down* departs from straightforward reportage or history, privileging instead a popular-fiction style of first-person action. As Bowden admits in the book's epilogue, "I wanted to combine the authority of a historical narrative with the emotion of the memoir, and write a story that read like fiction but was true" (331–332). Like Krakauer in *Into Thin Air*, Bowden aims to fuse the memoir's claims to authenticity and immediacy, the journalistic account's accuracy, and the popular novel's fast paced and omniscient narration. Given its subject and the assistance that U.S. military personnel provided to the author, readers might expect the book to serve an explicit, nationalistic political ideology. Bowden's book, however, offers less in the way of military-policy analysis than it does in vivid reconstruction of the sights, sounds, actions, and emotions of the event. The book's graphic presentation of small-arms combat contributes to some extent to a military mythology of battlefield excitement, but Bowden's emphasis on the participants' fear and confusion, and the high toll of death and injury on both sides of the conflict, disabuses readers of notions of mythic wartime valor.

In his choice of the memoir and the thriller as models for a comprehensive account of a historical event, Bowden acknowledges the captivating qualities of such popular forms. Moreover, the emphasis on first-person testimony allows Bowden to probe contradictory cultures and value systems without foregrounding his own prejudices. On one hand, Bowden frames U.S. soldiers' conventional, conservative statements about manhood and military power in ways that make the statements seem deeply felt and authentic rather than hollow clichés. For example, early in the book, Bowden presents the views of a member of an elite U.S. combat team, Delta Force:

> [T]he job demanded more. It demanded all you had, and more [. . .] because the price of failure was often death. That's why Howe and the rest of these D-boys loved it. It separated them from other men. [. . .] Victory was for those willing to fight and die. [. . .] If the good-hearted ideals of humankind were to prevail, then they needed men who could make it happen. Delta made it happen. (33)

To a great extent, such statements appear initially as macho bluster, evidence of the overconfidence and myopia of military indoctrination.

When located against a backdrop of unsuccessful battles and U.S. casualties, however, they acquire a different resonance, ironically indicting U.S. military policy and the volatile model of masculinity that such policy supports. In addition, because the bloodshed that Bowden records is so senseless— neither side's political agenda is advanced, and many of the Somali dead are noncombatants—the Delta Force member's "the job demanded more" ethos seems perfectly apt, as reasonable and useful a claim as any other offered on the conflict's front lines. Elsewhere, Bowden presents competing views about the conflict—for example, paraphrased quotes from Somali combatants and civilians—also without direct attribution. He thus presents readers with dueling subjectivities, competing perspectives that he does not explicitly reconcile. Through its reticence, though, Bowden's book ultimately proves sympathetic to the military perspective. He critiques the planning and execution of the U.S. operations in Somalia rather than the ideology of military activity itself. Nevertheless, in reconstructing events as a series of first-person narratives, he acknowledges that grasping the overall situation in some depth requires consideration of multiple viewpoints, not just the short-sighted "Delta made it happen" perspective. Amid these competing viewpoints and Bowden's narrative of the failed mission, acts of individual heroism and bravery redeem the operation for the U.S. military and government.

The Delta Force member's aggressive worldview suggests the complex ways in which nonfiction-adventure texts, and the events that inspire them, negotiate constructions of masculinity. Far from being inoperable, the uncomplicated Delta creed provides the modus operandi for real soldiers' often deadly excursions into the battlefield. In the logic of the Delta Force member, the likelihood of a sudden, violent death distinguishes an exemplary manhood. According to this logic, only men who risk their lives regularly can contribute actively to the maintenance of humankind's "good-hearted ideals." Paradoxically, the explicit lack of concern with personal longevity contributes to an exceptional male identity; the nearness of death enriches men's lives. Individualism supplies another foundation of the Delta Force ideology—fulfillment comes from activity that "separated them from other men." Contrary to tenets of individualism, though, the men's exceptionality grants them group membership in Delta Force itself. As in much military discourse, a stated desire for peace underwrites male militancy. In addition, despite the men's obvious position in the adult world of the international armed forces, the "D-boys" appellation signals the abnegation of adult responsibility. As in many other adult male groups, associations with youth or boyishness signify the temporary removal from the domestic order and liberation from conventional social strictures (and social morality as well). In this respect, the grimly realist, violent world of

Black Hawk Down overlaps with the *Treasure Island* milieu of globe-trotting boy's adventure.

Bowden's narrative model, then, corresponds with the nonfiction adventures already discussed as well as with the representations of male activity that dominate 1980s and 1990s popular cinema. As in cinema, print texts' representations of the right-minded actions of individuals supersede the potential contradictions of the texts' larger ideological positions. *Into Thin Air* locates readers alongside individual climbers, posing few explicit questions about the utility of climbing itself. *The Perfect Storm* accepts death in service to commerce, issuing no call for industrial reform. *Black Hawk Down* similarly makes only implicit arguments about U.S. military policy, focusing instead on the individual soldier's courage under fire. Krakauer's and Bowden's books in particular, while presenting contexts for social behavior, prefer narrative momentum to careful analyses of behaviors or institutions.

From Real to Reel Masculinity

Bestselling nonfiction accounts of male activity, such as Krakauer's and Bowden's, borrow not only the solitary heroes or tightly knit groups germane to action cinema but also their narrative techniques. They offer a series of rising actions with climactic violence or triumph; hastily sketched characters, often identified by a single, outstanding personality trait or visual signifier; minimal historical context; and subordination of issues and conflicts not immediately related to the story at hand. Because of the apparent camera-readiness of books such as *Into Thin Air* and *Black Hawk Down*, popular filmmakers in the late 1990s looked to nonfiction-adventure texts as sources for mainstream films. The IMAX documentary *Everest* (1998), despite its limited release at the small number of IMAX-equipped theaters nationwide, grossed nearly $75 million in the United States.[16] The fictionalized film version of *The Perfect Storm* appeared in summer 2000, directed by Wolfgang Petersen, a filmmaker known in the 1990s for semi-realist action dramas with middle-aged protagonists, including *In the Line of Fire* (1993) and *Air Force One* (1997). (Notably, whereas Junger resists the urge to build a fictional narrative for his disappeared protagonists, the star-driven Hollywood film wholly forsakes this restriction.) Likewise, Krakauer's book appeared as a fictionalized television movie, *Into Thin Air: Death on Everest*, in 1997. U.S. film studios, hoping to maintain or expand viewership, continue to seek potentially lucrative alternatives to muscular or effects-laden action films targeted at the reliable, but relatively narrow, adolescent-male demographic. The popularity of real-world male trials among the adult, book-buying public makes such texts obvious candidates for film adaptation. As films, both *Black Hawk Down* and *The Perfect Storm* were substantial hits, suggesting that their realist credentials helped attract viewers across categories of age and gender. Thus, the films successfully recuperated well-worn themes and narratives surrounding male achievements, both *Black Hawk Down*'s "war is hell" perspective and *The Perfect Storm*'s venerable "man versus the elements" narrative.

When bolstered by claims of authenticity, highly conventionalized visual representations of active masculinity can be promoted as gritty reality rather than stylized fantasy. Bowden served as a consultant for the film version of *Black Hawk Down*, which was moved forward from a planned spring 2002 release to a December 2001 release to capitalize on post-9/11 nationalist sentiment. The film applied realist conventions of tight and imbalanced framings and jittery hand-held cinematography, and featured graphic scenes of battlefield carnage and triage. Nonetheless, it still bore the simultaneously aggressive and mawkish stamp of producer Jerry Bruckheimer, known for high-concept action blockbusters such as *The Rock* (1996) and *Armageddon* (1998). In promoting the film, Bruckheimer and director Ridley Scott touted the film's supposed semidocumentary aesthetic. In one *New York Times* interview, for example, Scott asserts of the film, "It's as near to the edge of a documentary as I could make it."[17] Interestingly, Scott offers documentary realism as a standard of artistic achievement, despite the near-total absence of documentary films from commercial theaters, studio distribution rosters, or Scott's own resumé. Overall, given the evidence of the film's expressive color, frenetic editing rhythms, and casting of numerous well-known or rising Hollywood actors, "near to the edge" is a highly elastic term.

Early in this chapter, I quoted *Black Hawk Down* cinematographer Slawomir Idziak regarding the perceived authenticity of CNN's green-hued "TV nights." Idziak's statement acknowledges that media texts figure strongly in the signification of the real. Given this disconcerting power, along with the rapid consolidation of media and publishing industries in the late 1990s, these industry practices merit close scrutiny. Despite the proliferation of specialized niches in the book- and magazine-publishing industries, corporate control over the U.S.- and global-public sources of information, entertainment, and enlightenment increasingly limits political and cultural perspectives that are not explicitly mainstream. Compared to print media, popular cinema supplies the public with an even more circumscribed range of texts. The vast majority of U.S. theaters show only fiction films from major U.S. studios, eschewing nonstudio productions, foreign films, or documentaries. Studio films generally deal with fantasies of personal transformation or virtuous suffering and conclude unambiguously and completely, thereby discouraging viewers' critical reasoning. The more such texts dominate the global media landscape, and the fewer the alternatives to dominant narrative models, the more essential critical practice becomes. Popular texts' ongoing cannibalization of the category of documentary realism can ground these texts in social reality, but it can also rationalize irresponsible fabrications and distortions of world conditions. The books discussed here, and their film offshoots, work on both sides of that divide.

2

"I Married Rambo": Action, Spectacle, and Melodrama

The contemporary action film, the most profitable of global film genres, uses various formal and narrative strategies to respond to cultural crises about masculinity and male social roles. Since the codification of the action genre's dominant narrative conflicts and conventions of visual style in the early 1980s, the action film has been the most visible site of male conflict and identity formation in popular global cinema. The genre's visibility derives both from the widespread global distribution of U.S. action films and from the literal visibility of its films' protagonists, usually solitary (or highly individualized), athletic, white men. As contemporary capitalist society severely limits and codifies the bourgeois male's ability to establish his identity through physical activity, action cinema offers particular appeals to male filmgoers. Action films provide fantasies of heroic omnipotence and escape from, or transcendence of, cultural pressures. These escapes do not represent real solutions to the problems faced by members of capitalist societies, since action-film narratives necessarily displace the present-day contradictions of male identity into visual space, into spectacle. While violent spectacle has been a prominent feature of the genre since its inception, action films in the 1990s increasingly constructed stories around threats to domesticity, marriage, and the nuclear family. By presenting spectacular violence as the solution to domestic and familial conflicts, the genre displays the ideological contradictions between idealized masculinity and familial responsibility under contemporary capitalism.

The action film has historically been a "male" genre, dealing with stories of male heroism, produced by male filmmakers for principally male audiences. The genre's most intriguing development in the 1990s was the incorporation of formal elements associated with the "female" genre of melodrama.[1] This development is linked to crises of authority associated with contemporary capitalism and postmodernity: challenges to male power in both public and private spheres, the privileging of simulation over authenticity, and the corresponding distance between fictional texts and the social reality in which they appear. In response to these crises, the Hollywood action film proffers conventional narratives of male mastery, but modifies these narratives through reliance on other generic languages, particularly those central to film comedy and melodrama. This process of genre hybridization accomplishes the ideological work of male-dominated, multinational capitalism: 1990s action films celebrate the ingenuity and physical prowess of individual heroes, while also depicting such heroes as champions of women, children, and capitalism itself. At the same time, these films more often address women audiences narratively and formally. Action films in the 1990s and early 2000s present women characters in more substantive and less decorative roles than in previous decades. Relatedly, action films increasingly utilize a melodramatic mode of address, structuring narratives around a logic of spectacle and excess emblematic of the classical-Hollywood melodrama.

The action film's significance for film and cultural-studies critics lies in the ways the genre articulates prevailing ideological positions. By means of its hyperbolic genre conventions and its codified narratives, the action film displays the instability of cultural paradigms of race, gender, politics, and capitalist ideology. Action films, like Hollywood blockbusters in general, tend to present conservative narratives and prosocial iconography for a target audience of adolescent males. While action films occasionally display progressive overtones, the surface narratives of such films appear to reinforce patriarchal structures of white male authority, privilege, and omnipotence. At the level of plot, the vast majority of action films of the 1980s and early 1990s support conservative formations of militant, heterosexual, white masculinity.[2] To advance their preferred ideological positions, though, generic texts regularly invoke the competing ideological frameworks they seek to disavow.[3] Action films' use of exaggeration, parody, irony, and self-reflexivity indicates the anxiety that accompanies the insistence on preferred readings. At the same time, these strategic devices allow the engagement of different viewing positions and the texts' repudiation of their explicit, narrative meanings. Despite their masculinist overtones, contemporary action films formally and narratively follow patterns developed in popular media geared toward women rather than men. Such a cultural positioning indicates a shift in the rhetorical strategies of popular texts: whereas cultural discourses and texts of the 1980s promote militant masculinity as an explicit alternative to feminine or liberal weakness, 1990s discourses synthesize categories of feminine domesticity and sentiment with those of masculine discipline and strength. Evidence of this shift appears in the action film at the level of visual style, in narrative linkages of active and domestic spaces, and in the genre's contextualization of violence.

Action films present violence as a component of a spectacular visual style, using images of violence to thrill or excite rather than to shock. 1990s action films present graphic violence and pyrotechnic spectacle as exaggerated simulations of real violence and destruction rather than as credible, discomfiting representations of these phenomena, despite ongoing debates about the relationship between fictional and real violence, especially with regard to children. Throughout the 1990s, critics referred increasingly to action films' "cartoon violence" to suggest that viewers—especially younger viewers—would not find that violence objectionable. The phrase connotes the perceptible distance between cinematic representation and its social referent—in this case, a distance substantial enough that a child could recognize it. With screen violence distanced from reality by elaborate special effects and fantasy narratives, action-film violence appears legible and comprehensible to viewers. In his analysis of the social function of popular texts, John Fiske suggests that violent media images and texts appear as cultural responses to perceived social pressures.[4] The visibility of real violence in news media, inequitable distribution of wealth, and the diminished utility of physical strength for bourgeois males under multinational capitalism all indicate complex social conditions disadvantageous to many members of society. In the face of these social and cultural crises, action films, like other popular texts, retain their currency because they offer conventional, definitive solutions to otherwise insurmountable problems.

James Cameron's 1994 film *True Lies*, which serves as the basis for this chapter's arguments about the contemporary Hollywood action film, combines an action narrative involving terrorists with a romantic narrative about the action hero's marriage and family life. This combination allows the film to make extensive use of melodramatic formal elements and narrative situations.[5] Late in the film, following the resolution of the marital conflict and just prior to the climactic action sequence, the romantic leads embrace passionately while a nuclear bomb detonates in the background. The mushroom cloud offers a spectacular display of phallic power and a metonym for the sexual fulfillment the pair never achieve during the film. The scene aestheticizes destructive weaponry, as the kissing couple in the foreground lends a lyrical quality to the image. The excessive visual display also punctuates a rather unspectacular moment in the romantic narrative, an intimate exchange between husband and wife. In addition, the image announces the linkage of the film's romantic/domestic elements to its action environment while simultaneously heralding the demise of the domestic sphere. When the understanding wife tells her super-spy husband to "go to work," ceding to him the provider/protector role, the film sets aside its domestic plot in favor of an extended action sequence. The kiss scene locates the couple at the site of action but also necessitates the woman's departure from that space. The film's linkage of active and domestic realms follows a pattern established in Hollywood melodramas: as in melodrama, this action-film episode derives its impact from stylistic excess and from its conflation of social and personal spaces.

As *True Lies* demonstrates, the combination, through melodrama, of traditionally male spaces of action and female spaces of romance and domesticity makes the contemporary action film a synthesis of historically male and female cultural forms. The explosion scene transforms a display of nuclear weaponry into a sentimental framing device. Elsewhere in the film, spectacular representations of violence and destruction induce affective responses of excitement, fear, and, occasionally, anger. In complementary fashion, the film, like action cinema as a whole, transforms emotional situations into episodes of public violence. Action films consistently channel sexual and romantic conflict into physical, performative, and violent displays, transforming or displacing emotion into sensation.[6] Meanwhile, the genre's corresponding over-representation of active, masculine space, far beyond the physical or experiential capacities of men or women in postindustrial society, suggests that the cinematic spectacle of masculinity in the contemporary action film conceals real crises of male identity. *True Lies* uses a melodramatic plot and mode of address to work through issues understood in popular media as central to men in the 1990s: paternal responsibility, male anxiety surrounding female infidelity, the moral and civic value of white-collar or managerial occupations, and concerns about the banality of middle-class suburban life and the consequent demasculinization of those within it. Tellingly, *True Lies*, like the action film in general, proffers violence as the universal solution to contemporary sex-role and work-based anxieties.

Melodrama, long recognized as a women's genre in cinema, provides the operative mode of contemporary action cinema, by most standards an overwhelmingly male genre. Not only do action films periodically venture into the narrative and thematic space of melodrama, melodrama forms an essential formal component of the action genre, particularly in the spectacle-oriented mode of action cinema prevalent since the early 1980s. Action films' melodramatic elements—including moral legibility of plots and characters and spectacular, excessive mise-en-scène—link the action genre structurally to melodrama, in particular to the domestic-melodrama genre that has historically appealed predominantly to women audiences. Action films in the 1990s increasingly featured melodramatic narratives involving the home and family. Films such as *True Lies, Terminator 2: Judgment Day* (1991), *The Long Kiss Goodnight* (1996), *Face/Off*, and *Deep Impact* (1998) built stories around threats to family and domesticity while also presenting the action genre's traditional narratives of global terrorism or other threats to the human race. Like melodrama, the action film emphasizes archetypal characters and the nonpsychological development of those characters, displacement of conflict through hysteria and excess, unambiguous moral oppositions, and accessibility of meaning.

The action film's invocation of the domestic sphere represents a significant development in a genre that has largely set its conflicts against the backdrop of expansive public spaces such as large cities or exoticized foreign settings. The genre, traditionally a utopian space of action and individual freedom, incorporates melodrama's personal and social crises by making those crises reparable on the genre's terms. What a traditional melodrama might present as a problem of capitalism or family structure, an action film presents as a matter of action and inaction. *Armageddon*, for example, includes the subplot of a father–daughter relationship (Bruce Willis and Liv Tyler comprise the motherless family), in which the emergence of a young suitor (Ben Affleck) challenges the father's monopoly on his daughter's affections. The film resolves this conflict of triangulated desire when the father embarks on a solo suicide mission to save the planet. The incompatibility of familial and social roles, foregrounded in the melodrama genre, erupts throughout action films as decisive violence. Alternately, the action film uses violence, motion, and action to stave off the resolution of ideological problems. By incorporating family into cinematic narratives of ritualized heroism and combat, action films sustain the illusion that viewers may attend to pressing social concerns—that is, they may be good parents, spouses, or citizens—within the conventional terrain of a master narrative that puts a premium on individual autonomy and dominance.

The action genre uses melodrama's structures to repackage an anachronistic master narrative in a postmodern guise of accessible, viewer-friendly entertainment. Melodrama makes essential contributions to this rehabilitation project, particularly when coupled with comedy. Postmodern self-reflexivity and generic irony assure action-film viewers that they are "in on the joke," that the genre's distortions of gender, race, politics, and so forth are whimsical devices intended to gratify audiences. Visual or verbal references to star personas, action choreography that calls to mind sequences in previous films, and other citations of prior films position action films as metacommentaries on genre rather than as reactionary depictions of social reality. The subtle disavowal of the genre's overt ideological agenda allows action films to rely continually on master-narrative tropes. Significantly, the comic tone of many contemporary action films permits a recapitulation of familiar narratives of male mastery. Action films proffer male mastery as a necessary component of their generic narratives: the ability to assert control over threatening situations virtually defines the action hero. Yet 1990s action films often show men facing threats in areas previously outside their sphere of responsibility. This new generic category of "action fathering" locates the durable male-mastery narrative in a popular form that, historically, has disproportionately appealed to women audiences. This adaptation successfully reinforces patriarchal ideology (by assuring the reproduction of patriarchal narratives), but it also renders that ideology unstable. If narratives of male mastery can be transmitted only through texts structurally similar to those constructed for women audiences, the social order underpinning such narratives may also be under siege.

Ideological contradictions, though displaced, play a decisive role in most contemporary action films. So-called buddy films—such as the *Lethal Weapon* series (1987, 1989, 1991, 1998) and *Tango & Cash* (1989)—compensate for the threat of homosexuality with heavy doses of homophobic humor masked as male camaraderie. Films that include spies, terrorists, mercenaries, or other international figures pit iconoclastic (though idealized) heroes against stereotypical villains in interminable battles for cultural and national identity. With remarkable consistency, action films either exclude women from their narratives or soften their protagonists' misogyny by depicting villains as even more objectionable sexual sadists. *True Lies* makes each of these volatile elements particularly evident. Through its relatively complex treatment of a female character (though by no means making her equal to the male hero) and its emphasis on domestic relations and conflicts, the film highlights the functions of melodrama and comedy. In action films of the 1990s, invocations of these other generic discourses allow screen characters to move between the domestic realm, which corresponds loosely to the viewers' familiar real-life experiences, and the utopian space of action, where social limitations and the laws of physics only occasionally apply.

Action Violence, Male Bodies, and Racial Difference

Like many genre texts, action films tend to engage in dialogue most cogently with other genre texts rather than with social reality; to use Steve Neale's terms, they privilege generic verisimilitude over cultural verisimilitude.[7] Nonetheless, action films remain popular amid different cultural climates. Shifting social ideologies help determine what such films will or will not represent, although the principal cultural referents for action films are the stars, plots, fight sequences, stunts, and special effects (and to a lesser extent, dialogue) that appear in other films. While the action film constitutes a genre of its own, it draws from a variety of other established film genres. Its images of masculine authority and violence follow from earlier representations in the gangster film, the western, and the war film. The malleability of the form derives not only from the need to retain audience interest but also from a tendency to elide or displace the genre's ideological conflicts ever more spectacularly and decisively.

Increasingly graphic depictions of violence are a key site of elision and displacement. Spectacularly destructive hand-to-hand combat, gun battles, and explosions appeal to audiences familiar with the genre's existing formal conventions and special effects. Displays of violence also transfer violence's narrative and social meanings into the purely aesthetic sphere. Viewers learn to enjoy displays of violence as displays rather than as violence. Even films awash in violence need not necessarily represent conservative or nihilistic worldviews. Viewers may interpret action films as commentaries on violence or on cinema's propensity for violence, rather than as glorifications of social violence. Many Hollywood films that develop or reference action-film conventions surrounding violence, including the western *The Wild Bunch* (1969) and the blackly comic crime films *Natural Born Killers* (1992) and *Pulp Fiction* (1994), ostensibly represent ultraviolence to show its inimicality to social order.[8] The Schwarzenegger vehicles *Terminator 2* and *The Last Action Hero* (1993) use comic irony for a similar purpose. *Terminator 2* offers the narrative conceit of a "no killing" parameter for its robot hero, which results in his shooting an innocent man in the kneecaps, an event depicted as humorous. *The Last Action Hero* represents the gulf between fantasy violence and its real-world consequences, when an action hero finds himself in a "real" world where he is physically vulnerable.

Setting benchmarks for representations of violence and other subjects, many action-film conventions refer more closely to previous cinematic representations than to corresponding developments in the material world. With this in mind, the genre's anachronistic depictions of women, nonwhite ethnicities, and domestic and global politics become more comprehensible, though not more excusable. Action films' narrative conflicts are often not so much anachronistic as merely unreal: in the late 1990s, Hollywood action heroes were called upon to battle volcanoes (in *Dante's Peak* [1996] and *Volcano* [1997]), asteroids (in *Deep Impact* and *Armageddon* [both 1998]), aliens (in *Independence Day* [1996] and *Men in Black* [1997]), zombie legions (in *The Mummy* [1999] and its sequels), and Godzilla (in the eponymous 1998 U.S. revamping of the low-budget Japanese series). Even in films with contemporary, urban settings, an identifiable historical reality provides only a perfunctorily staged backdrop for spectacles of the impossible. This ever-increasing gap between action-film narratives and their referents in reality suggests, among other things, the estrangement that viewers feel from both normative institutions and mechanisms of social change.

Comic, stylized, or otherwise exaggerated treatments of violence in action films displace screen violence's obvious meaning: that it represents horrific pain and suffering and should repulse the viewer. Similarly, action films repress and displace other factors—paradoxes of masculinity and homoeroticism, and social and political ideology—through comedy, visual excess, and emphases on performativity or artificiality. In an essay on popular-film ideology, Robin Wood notes the difficulty of assigning discrete boundaries to film genres. According to Wood, different genres "represent different strategies for dealing with the same ideological tensions."[9] Privileging tempo and spectacle, the action film admits a vast array of settings and conflicts, and a correspondingly wide canvas for the articulation of ideological positions.

Action films use their suitability to hybridization to cope with contemporary crises of gender, race, political conflict, and social behavior. The genre addresses these conflicts by assimilating elements of melodrama, comedy, the western, the martial-arts film, and other genres. Still, like other genres, action films raise issues they cannot satisfactorily resolve, particularly issues surrounding male identity and gender construction. Action films negotiate their logical gaps and inconsistencies through visual spectacle, narrative excess, and the application of melodramatic and comic elements to existing genre conventions. Comedy, particularly, allows for discussion of gender and sexuality, if not resolution of conflicts involving those categories. Analyzing comic action heroes such as Bruce Willis and Kurt Russell, Yvonne Tasker argues that "comedy opens up a space for male and female drag, allowing a play with the 'boundaries' of gendered identity, with jokes about the male image and sexuality which are not permissible within the more earnest dramas of the action tradition."[10] Meanwhile, earnest action films such as *First Blood* (1982) and *Rambo* cast male predicaments in melodramatic terms, with emotion serving as a pretext for violent release.

The prevailing elements of contemporary action film merit definition despite their apparent self-evidence. On-screen action—particularly physical combat and gunplay, fast-moving bodies or vehicles, and destruction of property or landscape features—constitutes the genre's principal feature. Contemporary settings and urban locations also distinguish the genre; however, in hybrid form, action films overlap with war films, westerns, and gangster films, which situate their violent action in other culturally sanctioned or ritualized spaces (wartime, the historical past, and the underworld, respectively). The action film's generic hybridity depends on selective emphasis; action films with military or science-fiction settings, for example, often downplay the thematic appeals of these other genres. *Predator* (1987) deals less with military codes of group interaction or science-fiction questions of the limits of human knowledge than with muscle-flexing, bloodletting, and Arnold Schwarzenegger's monster-fighting credentials; in short, the action genre's fundamental tests of heroic masculinity. Even when located in familiar, contemporary settings, action typically occurs at a distance from or as an embellishment of events that might occur in lived, everyday reality. For example, audiences can see speeding cars on racetracks and highways, but only in action films can they regularly witness unsanctioned, destructive pursuits through city streets. Similarly, while most viewers observe real physical violence at some point in their lives, action films both locate viewers at a safe remove from conflict and choreograph action in a lyrical or spectacular style. Multiple camera positions and rapid cutting transform action from an approximate representation of reality into a rhythmic spectacle, appealing to viewers at a visual and physical rather than an intellectual or sentimental level. The use of extreme close-ups and computer-enhanced special effects further heightens the sensory appeal of action over its narrative or social relevance.

The representation of action and motion is a fundamental component of the film medium, and so, the birth of action film effectively coincides with the birth of cinema. Cinematic reproductions of action began with films such as Auguste and Louis Lumière's *Demolition d'un mur* (1896) and *Arriveé d'un train en gare* (1896). During the same period, actuality films of boxing matches also helped draw audiences to the new leisure attraction of Kinetoscope parlors and contributed to the growth of producers such as the Biograph and Edison companies. (Also, as many film historians have noted, boxing films often could be shown in cities that prohibited live boxing matches. Even in the earliest years of the medium, social groups treated the representation of violence differently than real violence.) Historical epics such as Griffith's *Birth of a Nation* (1915), Eisenstein's *Battleship Potemkin* (1925) and *October* (1928), and Abel Gance's *Napoleon* (1927) used overtly political narratives and melodramatic codes of performance, spectacle, and stylistic excess to frame their representations of small- and large-scale action. In the classical Hollywood era, the gangster film, the war film, and the western consistently provided screen action featuring male heroes and directed toward predominantly male viewers. Of these forms, only the western evolved substantially as a genre. The gangster film wilted under the threat of the Hays Production Code and opposition from religious groups, and the war film largely retained its prosocial function throughout the studio era (with some darker notes struck by films such as John Ford's *They Were Expendable* [1945] and Sam Fuller's *The Steel Helmet* [1951]). In both cases, extracinematic discourses surrounding representation of violence dictated the genres' dissipation or stasis. After World War II, cinematic action and violence appeared most prominently in other genres or modes: in westerns; in film noir, with its internalized, psychological violence; in youth-oriented swashbuckler films such as *The Crimson Pirate* (1952); and in spectacular male epics such as *Ben-Hur* (1959) and *Spartacus* (1960).

By the mid-1960s, themes of the western—including tensions between civilization and savagery, sanctioned authority versus vigilantism, and regeneration through violence—traveled to contemporary settings in criminal and police dramas such as *Bullitt* and *Dirty Harry*. While driven by dramatic, putatively realist narratives, these films also featured constructions of alternately prosocial and antisocial masculinity and extended sequences of spectacular action and violence. These latter elements achieved greater prominence in male-centered narratives such as *Jaws* (1975) and *Rocky* (1976). In the 1980s, films such as *First Blood* and its sequels signaled an emphasis on the solitary, muscular male hero, sending the Western male around the globe in search of spectacular violence. In the 1990s, the rise of directors familiar with the visual conventions and editing of music videos and television commercials led to entire films constructed around perpetual visual spectacle. Mid-1990s films such as *Strange Days* (1995), *The Rock*, and *Heat* (1996) choreograph even transitions and plot developments in the manner of action sequences, via performativity, an abundance of extreme close-ups, and terse dialogue. In the late 1990s, calculated blockbusters such as *Armageddon* and *Star Wars Episode I: The Phantom Menace* (1999) relied on brief shot durations and rapid edits to generate the sensation of persistent activity.

Accelerated films with close proximity to screen subjects correspondingly privilege particular viewing strategies. They reward immediate engagement but discourage depth of involvement. *Armageddon*, despite its two-and-a-half-hour running time, maintains the approximate rhythm of a thirty-second car commercial for much of its length. The film's prolonged astronaut-training sequence, for example, is composed of a multitude of very brief scenes, subordinating narrative progression to a series of snapshot-like moments of activity. Throughout the film, conventionally "American" images of rural children, as well as images of plaintive children in an indistinct Third World setting, serve as transitions between narrative events. The *Star Wars* series similarly maintains visual appeal through frequent changes in camera position and setting. Exposition often occurs in scenes of less than ten seconds' duration, with characters exchanging a few lines of dialogue in shot/reaction shot form, followed by abrupt cuts to different locations. Such editing, combined with the film's frequent use of swift wipe transitions, borrows conventions of fast-paced visual spectacle originating in the silent era and refined in the economical style of 1930s Republic serials. At the same time, the late-1990s films accelerate the pace of editing considerably. Brief shot durations, coupled with long running times, produce a sort of epic-length montage. In place of character interiority or the kind of linear narrative that requires viewers to connect disparate events, they offer a perpetual present, a space in which decisive action produces immediate consequences.

1990s action-film narratives, which usually focus upon a solitary hero or pair of heroes, often function simply to advance the protagonists from one dangerous predicament to another. These narratives generate suspense not by prolonging viewers' anticipation of upcoming action sequences, but by delivering a continuous flow of action as the narrative itself. *Speed* (1994), for example, extends a speeding-bus sequence over more than half the film's running time, and related action set-pieces comprise the film's opening and climactic sequences. The film pares down its story and the interactions among characters to the absolute minimum required to suture viewers into the rhythm of the action. Contemporary action films often reshape the familiar narrative pattern of stasis/conflict/resolution, bypassing the period of stasis almost entirely to focus on conflict that spreads across an entire film. Many 1990s action films commence in action, beginning with a modestly scaled conflict that introduces the lead players and provides cursory character development. An opening elevator-crash sequence in *Speed*, for example, establishes the virility and resourcefulness of an L.A.P.D. officer (Keanu Reeves) and the ruthlessness and vindictiveness of his mad-bomber adversary (Dennis Hopper). Similarly, the opening sequence of *Cliffhanger* (1993), in which Sylvester Stallone leads a failed rescue operation that results in a woman's death, establishes Stallone as a flawed male whose desire to regain control over his body and his physical environment motivates his confrontation with the film's villains. In both cases, male protagonists' actions are raised to a level of absolute significance; the films' conflicts train their male heroes for entry into or return to a pantheon of super-active masculinity.

The conventional action-film narrative deals with a solitary hero's tests of masculine identity. The struggles usually unfold across the male body or shift onto the body's typically phallic extensions in weaponry, machinery or larger symbols of power, authority or physical mass (from tanks and airplanes to large buildings to mountains or entire cities). Describing 1980s Hollywood action films, Susan Jeffords suggests that displays of the male body and complementary images of masculine spaces and events construct a visibly male narrative world:

> [T]he male body—principally the white male body—became increasingly a vehicle of display—of musculature, of beauty, of physical feats, and of a gritty toughness. External spectacle—weaponry, explosions, infernos, crashes, high-speed chases, ostentatious luxuries—offered companion evidence of both the sufficiency and the volatility of this display. That externality itself confirmed that the outer parameters of the male body were to be the focus of audience attention, desire, and politics.[11]

Writing in the early 1990s, Jeffords suggests that 1990s films, in contrast, provide a space for more interiorized and emotive male heroes. With the decade now complete, it seems that 1990s action films more frequently did narrate the exploits of psychologically and emotionally complex males but still privileged the exteriorized male body. Male characters and viewers continue to enjoy dominion over physical as well as emotional spaces.

The prevalence of the white male in action films highlights the genre's construction of stable, unassailable identities for its heroes. Action films routinely subject masculinity—through its metonymic representation as a male body, itself an approximation of the phallus—to rituals of combat and suffering. The triumph of masculinity occurs only when the screen male exhibits mastery over his own body. To generate conflict around the idealized space of the male body—and to discourage erotic contemplation of static or rigid bodies—action films threaten, test, and punish their heroes. The films subject their heroes to ritual or conventional obstacles that, once overcome, demonstrate the fantasy omnipotence of the action hero, usually a white male. Action films tend to present white maleness as sufficient evidence of stable self-identity, in opposition to other gender or racial formations. Jeffords notes in Hollywood films "a pattern of masculinity that necessitates defining men not by content but by opposition to an other."[12] Viewers recognize a male hero not entirely through a perception of the character's positive traits, but also in his opposition to representative villains, who often appear as characters of different races or ethnicities.

The almost complete absence of black or female protagonists from action films before the late 1990s appears partly to be a consequence of Hollywood's—and more broadly U.S. culture's—definition of blacks and women as already oppositional figures, counterparts or complements to the male ideal. Although stars such as Wesley Snipes, Will Smith, and Chris Tucker made inroads into the action genre in the 1990s, filmmakers routinely paired them with partners or mentors who were white (or Asian, for

Tucker in the *Rush Hour* series [1998, 2001]).[13] Mixed-race duos populated many successful action "buddy movies" of the 1980s and 1990s, and the films regularly defined the white male hero in relation to his black counterpart. In an analysis of racial pairs in buddy movies, Cynthia Fuchs notes a pretext of avowedly race-blind masculinity that transforms racial difference into male camaraderie. In such films, she traces "a narrative continuum which contains initial axes of racial, generational, political, and ethnic difference under a collective performance of extraordinary virility."[14] Nevertheless, in most cases only the white male partner gains access to real, that is, visible and narrated, virility.

Throughout mixed-race buddy films, such as the *Lethal Weapon* series and *Die Hard with a Vengeance* (1995), the black partner's pragmatic skepticism and caution render him a comic foil for white male heroics. The *Lethal Weapon* series establishes a dynamic between the reckless—and in the first film, suicidal—Riggs (Mel Gibson) and the sensible, aging Murtaugh (Danny Glover). The films transfer the symptoms of midlife crisis, a common enough anxiety among white males, onto the body of Murtaugh, leaving Riggs free to demonstrate a version of masculinity that consists of physical autonomy, lack of inhibition, and freedom from the burdens of women and family. The series underscores the childish nature of this masculinity by showing Riggs moving into Murtaugh's home and flirting with his partner's teenage daughter. Riggs's youthful masculinity, though, repeatedly proves superior to his partner's mature but diminished gender identity. Riggs performs many acrobatic feats and fights in a showy martial-arts style, while Murtaugh displays little agility and minimal prowess in hand-to-hand combat. Riggs also possesses a reservoir of knowledge about policing and science that Murtaugh lacks. Finally, Riggs's sexuality is defined and glamorized in lovemaking scenes (in the second and third films) that show his nearly naked body, while the display of Murtaugh's exposed body occasions the black character's mockery or humiliation. The series successfully defuses the stereotype of the wholly physical, hypersexual black male, but only by parceling out those traits to the white hero and leaving the black counterpart inept and impotent. The *Lethal Weapon* series, like numerous other black/white pairings in action films and in other genres and media, displaces crises of masculine identity from the white hero onto his perpetually suffering black partner, who becomes a degraded mirror or a negative image of the white lead.

Action films consistently naturalize racial, ethnic, and gender differences through self-reflexive comedy. Late-1980s and 1990s action films used comedy simultaneously to retain and critique conventions of heroic masculinity. *Die Hard* and its sequels combine Bruce Willis's comic timing with the genre's solemn tests of masculinity. Arnold Schwarzenegger's tongue-in-cheek persona gives free rein to his many roles as phallic superman. His character in *True Lies*, for example, conceals his identity by pretending to be a computer salesman. This conceit permits the film to contrast the character's masquerade as an ordinary husband and father with the fantasy representation of his "real," heroic identity. Even stereotypically masculine performers like Stallone manage to gain comic mileage by tweaking their previous images: His character in *Tango & Cash* declares early in the film that "Rambo is a pussy," mocking the ultraconservative Rambo character in sexist and homophobic terms.[15] In these and other cases, action films rely on postmodern self-reflexivity, or what Jim Collins calls "hyperconsciousness": "[A] hyperawareness on the part of the text itself of its cultural status, function, and history, as well as of the conditions of its circulation and reception."[16] By presuming to offer audiences a meta-commentary on media culture, action films can rearticulate conservative ideologies that other contemporary texts and discourses have challenged. At the same time, such intertextual references offer the possibility that the conservative discourses they invoke can only function in this intertextual relay, and are correspondingly inoperable in social reality.

The genre's codes of visual style complement male heroes' comic self-aggrandizement. Action films consistently foreground their protagonists as the camera follows the hero's movements through space and frames him at the center of the visual spectacle. In action sequences, cameras track the protagonist, whether he is the pursuer or the pursued, the attacker or the defender. Multiple camera positions during fight sequences present a variety of male selves that converge toward a singular masculine ideal. Fragmented shots of the hero's body in action and multiple-angle views of the same body signify the hero's threatened or fractured masculinity. These films visually represent a hero's successful combat by reviewing the image of the solitary, whole male. Such a presentation adheres generally to principles of classical cinematic narrativity. Conventions of analytical editing call for fragmented close-ups to draw attention to significant components of a larger image. In action films, though, close-ups of male heroes' limbs and muscles often emphasize these body parts' contributions to a functional male whole rather than their relevance to a particular scene (just as fragmented shots of the female body typically highlight the object status of that body over its narrative relevance). The centrality of the protagonist in shot compositions both activates the viewer's voyeuristic gaze and promotes identification with the screen protagonist.

Action films' consistent incorporation of visual spectacle also fetishizes the male hero, not as an object of erotic contemplation, but as a component of a full-screen spectacle.[17] Steve Neale observes that repetitive close-ups of the male body and its extensions in weaponry encourage fetishistic looking, "by stopping the narrative in order to recognize the pleasure of display, but displacing [the display] from the male body as such and locating it more generally in the overall components of a highly ritualized scene."[18] In addition to offering their heroes as objects of voyeuristic admiration, action films diffuse the boundaries of their protagonists' bodies so that the figures transcend the physical specificity of their representations. The male body becomes a connotative visual element in the genre's presentation of spectacular action. In turn, action-film spectacle serves as a bombastic representation of masculinity, a representation that can exist only in visual abstractions. The spectacle of action, and the fantasy of masculinity it represents, finds no parallel in the domestic or personal sphere. Action films, through their overemphasis on the terrain of action, suggest the threat to male dominance that lurks at the edges of spectacle-oriented narratives.

Digital effects further dilute the boundaries between the male body and the surrounding spectacle. *Terminator 2* offers a paradigmatic case through its presentation of a villainous, shape-changing man/machine. This creature, dubbed the T-1000 (Robert Patrick), uses its powers to blend into the film's physical environment (e.g., by "morphing" into a checkerboard floor pattern) and to bypass physical barriers (as it does by partially liquefying to slip through prison bars). Later films also substitute digital reproductions of characters' bodies during action sequences. *Mission: Impossible* (1996) achieves its most stunning effects with a digitally composited scene with its hero in midair between an exploding helicopter and a speeding train. Similarly, in *True Lies*, the airborne hero's effects-enhanced battles with terrorists excite viewers through sheer visual excess, disengaging the viewer's desire for credibility or realism. As in other 1990s films, some of *True Lies*'s action sequences locate filmed characters in environments that include digitally generated elements.[19] (In *True Lies*'s climactic battle, long shots of Tasker piloting a Harrier jet amid downtown skyscrapers use filmed backgrounds, but the jet itself is a computer-graphic effect.) More recent films, including the later Schwarzenegger vehicle *The 6th Day* (2000) and the disaster film *The Day after Tomorrow* (2004), digitally superimpose film footage of characters onto computer-generated backgrounds. Action scenes that once highlighted the virtuoso performances of stunt people now acquire their chief appeal through the technical sophistication of the images themselves. Ironically, contemporary action films' exaggerated narratives of male activity include physical feats that can no longer be staged before the camera. Digital visual effects privilege arresting simulation over profilmic reality, and the human body becomes another manipulable element in digitally enhanced representations of scenographic space.[20] Images of the literal body of the actor—usually male—lend scale to the simulated world and establish narrative continuity. Just as spectacle and the visual landscape define the hero, the hero's presence defines the landscape, reconfiguring it into a grandiose emblem of masculinity and control.

Action Cinema as a Melodramatic Mode

The action film's emphasis on spectacle, rhythm of action, spatial properties, performance, and music links the genre to melodrama, both in its narrative structure and its formal properties. The action genre's association with masculinity and male audiences parallels the melodrama's linkage to female audiences and femininity. Such gender associations have resulted in critical disparagement for both genres: the contemporary action film, like nineteenth-century stage melodrama and the classical-Hollywood melodrama, is regularly pilloried for its visual and performative excesses and lack of narrative realism. Moreover, 1970s feminist critics' recuperation of the melodrama—challenging its denigrated status as a vehicle for low pleasures and artificial evocations of sentiment—parallels the 1990s (and ongoing) feminist project of revisiting traditionally male genres for representations of conflicted masculinities. Feminist analyses of the melodrama identify the social conflicts the genre exaggerates or displaces into personal space. Theorists of melodrama also examine the spectatorial pleasures that coincide with affective entertainment—in melodrama, usually pathos rather than elation. Contemporary feminist analyses of "masculine" genre films have also recognized the ideological conflicts that these films generate or elide. However, analysis of this sort often fails to account for the spectatorial pleasures associated with such texts. Action films present physical strength and dexterity as the solution to social conflicts, an attractive proposition for male viewers socialized to rely on physical force despite increasingly limited opportunities to make use of such force. Mechanisms of disavowal notwithstanding, action films also showcase the eroticized, objectified male body, offering straightforward or ironic pleasures to men and women across categories of sexual preference. For both male and female viewers, action films also offer uncomplicated oppositions between good and evil in a morally lucid world.

The term melodrama designates particular film genres and subgenres as well as an aesthetic mode popular since the eighteenth century. Linda Williams begins her article "Melodrama Revised" with the statement, "[m]elodrama is the fundamental mode of popular American moving pictures" (42). She argues that melodramatic codes of moral legibility, as well as combinations of pathos and action, are not the province of specific genres such as the family melodrama or the action film. Instead, she identifies melodrama not as a discrete genre but as "a modality of narrative with a high quotient of pathos and action" (51). Supporting her historical argument, she cites exhibitors' categories of film genres—including western melodrama, crime melodrama, action melodrama, and romantic melodrama—that use the term melodrama to refer to "a form of exciting, sensational, and above all, moving story that can be further differentiated by specifications of setting or milieu" (50–51).[21] Williams's goal is partly to align previous understanding of the melodrama genre with a broader conception of melodrama as an aesthetic mode, a conception based on the term's use in the U.S. trade press in the 1920s and later.[22] Williams does admit the legitimacy of generic categories such as the family melodrama and maternal melodrama but argues that many male-oriented genres, for example, the western and the crime film, have been defined apart from or in opposition to the category of melodrama, despite their reliance on melodramatic principles. Christine Gledhill extends Williams's argument, observing as well that "[i]f male-oriented action movies are persistently termed 'melodrama' in the trade, long after the term is more widely disgraced, this should alert us to something from the past that is alive in the present and circulating around the masculine."[23] Both Williams and Gledhill effectively challenge the earlier critical equation of action with realism (as other commentators on the action genre have done). Affirming the compatibility of action and emotion, Williams argues: "If emotional and moral registers are sounded, if a work invites us to feel sympathy for the virtues of beset victims, if the narrative trajectory is ultimately more concerned with a retrieval and staging of innocence than with the psychological causes of motives and action, then the operative mode is melodrama" (42). (Despite her carefully argued if sweeping reassessment of melodrama's significance in popular cinema, Williams cites as contemporary examples a range of films that fits previous critical understandings of the melodrama genre, including *Philadelphia* [1993], *Schindler's List* [1993], *Malcolm X* [1992], *Silkwood* [1983], and *Norma Rae* [1979].)

Williams, like Gledhill, identifies melodrama as a mode rather than a genre, though her most detailed contemporary examples concern melodramatic codes in a discrete body of films recognizable as part of the action genre. She observes, "we have only to look at what's playing at the local multiplex to realize that the familiar Hollywood feature of prolonged climactic action is, and I would argue has always been, a melodramatic spectacle" (57). She continues: "Nothing is more sensational in American cinema than the infinite varieties of rescues, accidents, chases, and fights. These 'masculine' action-centered multiple climaxes may be scrupulously motivated or wildly implausible depending on the film" (57). Williams does not define the action film as a genre itself, but she clearly invokes the conventionally male world of action cinema. She defines *First Blood* and *Rambo* as "male action melodramas," noting both films' emphasis on their protagonist's victimhood and pathos. While such elements support Williams's argument about the melodramatic mode, genre differences do exist, and attention to those differences illuminates the significance of emotional displays in the action genre. Whereas domestic, affect-centered melodramas—for example, the maternal melodrama *Stella Dallas* (1937) or the male melodrama *Written on the Wind* (1956)—represent pathos and suffering in order to maintain and satisfy viewer expectations, action films such as *Rambo* use pathos as a pretext for cathartic, explosive violence. In action cinema, suffering is a catalyst for action, not its endpoint. For my purposes, melodrama's relevance to the action film lies not only in the action genre's general use of the melodramatic narrative mode (and a correspondingly spectacular visual style) but also in its increasing turn to melodrama's domestic settings and conflicts in the late 1980s and 1990s. At work is a process of genre hybridity, or in other terms, what Gledhill calls "boundary encounters and category mixing" (225). This intersection, she continues, "permits the exploration of one social gender in the body of another," precisely the effect of the contemporary collision of action and melodrama (225).

Action-film violence, like the genre's other predominant elements, operates according to melodramatic codes of representational excess. Mary Ann Doane argues that generic prescriptions in U.S. film situate violence and emotion in correspondingly "male" and "female" spheres, adding that "[i]n the Western [*sic*] and detective film aggressivity or violence is internalized as narrative content. In maternal melodrama, the violence is displaced onto affect."[24] By synthesizing traditionally male and female genres, contemporary action films shape violence into affect and reconfigure emotional displays as violent spectacles. Action films, traditionally addressed to male viewers, produce emotion through violent rather than sentimental images. Sharon Willis's reading of *To Live and Die in L.A.* (1985) traces the convergence of violence and affect: "By its very excessive violence, *To Live and Die* manages to maintain both levels of intensity; it thematizes violence and it produces bursts of affect channeled as spectator horror."[25] The relation between violence and affective intensity constitutes a prevailing convention in contemporary action films. With each passing year, technical developments in the action cinema permit increasingly graphic displays of violence and trauma inflicted on the body. To temper the affective power of such images, action films typically surround episodes of graphic violence with comic dialogue or plot elements. Thus, the films generally offer viewers an escape valve, a means to engage with the narrative at a different level if certain images or situations become too unsettling, or in other words, if viewers respond too emotionally. Melodramatic codes also determine the action film's available content and its manner of presentation. Thomas Elsaesser notes that in melodrama, "significance lies in the structure and articulation of the action, not in any psychologically motivated correspondence with individualised experience."[26] Since the experience of action films—shootouts, chases, international intrigue—bears little relevance to viewers' everyday realities, the films promote viewer engagement based on performative and gestural codes, and on motion, rhythm, and visual excess. Genre conventions situate action-film characters and narratives outside lived reality. This disjunction liberates characters and plots from encroachments of "real" social and political conditions while limiting the available range of narrative responses to particular situations.

Melodramatic excess engages the viewer both formally and at the level of visceral appeal. In the action genre, excess also signals the failures, limitations, or contradictions of films' manifest ideologies. 1970s commentators regarded the classical-Hollywood melodrama as producing ideological contradictions through stylistic excess and narrative discontinuity, disrupting the ideological positions that films might appear to enforce.[27] In action films, pyrotechnic or violent excess substitutes for pragmatic solutions to real-world problems. Combat replaces diplomacy, solitude and alienation replace personal bonds, muteness and stock phrases preclude communication, and ritualized male camaraderie stands in for dialogue between the sexes. Action films regularly recode male anxieties or traumas as hysterical symptoms, displaced from the active male persona.

As noted above, the audiovisual qualities of action sequences often subsume the sequences' logical narrative function. Geoffrey Nowell-Smith argues that in melodrama, "music and mise-en-scène do not just heighten the emotionality of an element of action: to some extent they substitute for it."[28] He links this stylistic device to the psychopathology of hysteria, in which repressed ideas or emotions reappear on the body as displaced symptoms. For Nowell-Smith, melodrama's manifestation of inexpressible ideas through visual or performative devices indicates the genre's resistance to normative ideologies. Melodrama operates according to social norms, but exaggerates social conventions to expose the artifice and limitations of prevailing codes of behavior. Action films, through a similar use of visual excess in place of logical resolution, may share this resistance to social repression. Visual excess transforms otherwise logical actions—that is, logical within the framework of an action-film narrative—into absurd posturing or impossible physical feats. Moreover, the notion of action-film spectacle as hysterical symptom problematizes the genre's distinct associations with masculinist ideologies. The action film thus situates itself in an already feminized mass-cultural space.[29]

Action films' distance from realism also situates the genre outside historically male—and thus esteemed—categories of cultural expression. In classical-Hollywood cinema, the visual, narrative, and thematic conventions of male-dominated genres such as the gangster film and the western contributed to associations between male action and the critical category of realism. Notwithstanding the pulp-fiction qualities of their plots and dialogue, gangster films and westerns often featured restrained acting, the pictorial realism of open landscapes or characteristically gritty urban locales, and, for gangster films, ostensible attention to social context. In their depictions of violent action, classical westerns, war films, and gangster films also tended toward realism rather than exaggeration, with violence reduced to frequent but emotionally understated displays (i.e., swift and bloodless episodes, not protracted and anguished ones). Since at least the 1980s, though, action cinema has been marked by an overt and increasing disruption of realist codes. Appeals to adolescent viewers partly motivate such disruptions. Youth appeals motivate too the genre's creation of utopian or fantasy settings such as outer space or the supernatural world. Similarly, action films based on video games provide adolescents with fantasy narratives removed from the contested familial, educational, or social spheres. In the mid-1990s, a wave of such films appeared, including *Super Mario Bros* (1993), *Street Fighter* (1994), and *Mortal Kombat* (1995). The early twenty-first century has seen a second wave with two *Tomb Raider* films (2001, 2003), two *Resident Evil* films (2002, 2004), and *Alien vs. Predator* (2004), among others. These newer films mix codes of action and horror, but in place of horror cinema's abiding interest in sexuality, these texts emphasize their protagonists' ability to ward off bodily threats through physical action.

The contemporary action cinema's relationship to realism bears additional scrutiny. This relationship is not one of opposition but of selective engagement. Selective critical reception also plays a role, as a further comparison with the classical gangster film makes clear. During the early sound era, the gangster film, a genre invested in male action and violence as well as male relationships, appealed to proponents of realism on multiple levels. It offered photographic realism in the form of urban, often working-class settings (albeit settings represented by studio sets rather than location shooting) and featured characters dressed in contemporary and often shabby clothing. Also at the formal level, synchronous dialogue and sound effects constructed a dense, coherent aural world. With its often bleak stories and unhappy endings, the genre fulfilled accepted narrative criteria for realism. Its actors typically eschewed the broad gestures and visible emotions of earlier silent films and of other sound-film genres such as maternal melodrama, comedy, and the musical. (These performative codes had already become more understated than in early cinema, which owed more to stage-acting styles such as pantomime.) In addition, the gangster film usually supplied both psychological and social motivations (e.g., insanity or greed, and poverty or class hatred) for its characters' misdeeds. For all these historically realist attributes, though, the gangster film, like the action cinema of the 1980s and thereafter, also departed from realism in many ways. These departures were characteristic of popular genre cinema: circumscribed narrative worlds, rigid causality, ritualized and performative interactions among men, exaggerated sound recorded in postproduction, and sensational depictions of violence and destruction. Julia Hallam and Margaret Marshment refer to this latter tendency as "realisation": "in the sense of reality stimulation, of 'making realistic' the fantastic, spectacular effects of storytelling through visualization and auditory effects."[30] "Real-isation" provides the foundation for expressive spectacle by anchoring viewers to a coherent visible and audible world. Even films adapted from comic books or fantasy video games ground their so-called alternate realities in an unstated logic of physical laws, behavioral codes, and spoken language. In particular, films' constructions of gendered identities refer to the gender biases of their producing cultures. Male psychological pain, for example, underwrites countless texts ranging from the unflinchingly realist to the utterly fantastic.

Action heroes embody generic and melodramatic attributes, attributes that are wholly fabricated, the products of intertextuality and a history of mediated performance. Narrative excesses and disjuctures characterize the action genre. The genre also depends upon performative, excessive masculinity, further eroding the long-standing equation of male texts with realism. Spectacular displays of the male body and exaggerated male behaviors extend beyond narrative requirements and beyond the limits of realist convention. Incoherence and ambiguity often results from this exaggeration. For Nowell-Smith, "the 'hysterical' moment of a text can be identified as the point at which the realist representative convention breaks down" (74). Regarded in this fashion, the contemporary action film consists of a nearly uninterrupted series of hysterical moments. Redundant footage of spectacular destruction—for example, the replaying of the bus/train collision in *The Fugitive* (1993) or the repeated long shots of the climactic explosion of a Russian attack helicopter in *Rambo* from multiple camera positions—supersedes the essential requirements of narrative and encourages viewers' differing interpretations of the sequences and the films in which they appear. Also applying the notion of hysteria to film, Chris Holmlund locates similar pathological symptoms in two Stallone vehicles, *Lock Up* (1989) and *Tango & Cash*, which she interprets as displays of male masquerade. The two films, she argues, exalt masculinity through the pairing of Stallone with "the Stallone clone," a virtual copy of the hero who may safely idealize (through behavioral similarities) and challenge (through verbal barbs) the original.[31] This sort of pairing demands recurrent homophobic disclaimers on the part of the characters, which they combine with deliberately stunted assertions of their own physical superiority. As Holmlund suggests, this nervousness suggests a corresponding uneasiness about gender norms. The action hero's overstated masculinity denotes the constructedness of conventional gender paradigms. Viewers' pleasure in such performative displays suggests a further contradiction between action-film narratives and the genre's aesthetic excess. Though at some level action films require viewers to take male performance seriously (seriously enough to generate suspense or promote superficial identification), at another the films allow viewers to enjoy the artifice of men masquerading as supermen.

By presenting male performance and visual spectacle as hysterical excess, action films promote negotiated viewing positions for both male and female viewers. Tania Modleski argues that conventional melodramas may appeal to men "because these films provide them with a vicarious, hysterical, experience of femininity which can be more definitively laid to rest for having been 'worked through.' "[32] Action films, through their exaggerated representations of heroic masculinity, offer this vicarious, hysterical experience to viewers of both sexes. Though films periodically offer cinematic masculinity as an ideal toward which male viewers might strive, the excessive nature of this masculinity mediates viewer involvement with the screen image. Because of their representational distance from reality, contemporary action films do not call upon their male viewers to enact the fantasies of masculinity that appear onscreen.[33] Similarly, female spectators may use experiences of hysterical masculinity to negotiate their own positions within patriarchal power structures, aided by the awareness that sufficiently exaggerated masculinity is indistinguishable from the female pathology of hysteria. Action films transform masculinity into spectacular abstractions and performative exhibitions. Such presentations may neutralize the threat that hegemonic masculinity poses for male viewers, who face social pressure to live up to the masculine ideal, and female viewers, who must live in its long shadow.

True Lies and the Struggle between Activity and Domesticity

Film, literature, historical texts, and other media typically represent male activity occurring in public or open spaces. Such spaces offer a privileged setting for autonomous male action or visually arresting male conflict.[34] Through the mid-1980s, most action films chose settings far removed from domestic space. Homes, wives, and children, if represented at all, usually were entirely separate from violent action. The lone-hero focus of films such as *Rambo* and *Predator* could not accommodate romantic interests or family narratives. However, in the late 1980s and 1990s, many action films dramatized domestic space and transformed it into a setting for action. Domestic settings may appeal to aging male viewers who, through marriage and fatherhood, play more central roles in the domestic economy and for whom domesticity heightens anxieties about masculinity. These viewers may take pleasure in paternal heroes' resolution of domestic conflicts. Emphasis on home and family also indicates Hollywood's attempts to draw female viewers to action films. Action films centered around families and the home attractively domesticate the aggressive male action hero, rendering him an object of romantic fantasy rather than a threatening supermale. Typically in domestic action films, a male hero or a hero and his partner defend the domestic space against an outside threat, and this defense partially defines their masculine identities. In each of the first three films in the *Lethal Weapon* series, for example, killers attack the heroes in their respective homes. Throughout the series, domestic space is foregrounded. The first film stages its climactic battle on the front lawn of Murtaugh's home. The second features the destruction of Riggs's home and a near-fatal explosion in Murtaugh's. In the third film, domestic tragedy ensues when Murtaugh kills his son's friend, a gang member. The third film concludes with an extended shootout in an unfinished domestic space, a housing development under construction that serves as a front for arms dealers. The action genre previously demonstrated its protagonists' heroism in public spaces—such as cities, the jungles of South America and Southeast Asia, and outer space—and often characterized these men as iconoclastic loners with no connections to family. By the late 1980s, though, many films presented male action as essential to the preservation of bucolic, suburban settings and the families inhabiting them.

Moving away from the *Rambo*-era convention of the solitary male with no social or familial ties, films such as those in the *Lethal Weapon* series reposition the male hero as the protector of domestic space.[35] (In the *Lethal Weapon* and *Terminator* series, the white male protagonist is both a protector of domestic space and an iconoclastic loner, defending a family of which he has become a surrogate member.) Conversely, threats to domestic space occur because of preoccupied or inattentive patriarchs. In this respect, *True Lies* and other films anticipate the rhetoric of groups such as Promise Keepers, suggesting that the father is both cause of and solution to intrafamily conflict. In *True Lies*, for example, the hero's neglectful parenting leads to his daughter's kidnapping by terrorists. (Curiously, it is his earlier kidnapping of his own wife, in an attempt to repair his failing marriage, that leaves the daughter alone.) In rescuing the child, the male hero usurps the parental care-giving role traditionally assigned to women. The apparent violation of the action-film convention of the heroic loner occurs through a framework that Jeffords calls "individualism as fathering" (258). When paternal duties beckon, the male hero does not abandon his dominion over public space. Instead, the family, represented by the endangered woman or child, intrudes into the space of action. In many cases, an inadequate family structure suffices to generate narrative conflict: poor parenting literally endangers children's lives. Jeffords argues that, given challenges to male power in the workplace and the U.S. political system, paternal heroes work to reclaim the world of the family as a realm of male authority:

> [T]he Terminator films are offering male viewers an alternative realm to that of the declining workplace and national structure as sources of masculine authority and power—the world of the family. It is here, this logic suggests, that men can regain a sense of their expected masculine power, without having to confront or suggest alterations in the economic or social system that has led to their feelings of deprivation. (258)

Action-film fatherhood thus offers a fantasy of autonomy, requiring no substantial behavioral change from men.

In an examination of the prevalence of families in action films, Karen Schneider notes the genre's tendency in the late 1990s to "introduce the family as the central narrative concern in a genre that previously had focused on the isolated individual—often an outsider—and/or on simple heterosexual romance."[36] Additionally, she argues, such films "effect a coalescence of the 'natural' elements of the traditional family—heroic father, supportive mother, vulnerable children—again and again" (4). These narrative shifts partly represent studios' attempts to lure families and younger viewers to theaters, offering mothers and children as supplementary, though subordinate, points of identification alongside the films' male heroes. Films such as *Lost in Space* (1998), *Batman & Robin* (1997), *The Lost World* (1997), and *Independence Day* (1996) locate families amid comic-book or science-fiction scenarios: the ostensible realism of the family structure anchors the films' extensive fantasy elements. In other films, such as *Air Force One* and *Dante's Peak*, the male protagonists' family connections denote their integrity while offering active, life-saving roles to male characters who may appear past their physical prime. In the films she analyzes, Schneider finds "a lack of faith in the rearticulation [the films] worked so hard to achieve" (5). Schneider notes the contradictions of using violent, public activity—the action film's principal convention—as a means for maintaining or repairing family ties. "Violence," she observes, "is the catalyst for and the means of rearticulation" of the family (11). She notes as well that, with the exception of *The Long Kiss Goodnight*, the films she analyzes present traditional formations of male patriarchs defending their wives and children. At one level, the incorporation of threats to the family expands the genre's narrative possibilities to include subject matter previously relegated to the private, domestic world—a sphere the genre historically neglects. At the same time, the inclusion of families facilitates the transmission of conservative principles of family structure alongside the genre's largely conservative representations of male agency. Only the *Spy Kids* trilogy (2001, 2002, 2003) upsets this arrangement, granting agency to both parents and children, and distributing this agency roughly equally among male and female characters.

Threats to children usually allow solitary, male heroes to act as guardians of the family while they engage in destructive violence. Schwarzenegger's characters in both *Terminator 2* and *The Last Action Hero* function not only as autonomous heroes but also as compelling father figures, providing fantasy alternatives to absent or inadequate parents. The two films justify their male heroes' emergency fathering by placing the threatened children in splintered families. In *Terminator 2*, young John Conner's mother first appears in a mental asylum, and when released, she devotes her energies to the film's action plot, leaving Schwarzenegger's Terminator character to spend quality time with her son. *The Last Action Hero* teams Schwarzenegger with another young waif who lives with a negligent single mother. The films combine a father–son dynamic with familiar buddy-movie conventions, making the boys both comic foils and dispensers of precocious wisdom. The adult male protagonists of *Terminator 2* and *The Last Action Hero* learn rudimentary fathering skills in their relationships with their young cohorts, but this learning occurs in public space and amid narrative action rather than in the contained domestic environment. Similarly, in *True Lies*, Harry's rescue of his daughter redeems him as a father without requiring him to deviate from his public, physical role.

Most action films negotiate domestic and family concerns by mapping these issues cursorily onto the active, public, male sphere. In *True Lies*, which begins with the domestic and the active spaces rigidly separated, the active sphere eventually subsumes the domestic. While the domestic world recedes from the narrative, its representatives, the hero's wife and teenage daughter, cross into the active sphere. The film enforces the separation of the familial and active spheres by presenting its few female characters as traditional melodramatic types: the dissatisfied wife, the wholesome but quietly rebellious daughter, and the greedy temptress. Meanwhile, male characters operate according to melodramatic, nonpsychological principles of action, and the film repeatedly substitutes visual spectacle for emotional outbursts. Notably, though, the film's interplay between the active and familial realms includes some seepage between the two spaces, which occurs because of the hero's marital crisis and because of the intrusive behavior of his misogynist partner. The partner stresses the importance of events in the active sphere (regularly citing national defense and presidential authority) while zealously monitoring and constraining the hero's domestic conduct.

The action narrative of *True Lies* concerns a dashing super-spy, Harry Tasker (Schwarzenegger), and his battle against a group of Middle Eastern terrorists. This plot is relatively conventional, but the film integrates the story of Harry's wife, Helen (Jamie Lee Curtis), who is unaware of her husband's secret identity. The film's first act comically juxtaposes Harry's spectacular exploits against his banal home life, in which he fabricates an identity as an exceptionally dull computer salesman. The couple's relationship is threatened when a used-car salesman (Bill Paxton) tries to seduce Helen by masquerading as a gallant secret agent. Harry mobilizes government forces to prevent her possible infidelity, and shortly thereafter, Harry's enemies kidnap him and his wife, at which point she discovers his real identity. Following the couple's hasty reconciliation, Harry flies off to rescue their kidnapped daughter and to prevent nuclear war. At the film's conclusion, the family appears briefly to exude domestic bliss—though the film foregrounds the relationship between the married couple rather than the family threesome—and Helen joins Harry as a secret agent.

Melodrama informs the narrative through comic references to domesticity during action sequences and through spectacular displacement of psychological crises. The film's opening sequence, in which Harry infiltrates a party at an enormous villa, places action in a melodramatic context. Harry's first line of dialogue is "Honey, I'm home," a code phrase he whispers to his nearby support team through a hidden microphone.[37] To accomplish his mission, he maneuvers through a crowded reception area, then proceeds upstairs to a bedroom, where he begins stealing computer files. As in a traditional melodramatic narrative, the sequence uses the home as a site of conflict and recognizes the residence's public/private boundaries. The notion that a male hero needs a team of hidden associates to guide him through social space recurs throughout the film: Harry's partner Al "Gib" Gibson (Tom Arnold) provides him with a cover story to explain Harry's absence to his wife and daughter, and in a later sequence, Gib phones Helen to account for Harry's late working hours as the hero sets out to pursue his foes. This later episode prevents Harry from attending the birthday party his wife and daughter have prepared for him. The film briefly shows his family's disappointment, then abandons the domestic conflict entirely by cutting away to an extended chase sequence. At the thematic level, Harry's choice of work and action over family duties exemplifies his paternal shortcomings, but the film's maintenance of viewer interest depends on such character traits. The film's adherence to genre conventions such as fast-paced narrative events, visual spectacle, and violence requires evasion of visually static domestic space. Later, the film literally activates (i.e., makes active) another domestic space, when Harry musters a commando team to intrude upon his wife at the car salesman's home, which is destroyed in the process.

The possibility of Helen's infidelity produces further opportunities for the convergence of the active and domestic spheres, figured around melodramatic representations of personal intimacy and male hysteria. In place of the heterosexual couple, the film's first third foregrounds Harry's partnership with Gib, who is a conspicuous presence in Harry's personal life. Gib appears throughout as a surrogate mate for Harry, sharing his confidences and narrating his exploits. In addition, the film thoroughly emasculates Gib's character: he rarely uses a gun or participates in action; he complains frequently about his passive, subordinate role; he chides Harry about his bravura (i.e., hypermasculine) behavior; and at one point he dances an impromptu tango with another of Harry's male cohorts. Gib's character embodies the hysterical residue of Harry's oversufficient masculinity. Harry is largely silent when he learns of Helen's possible affair, but Gib uses the situation to discourse at length about his own marital failures and his misogynist attitude toward Helen and women generally. The film presents each of these situations as comedy, relying on Tom Arnold's comic persona to soften its displays of sexism, homophobia, male hysteria, and fear of impotence. Gib verbalizes the conflicts that Harry's position—locked into conventions of action-hero autonomy—tries to conceal.

True Lies makes clear the contradictions between domestic melodrama, with its emphasis on conflicts in the personal sphere, and the action film's spectacular appropriation of melodrama. Domestic melodramas bring sublimated social and personal conflicts to the surface. Conventions of action-film heroism, however, make no allowance for family crises. The genre's emphasis on taciturnity and action leaves few options for intimate communication, a problem that informs *True Lies*'s most disturbing sequence. After removing Helen from the car salesman's clutches, Harry and Gib imprison her in a windowless room and interrogate her through a voice synthesizer that transforms their voices into a bass-heavy monotone (notably too, Harry's and Gib's voices become indistinguishable, blending into a singularly oppressive patriarchal timbre). Only with this chilling mediating device can Harry discern his wife's feelings. Immediately following this episode, Harry adopts the guise of a shadowy voyeur who forces Helen to perform an erotic dance. Here Harry again becomes voiceless, masking his identity with tape-recorded phrases spoken in a soft French accent. This scene, the only erotic interlude between Harry and Helen, appears more perverse than tender on-screen. The scene exaggerates familiar cultural conventions of gender, presenting a silent, enigmatic man, and a woman who displays her body for the male onlooker and the camera. In the scene, Helen performs a masquerade of sultry femininity to a non-diegetic rock-guitar accompaniment that stresses melodrama's musical component (and the action film's reliance on bombastic music to create intensity). The scene's narrative justification as Helen's secret-agent debut situates her in the action film's compulsory role for active women, that of the erotic but physically capable sex object (a staple of the James Bond series, for example). Significantly, Helen is mobile in the scene, dancing around the hotel room, while Harry remains static, sitting in the shadows. His inactivity sanctions her movements, as ostensibly, her dance is intended to arouse him to sexual passion. At the same time, Harry's immobility indicates his abrogation of the preferred, active male role, which results in his and Helen's subsequent capture by the film's villains. Consequently, the film calls attention to the action-hero persona's incompatibility with the responsibilities of domestic life, whether parental or sexual. In another scene, Gib temporarily dispenses with his misogynist diatribes to observe that "Helen's a flesh-and-blood woman and you're never there."

True Lies demonstrates the fallacy of omnipotent masculinity, observing that men of action make unreliable husbands and fathers. Still, the film recuperates the ideal of active masculinity by narrating domestic, usually female, characters' halting aspirations to the active realm. Comparatively, *Terminator 2* and *The Last Action Hero* both depict ideal masculinity's connection to ideal fatherhood but elide issues of paternity. The heroes of these two films serve as exemplary father figures but lack blood ties to the children they protect.[38] *True Lies* resolves the dilemma of men's lack of control over the domestic realm by subjecting Helen to action-film conventions, altering her character's previous affiliation with domesticity. During the interrogation scene, Helen exhibits traditional melodramatic characteristics, displaying an intense rage about her predicament that elicits the viewer's sympathy. Here the film operates in the melodramatic mode of recasting an overarching social problem onto an individual character. Helen's desire for adventure and excitement, manifest by her own quotidian office job and her susceptibility to the "false" secret agent's advances, mirrors the concerns of women generally relegated to subordinate or undervalued roles in patriarchal society. Notably, the film—more specifically, Helen's husband—sanctions her entry into the active realm by invoking her duty to her family, not by capitulating to her plea for a more vibrant life. (With his disguised interrogator voice, Harry tells Helen that her family will be killed if she does not become a secret agent.) When Helen finally witnesses her husband in action, she realizes that "I married Rambo" and decides to become a suitable action-hero spouse. Since the action-film structure cannot accommodate conventional marital or familial relations, *True Lies* shows Helen acquiescing to her husband's active role and eventually stepping into this role herself.

If the melodramatic mode relies on what Peter Brooks calls "moral polarization," a Manichaean distinction between personified good and evil, *True Lies*'s action milieu represents a slightly different moral universe.[39] The film identifies its villains as anti-family because of the immediate, physical threat they pose to the hero's wife and daughter. Most of the film's characters are removed from the domestic economy; like most action films, *True Lies* does not represent their personal lives. Character development functions principally to delineate characters as good or evil. Although the action film strongly associates principles of good and evil with specific characters, its moral oppositions do not bear the sharp relation to real social conditions that family-centered melodramas offer. In *True Lies*, the moral frameworks of the melodrama and the action film initially compete but are ultimately reconciled. The film first depicts Harry as a distant father and inattentive husband, but a good spy and a staunch defender of "national security." Just as Helen is oblivious to her husband's achievements, Harry cannot perceive Helen's fidelity from his position within the active sphere. Relying on surveillance technology and spy-movie logic, he interprets clandestine phone calls and secret meetings as adulterous deception (never mind that he regularly practices a similar deception), so Helen's real motives become unclear. The film's middle sequence, featuring Helen's kidnapping, interrogation and erotic dance, enters a moral gray area, representing Harry's obsessive concern with his wife's fidelity as a character flaw but also presenting viewers with the spectacle of a terrorized female protagonist. Nevertheless, at the film's conclusion, when Harry rescues his kidnapped daughter and subdues the terrorists, the film unambiguously conflates protection of the family and service to the nation.

Elements of the film's active sphere that do not engage the domestic space are clearly coded as either good or evil. The prosocial trappings of Harry's organization—the insignia carved into a marble floor reads "Omega Sector: The Last Line of Defense"—and the dutiful technocrats who appear at its headquarters connote goodness and incorruptibility. The broadly sketched characterizations of supporting characters adhere to Brooks's dictum that "melodramatic good and evil are highly personalized: they are assigned to, they inhabit persons who indeed have no psychological complexity but who are strongly characterized" (61). The iconic presence of Charlton Heston as the organization's leader and the film's recurrent displays of military pageantry similarly locate the heroes on the side of virtue. Meanwhile, the film's villains appear in luxurious settings revealed as nefarious terrorist fronts: the sexual, duplicitous villainess works in an antiquities import–export firm, but lurking in the rear of the modish office space is her sadistic male leader, clad in army fatigues. The villainess also favors evening gowns and dies in a limousine crash. As in the melodrama genre, the film scorns ostentatious wealth while displaying it extensively.

Just as *True Lies* unambiguously presents the fictional "Omega Sector" as an essential government agency, the film, like most of its generic counterparts, divorces political ideology from its complex relation to issues of race, history, and imperialism. *True Lies* recasts global political conflicts as challenges to the male hero, challenges that obscure questions of gender and domesticity. Foreign cultures and politics are relevant only as proof of the hero's omnipotence. In an article on reporter films set in the Third World, Claudia Springer suggests that the real project of such films is the construction of white male subjectivity, defined in opposition to the exoticized Other: "[W]hat the Western protagonist sees around him is often a metaphor for qualities he must confront and deal with in himself. [. . .] [T]he reporter will find himself when he understands the confusion surrounding him."[40] In *True Lies*, the hero's task is simpler still: rather than attempting to understand his enemies, he need only exterminate them, clearing away the residue of disorderly, non-Western masculinity that the terrorists represent.

By defining the hero in relation to stereotypical foreign villains, the film denotes the righteousness of his cause and neutralizes the threat of the encroaching, unstable domestic sphere. Harry's inability to communicate with his wife contrasts with the multiple languages and epigrammatic wit he brings to the active sphere. Similarly, the physical power, fluidity, and kineticism he demonstrates in combat with his Middle Eastern foes compensates for his lack of control in the domestic sphere.[41] The terrorists, particularly their leader, Saleem Abu Aziz (the only male villain the film actually names, played by Art Malik), appear as brutal fanatics, more visibly misogynist than the heroes and adherent to an unintelligible political cause. The film denies the villains any substantial historical or political foundations and presents them merely as unsympathetic killers. Their largely untranslated Arabic—Harry translates part of one speech for Helen, then reduces the rest to "blah, blah, blah"—also promotes the superficial clarity of the active sphere's moral world. Viewers need not look beyond the hero for an understanding of the alien culture. The film confirms Ella Shohat and Robert Stam's observations about the colonizing impulses of Western cinema. In *Unthinking Eurocentrism*, they argue that "the spectator, identified with the gaze of the West [. . .] comes to master, in a remarkably telescoped period of time, the codes of a foreign culture shown as simple, unself-conscious, and susceptible to facile apprehension."[42] Further support for this idea occurs in a later scene in the film in which Aziz is videotaped expressing his demands, condensing his entire political history and position into a brief, high-pitched statement. Even this episode degenerates into comedy, as a failing camera battery prevents Aziz from completing his polemic. Since the film does not allow viewers to grapple with the political conditions that motivate international terrorism, the villains' malevolence never need be questioned. The decorative (and unmistakably pejorative) application of Middle Eastern politics and ethnicity clarifies the film's moral dimension but obscures the real-world significance of politics and ethnic identity.

The film's climactic focus on the utopian space of action transforms both political and domestic conflict into visual spectacle. Viewers may take pleasure in computer-enhanced images of Harry piloting an Air Force jet and machine-gunning terrorists in a downtown office building without troubling over the scene's consequences. By foregrounding spectacular action, the sequence displaces concerns about the disproportionate use of force, property destruction, and loss of life. The scene also plays on the fantasy of demolishing the corporate infrastructure, appealing to viewers disenchanted with multinational capitalism. *True Lies*'s spectacular episodes produce substantial contradictions as well. The climactic battle sequence both validates the prosocial uses of military weaponry and celebrates mass destruction. Harry's appropriation of the fighter jet reinforces the action genre's masculinist fantasies (through his skillful operation of the jet in downtown Miami and his familiarity with its weapons systems) and lampoons those fantasies (through his clumsy takeoff, which damages a police car, another icon of authority). Another spectacular image, the nuclear blast noted earlier, celebrates reconciliation in the domestic arena but punctuates the couple's embrace with a disconcerting icon of militant male aggression.

The film's combination of the fantasy space of action with the familiar sphere of marriage and domesticity makes apparent the multiple contradictions between the two realms, even within the conventional territory of the action film. Structurally, the film makes viewers long for the realm of action by periodically depicting its bland antithesis. Despite the novelty of seeing Arnold Schwarzenegger and Jamie Lee Curtis masquerade as an ordinary couple, the scenes of domestic relations are relatively static, visually and narratively. Compositions and color choices are routine, motion is limited, and dialogue is less memorable than in action scenes (even the screwball husband–wife repartee flourishes in active rather than domestic space). To avoid an overrepresentation of middle-class monotony, the film refines the spectacular and performative qualities of melodrama while limiting melodrama's presentation of domestic life. In Richard Dyer's formulation of generic pleasures (developed in relation to the film musical), the utopian promise of intensity—which he defines as "excitement, drama, affectivity of living"—overcomes the real social experience of dreariness or monotony.[43] The presentation in *True Lies* of both dimensions, the dreary and the intense, makes evident the difficulty of negotiating between them. While the film is deeply misogynist and clearly valorizes the active sphere over the domestic, it also recognizes the masculine sphere's inability or unwillingness to accommodate domestic rituals.

Nevertheless, the domestic sphere remains here as a cherished ideal, albeit one defined through crises within it and through its vilification by the film's antagonists. The terrorists' threat to Tasker's wife and daughter indicates the nuclear family's fragility and importance. The strongest denunciation of domesticity comes from the greedy Asian American villainess, Juno Skinner (Tia Carrere), who dubs Helen "Suzy Homemaker."[44] In the action film's binary logic, villains conventionally damn the virtues that the film extols. The film's conclusion shows that women need access to the active space to achieve satisfaction and, implicitly, to prevent their husbands' flirtations with non-Western women. With the heroine's accession to a space previously reserved for men, the film synthesizes the traditional melodrama's moral clarity and the action film's logic of spectacle.

Action Cinema at the Turn of the Millennium

The masculine utopia of the action film is fraught with contradictions that become more apparent as filmmakers seek new territory onto which to graft its basic structures. Genre narratives offer a means of compartmentalizing and ordering cultural experiences, providing accessible maps of social conflicts and ideological tensions. Action films in the 1990s resolved conflicts surrounding gender in multiple ways, each of which reveals the genre's adaptability as well as the underlying repressions and evasions it practices. The genre's continued investment in paradigms of masculinity helped shape its representations of women. One approach was to remove women entirely from the narrative, as in *The Rock* or *Armageddon*. In an all-male world, gradations of masculinity appear prominent, and characters are defined through their relations to offscreen women or to feminized male characters, whether partners or villains.[45] Alternately, women sometimes retained their anachronistic function as decorative objects or impediments to masculine freedom, roles already conventionalized in gangster films and westerns as early as the second decade of the twenty-first century. Finally, action films such as *True Lies* have responded to gender issues by situating women as both heroes and villains, allowing gender conflicts to erupt into narrative. In later 1990s films with female protagonists, including *The Long Kiss Goodnight* and *G.I. Jane* (1997), women's assumption of conventionally masculine roles appears as the central narrative conflict, emphasizing gender imbalances but also limiting the narrative autonomy of women characters. *The Long Kiss Goodnight* connects the sexy assassin, a type iconized in the French thriller *La Femme Nikita* (1990), to an exaggerated version of a detective-film femme fatale. *G.I. Jane*, as its title suggests, is largely an issue film built around the subject of women's suitability for combat roles in the military. In both films, female protagonists' assumption of active roles leads to scenarios in which they are threatened with or subjected to sexual violence. Geena Davis's character in *The Long Kiss Goodnight* endures a water-torture sequence in which she is stripped to her lingerie, and in *G.I. Jane*, fellow Navy SEAL trainees sexually assault Demi Moore's character during a training exercise. In both films, women's ability to succeed in the violent, male world is measured partly through their responses to sexual threats. Action films with male protagonists, in comparison, routinely subject their heroes to torture or beatings, but without the overt threat of sexual violation. (The more female-targeted *Charlie's Angels* [2000], in contrast, presents male villains as poor romantic choices rather than sexual aggressors.) The genre's orientation toward male viewers continues to produce conflations of violent activity and sexual threats.

Another way to integrate women into action narratives is to locate them in the more traditional role of the romance heroine, with a love story situated amid explosive historical conflict. The Chinese martial-arts romances *Crouching Tiger, Hidden Dragon* (2000), *Hero* (U.S. release 2004; originally 2002), and *House of Flying Daggers* (2004) have attracted large audiences in the United States and globally through such hybridity. In Hollywood cinema, the 1997 film *Titanic* uses this combination as an alternative to the action genre's polarization between muscular, active men and hypersexualized women, offering a marginally feminist variation on the classical damsel-in-distress narrative. *Titanic*, director James Cameron's first feature after *True Lies*, operates in the narrative mode of melodrama while importing the spectacular action and visual effects germane to the action genre. Earning comparisons to *Gone with the Wind* through the marriage of star-crossed romance and spectacular destruction, but surpassing even that 1939 film's great popularity, *Titanic* became the most successful international release of all time.[46] Through its combination of a female protagonist who faces romantic and family conflicts, the presence of teen idol Leonardo DiCaprio, a historical narrative about stalwart men of honor, and elaborate production design and visual effects, the film drew huge audiences across age and demographic categories. While the film's extravagant merger of period melodrama and the action subgenre of the disaster film has not yet been replicated memorably, popular response to *Titanic*, particularly the phenomenon of repeat viewings by preadolescent girls, indicates the malleability of the action form.[47] Similar to *True Lies*, *Titanic* grants agency to a female protagonist and represents spectacular destruction as an obstacle to romantic fulfillment. The film foregrounds the emotions and experiences of its female protagonist and reimagines conventional action-film themes such as male honor and treachery in terms of their relevance to its romance plot. Similarly, formal conventions of the contemporary action blockbuster, particularly computer animation, function in *Titanic* to enhance the scope and tone of its romantic narrative. The film's kinetic visual style and lavish mise-en-scène enhance its sweeping romance as well as its propulsive action. Significantly, the film's historical setting justifies the inclusion of hoary stereotypes of male virtue: the noble captain, the sentimental but steadfast band members, the selfless working-class hero. Though none of the film's male characters fit the action-hero persona—DiCaprio's protagonist, a scrawny artist and romantic, engages in modest boy-adventurer antics but shows no exceptional physical prowess—the film supplies sufficient evidence of upright patriarchs to promote identification among male viewers less committed to the film's romance narrative. Interestingly, the film's representation of spectacular action—the sinking of a mammoth ocean liner and the corresponding human calamity—is not linked specifically to the actions of particular heroes or villains. Destructive spectacle thus proves compelling even without an identifiable human agent to set that spectacle in motion or to resolve the conflict it represents. *Titanic* suggests that the spectacular destruction characteristic of the action cinema can also punctuate romance narratives, providing emotional weight in addition to visceral pleasures.

In a decade of both superficial and real movements toward gender equality, *Titanic* used its romance-plot adornments to introduce legions of preadolescent girls to the pleasures of spectacular destruction. Action films' shifting narrative emphases may represent ideological containment strategies manifest in textual form: while *G.I. Jane*, for example, challenges the action genre's conventions of female representation, the film requires women—both as viewers and as screen subjects—to subscribe to masculine models of behavior. Heroine Demi Moore's quotable "suck my dick" taunt in the film strikes a weak blow for feminism, as it tethers her character to the legions of screen males who have used the same phrase in countless sexist and homophobic ways. *G.I. Jane* also shackles its heroine to highly conventional conflicts for women in film, including the rape threat and the need to choose between career and heterosexual romance, but represents her too in terms of the often-empowering "musculinity" Yvonne Tasker finds in many action films with women protagonists. In comparison, action films' increasingly unstable figurations of heroic masculinity in the 1990s denote texts' and viewers' growing receptivity to perspectives that do not correspond to dominant ideologies. Contemporary action films, unable to contain representations of masculinity within actors' physical bodies, channel excess masculinity into visual spectacle. If both male and female spectators recognize combat sequences, pyrotechnics, chases, and other forms of spectacular action as the hysterical residue of unstable masculinities, viewers and scholars can reclaim the action genre as a progressive cinematic form that reveals the transparent operations of the patriarchal system. Even viewers inclined to understand action films as validating conservative fantasies of male behavior may acknowledge the films' precarious logics. Ultimately, these popular texts can encourage viewers to question rather than merely celebrate conservative masculinity.

Superficially, action cinema displays no visible crisis of masculinity. Its narratives and images are overwhelmingly triumphalist, apparently signaling the unimpeded power of traditional, heroic masculinity. These triumphs are rather transparent, though; they are staged postures of utility that scarcely conceal their obsolescence. They depend upon the manufacture of a host of adversaries displaced from existing, systemic conflicts. Neither male nor female viewers can directly confront the structures of class inequity, capitalism, or the political system. Action cinema offers only avatars of these systems—wealthy terrorists, megalomaniac businessmen, malevolent politicians—and fabricates other enemies whose defeat validates traditional masculinity. Conservative male action heroes succeed most gloriously against impossible foes such as invading monsters, statistically unlikely natural disasters, and those post-Soviet Eurovillains who are inevitably bent on world domination. Antirealist Hollywood action films superficially ignore challenges to traditional constructions of manhood, but the genre's shifting narrative and thematic interests represent defensive strategies. For every action narrative claiming unsurpassed realism—*Saving Private Ryan* and *Black Hawk Down* are prominent examples—another achieves greater popularity with the antithesis of realist claims. For every *Saving Private Ryan* there are many *X-Men* (2000); for every *Black Hawk Down* there is a *Spider-Man* or *XXX* (both 2002). Realist claims and nostalgia offer powerful appeals, but so do forward-looking and fantastic screen worlds populated by correspondingly weird, wondrous, or absurd men and women.

Still, action-film narratives' artifice and exaggeration can tacitly assure viewers that "real," immutable masculinity exists somewhere beneath the gunplay and pyrotechnics. This putatively authentic masculinity is made evident through a network of narrative conventions, particularly sur-rounding the spaces apportioned to male and female characters. As action-film narratives adapt to incorporate the spheres of home and family, they consequently grant less conditional access to female viewers, who have his-torically managed those spheres. Even when patriarchal norms dominate at the narrative level, visual evidence regularly contradicts the familiar logic of action-film plots. To displace the challenges and contradictions of hysterical imagery, action films showcase militaristic pageantry and weaponry and deploy a nostalgic rhetoric of male pride and agency. In asserting patriotic or militaristic power, though, the films produce further spectacle, further hysterical disavowals of lived reality.

Early in the twenty-first century, filmmakers continue to supply viewers with nostalgic constructions of masculinity, however distant such con-structions might be from prevailing social behavior. Frequently, media discourses frame commercial revisitations of the past as necessary exami-nations, attempts to recall historical conflicts for a productive, didactic, or cathartic purpose. The flurry of military and war films released in the months following the 9/11 terrorist attacks on the United States set mostly amid earlier military conflicts—including *Black Hawk Down, Behind Enemy Lines, The Last Castle* (2002), *Windtalkers* (2002), *Hart's War* (2002), and *We Were Soldiers* (2002)—can be understood as a relevant interrogation of military culture and the nature of warfare. However, these releases also allow viewers to evade the complexities of the present and give themselves up to a global culture of militancy and aggression rather than envisioning one of diplomacy and peace. In hindsight, the promotion in 1998 of *Saving Private Ryan* and in spring 2001 of *Pearl Harbor* now resembles a media culture in search of a popular war. At the turn of the millennium, melodramatic action films and a body of related commercial discourses helped mobilize nationalistic sentiment well in advance of the 9/11 outpourings of patriotism. Even in the pre-9/11 cultural climate, popular media clearly envisioned the prosecution of a protracted war, and action films were central to this vision.

Omega Men: Late 1960s and Early 1970s Action Heroes

This chapter examines films of the late 1960s and early 1970s that reconstruct cinematic masculinity in response to the cultural destabilizations set in motion by the Vietnam War, the 1960s women's movement, and the 1960s critiques of managerial capitalism. The films call attention to the contradictions of heroic masculinity within this shifting cultural context. They also suggest, however, that men can navigate the changing cultural landscape with only minor adjustments to the violent behavior and laconic mien that characterize traditional U.S. masculinity. Many films of the period pursue this strategic realignment of traditional masculinity. I offer here close cultural readings of three in particular: John Boorman's *Point Blank* (1967), Boris Sagal's *The Omega Man* (1971), and Sam Peckinpah's *The Getaway* (1972). These films do not function immediately as signposts of the Vietnam War era in the ways that *Rambo* and *Terminator 2* brazenly signify 1980s and early-1990s cultural values. Still, these three films bear consideration because of their distillation of particular qualities of male activity and comportment during a volatile era in U.S. culture. With civil rights legislation, feminist activism, and popular opposition to U.S. military involvement in Vietnam eroding faith in traditional social and cultural institutions, Hollywood films struggled to construct characters and narratives that both mirrored the era's shifting values and preserved time-honored ethical codes and models of interpersonal relations. Films of the late 1960s and early 1970s repeatedly depicted masculinity through stoic, physically or emotionally isolated figures who combined slow-burning aggressiveness with an innate suspicion of authority, thus appealing interchangeably to militant, prosocial, and antiauthoritarian tendencies among viewers.

Point Blank, based on a 1962 novel by Richard Stark (aka prolific thriller author Donald Westlake), identifiable in many ways as a gangster film or film noir, features Lee Marvin as a surly but principled outlaw who exacts revenge on a group of corporate-style criminals. *The Getaway*, based on Jim Thompson's 1959 novel of the same title and working within the crime or heist genre, presents Steve McQueen and Ali MacGraw as a bickering criminal couple in conflict with police, corrupt prison officials, and dishonorable thieves. *The Omega Man*, based on Richard Matheson's short story "I Am Legend," depicts Charlton Heston as a gun-toting scientist who battles technophobic zombies after a deadly plague kills most of the Earth's population. In all three films, a conservatively styled, middle-aged white man—both Marvin and McQueen were in their early forties when their respective films were made, and Heston was approaching fifty—pits himself against conformist, amoral representatives of modern capitalism. *Point Blank* and *The Getaway* explicitly present white businessmen as murderous villains, while *The Omega Man*'s narrative sleight-of-hand recasts black militants as a repressive, organizational mass, led by a former television newscaster, who attempt to eradicate the new community fostered by Heston's Christ-like protagonist.

Although the three films' emphases and appeals differ, all construct prototypes for the contemporary action hero, particularly in their relative positioning of men and women. Of the three, *The Getaway* was the greatest commercial success, relying largely on the star power of McQueen and MacGraw. One of few Peckinpah-directed films set in the present, *The Getaway* merits close attention for its depictions of gender relations, its conflation of sex and violence, and its montage aesthetic. This combination of attributes occurs with some regularity in early-1970s filmmaking and U.S. culture, and anticipates as well the sensibility of subsequent films such as *Pulp Fiction*. Similarly, *Point Blank*, with its modernist narrative, pronounced visual style, and revision of the structures and motifs of 1940s and 1950s film noir, reflects prevailing attitudes toward gender and genre in its own era while prefiguring developments in contemporary Hollywood film. The Charlton Heston vehicle *The Omega Man* memorably foregrounds spectacular violence and destruction, features that most other action films of the era, including *Bullitt*, *Dirty Harry*, and *The French Connection* (1971), subordinate to elaborate narrative development, character psychology, and technical operations such as police investigations and medical procedures.

Analysis of late-1960s and early-1970s Hollywood film poses some methodological problems for the contemporary scholar. With the breakdown of the Production Code and filmmakers' increasing experimentation with film form, narrative, and genre, we might designate many films of this period as "Art Hollywood" productions (the term "New Hollywood" once referred to films of this period, but critics later began to apply it to the blockbuster era that *Jaws* initiates).[1] Because many significant late-1960s and early-1970s films operate at the margins of traditional genre schema and other broad classification methods, they elude critics' efforts to identify them as markers of cultural and industrial change. Gender-based critiques present a particular challenge, given the changing or inconsistent paradigms of masculinity that appear in Hollywood films of this period. The haziness of genre boundaries during this era, combined with films' appropriations of models of masculinity prevalent in the European art cinema, further complicates analysis of male representation. Still, we can clarify the particular strategies of gendered behavior through comparison to the more rigidly codified genre films of previous and subsequent eras. The generic frameworks of the gangster film, the crime film, and the action film—all genres originating in or developing to prominence in the United States—allow for a culturally specific analysis of U.S. films of the Vietnam era. Their borrowings from Europe aside, Hollywood films remained principally directed at U.S. audiences through the early 1970s. This chapter strives to understand Art Hollywood films—in particular, *Point Blank* and *The Getaway*—and less self-conscious texts such as *The Omega Man* in their particular social and historical contexts as well as in relation to contemporary cultural environments, both in film studies and in the U.S. film industry.

Experimentation in late-1960s and early-1970s Hollywood films derives less from studios' deliberate encouragement of creativity than from attempts to capitalize on the unanticipated success of films such as *Bonnie and Clyde* (1967) and *Easy Rider* (1969).[2] When aging studio executives found themselves at an increasingly greater remove from the emerging youth market, studios looked to young directors or those whose departures from established formulas could appeal to younger audiences.[3] Studios made further appeals to youth markets through the casting of young or nontraditional actors, men such as Warren Beatty, Al Pacino, Dustin Hoffman, Elliott Gould, and George Segal. Films also paid attention to counterculture or youth-culture interests, including popular music, fashion, sexuality, and drug use. Corporate-controlled film studios' appeals to "hip" sensibilities in the late 1960s paralleled a larger trend in U.S. business and advertising of the period: the construction of mass-produced consumer products as signifiers of nonconformity.[4] Similarly, many mainstream Hollywood films openly represented antisocial or antiauthoritarian impulses narratively and thematically. In addition to the films noted above, the works of directors such as Arthur Penn, Sam Peckinpah, and Bob Rafelson undercut prevailing notions of heroism, justice, and morality. Similarly, blaxploitation films such as *Shaft* (1971) and *Superfly* (1972) gave voice to marginalized groups and viewpoints. Such impulses would eventually be reduced to conventional devices, but in the late 1960s and early 1970s they still connoted discontent, fatalism, and rebellion. Antiauthoritarian appeals served as a lure to disaffected youth and, particularly in the case of blaxploitation, to largely unacknowledged groups such as the urban, African American working poor. In addition, such appeals distilled widespread cultural confusion and cynicism related to U.S. involvement in Vietnam and to associated popular dissatisfaction with political and corporate institutions. Nevertheless, the films of the period, and the studios responsible for them, ultimately posed few challenges to established authority. Countercultural appeals in late-1960s and early-1970s film typify the industry's efforts to exploit images of dissent for profit. Indeed, the era of putatively radical filmmaking coincided with studios' growing reliance on major international banks and the widespread purchase of film studios by major corporations such as Gulf & Western and the Transamerica Corporation. Still, even in films produced by an industry increasingly under the sway of multinational corporations, the deployment of countercultural signifiers promotes a breadth of viewing positions. However cynical their producers' motives, the films of the marginal Art Hollywood and the emerging New Hollywood offer a remarkably indeterminate range of meanings for viewers.

As numerous film historians have noted, U.S. film form and narrative from the mid-1960s onward showed the influence of the imported films from Western Europe (and to a lesser extent from Japan and Soviet countries) that attracted growing art-house audiences. Foreign films such as *Blow-Up* (1966), *A Man and a Woman* (1966), and *The Discreet Charm of the Bourgeoisie* (1972) were box-office successes in the United States. In contrast to the classical-Hollywood model of linear causality, muted sexuality, and unobtrusive visual style, European films—from directors such as Bergman, Truffaut, Bertolucci, and Fassbinder—privileged character psychology, disjunctive editing, self-conscious camerawork, and often explicit sexual behavior. European films offered models for Hollywood studios hoping to halt declines in attendance. Buoyed by these models, many major U.S. films explicitly challenged long-standing genre conventions or resuscitated supposedly exhausted genres. Robert Altman's *M*A*S*H* (1970) and Arthur Penn's *Little Big Man* (1970) updated the war film and the western, respectively, while Francis Ford Coppola's *The Godfather* (1972) revived the long-ignored gangster genre. While each of these films achieved commercial and critical success, each also occupies a genre principally invested in male experiences. Despite the ostensible sexual liberation of the late 1960s and the visibility of the feminist movement, Hollywood's experimentalism offered new possibilities mostly for male characters, filmmakers, and audiences. The woman's film did not undergo a substantive rebirth in the late 1960s and early 1970s. Instead, such films as *The Graduate* (1967) and *Shampoo* (1975) repeatedly figured female power and sexual freedom as emblematic of duplicity, treachery, and manipulativeness. U.S. films, like many of their European counterparts, continued to regard woman principally as complements or barriers to consummate masculinity.

While the gender politics of Vietnam-era films appear objectionable by the somewhat more progressive standards of the new millennium, these films' male heroes remain a point of reference for contemporary cinema culture. Tough vigilante and outsider heroes were a staple of Vietnam-era cinema, and studios retrofitted these figures for the 1990s and the following decade. The populist vigilante of *Walking Tall* (1973) was revamped for a 2004 film starring Dwayne Johnson (aka The Rock). In the 1990s, both *The Getaway* and *Point Blank* were remade, the former in 1994 with the same title and the latter in 1999 as *Payback*, a commercially if not critically successful Mel Gibson vehicle. At least among film producers, nostalgia exists too for the avowedly hardened, authentic male stars of the 1960s. Prominent talent agent Robert Newman observed in 2004:

> We have a lot of pretty guys running around with six-pack abs, but they lack authenticity and credibility. [. . .] In the 1950s a lot of men had been in the war; some of them became actors. They lived hard lives. There was a weight that came out of it. [. . .] When Steve McQueen took his shirt off, he's thin, he's not ripped. There's a hardness and danger about him because of who he was.[5]

By the early 1970s, of course, there were no young veterans of World War II or Korea, so Hollywood necessarily modeled male stars' personas on different attributes. Yet popular cinema remains in dialogue with this earlier, iconic brand of masculinity.

None of the three films studied here poses substantial challenges to prevailing cultural and cinematic models of heroic masculinity. Instead, each film, while modifying genre conventions in ways that threaten their protagonists' command of narrative space, shows the adaptability of hegemonic formations of idealized masculinity. *Point Blank*, which intimates that its protagonist is basically dead for the entire film, presents aggressive, antisocial masculinity as simultaneously timeless and anachronistic, out of step with the modern world yet still able to overcome obstacles and attract women. *The Getaway*, while acknowledging that male taciturnity and non-communicativeness pose problems for heterosexual relationships, nevertheless privileges such qualities in other contexts, particularly in the male-on-male conflicts on which action-oriented genres depend. Finally,

The Omega Man constructs its protagonist, a virile scientist, as both the cause of and solution to global suffering. Set against a postapocalyptic backdrop, the film anticipates the structure of futuristic action narratives of the 1980s and 1990s—from the initial *Star Wars* trilogy (1977, 1980, 1983) to *Terminator 2*, *The Fifth Element* (1997), and the *Matrix* series (1999, 2003)—in which the fate of humanity depends on the successful adventure of one white male. *The Omega Man* foregrounds racial conflict, but does so largely in terms of a narrative struggle between two white men, following patterns of racial discourse articulated in mainstream U.S. cinema since its inception. Each film preserves and revitalizes paradigms of masculinity that might otherwise appear incompatible with the conditions and values of contemporary Western society.

Point Blank: Modernist Noir and the Hard-Boiled Hero

Point Blank illustrates many of the characteristic features of the mainstream art cinema that develops in Hollywood from 1967 onward, a category that includes films such as *Bonnie and Clyde*, *Easy Rider*, *Five Easy Pieces* (1970), *Straw Dogs* (1971), and *Deliverance* (1973). Like many films that follow it, *Point Blank* dispenses with or self-consciously refigures genre conventions, displays considerable directorial autonomy relative to classical-Hollywood style or the highly market-conscious films of the blockbuster era, and shows the influence of the European art cinema in its unconventional narration and editing. Each of these factors accounts for the growing appeal of Art Hollywood films among younger audiences, who Hollywood recognizes as a profitable market during this period. Similarly, *Point Blank*'s defining features contribute to shifting cinematic representations of masculinity and screen violence. In its attention to genre elements and its preoccupation with codes of male behavior, *Point Blank* exemplifies the alternately stagnant and fluctuating cultural preferences surrounding the attributes of exemplary masculinity.

Point Blank features a protagonist, Walker (Lee Marvin), whose self-assured, heterosexual masculinity offers viewers a stable position from which to experience the film's substantial visual, temporal, and narrative disjunctions. The film deals with Walker's attempt to retrieve his share of the profits from a robbery in which his partners betray him by shooting him in the chest ("point blank," as the title denotes). The story, which begins in disjunctive fashion before settling into a principally linear narrative, follows Walker as he is shot and left for dead by his erstwhile partners, his wife and best friend, in a robbery at the decommissioned Alcatraz prison. With the aid of the enigmatic benefactor Yost (Keenan Wynn),

Walker is an accessory to the death of those with connections to the robbery, and during his campaign of vengeance, he becomes romantically involved with his dead wife's sister. At the film's conclusion, Walker learns that he has served merely as an unwitting henchman for his benefactor, who reveals himself as Fairfax, a member of the criminal organization who has schemed to eliminate his rivals. Instabilities abound in the film, even at the plot level: Walker's wife abandons him for his best friend, the wife's sister makes herself available sexually to both Walker and his nemesis, the film reveals Walker's benefactor to be the story's enigmatic villain, and perhaps most significantly, the film does not explain how Walker survives an apparently fatal gunshot wound. The film consistently undermines categories such as love, romance, villainy, loyalty, and morality. Nevertheless, in narrating Walker's determination to retrieve his money, the film depicts masculine will as an unflagging, inviolable condition. His single-mindedness appears also to account for his presumed immortality. The film reminds viewers of Walker's state by having many characters, upon meeting him, express astonishment that he remains alive. The film delays Walker's relentless forward momentum through flashbacks and frequent repetition of individual shots, both of which signify Walker's reminiscences. Still, the film presents the viewer with reliable narrative schema: whether dead or alive, in past or present, Walker's actions and motivations never diverge from their initial trajectory. The viewer largely shares Walker's point of view in the film, with few scenes occurring outside his immediate perspective. His steadfastness assures viewers of the film's ultimate coherence.

Unyielding determination and deathless detachment have long been hallmarks of heroic masculinity. U.S. culture—in military, corporate, political, and other realms—lionizes tenacity, endurance, and intractability as means to overcome adversity and achieve greatness. In *Point Blank*, such qualities carry Walker through his mission and render him threatening to men and alluring to women. While the silent, animated corpse would logically be neither a powerful figure nor a love object, popular cinema often figures ideal masculinity as taciturn and deathlike. Iconic figures such as Clint Eastwood's Harry Callahan character in films from *Dirty Harry* to *Sudden Impact* (1983)—and this character's many variants in Eastwood's other police films—and Sylvester Stallone's Rambo character of the 1980s embody these characteristics.[6] In each case, silent, aggressive individualism appears as a means to combat deviant behavior—whether urban crime or Third World Communist occupation—in the name of the weak and oppressed. Taciturnity similarly accounts for the ruggedly blank appeal of stars such as McQueen, whose laconic persona serves as a *tabula rasa* onto which male viewers can project themselves and female viewers can imprint the desirable qualities of their choice. Similarly, the notion of the walking corpse as male icon simultaneously mobilizes authoritarian and antiauthoritarian impulses.[7] In *Point Blank*, the undead male appears as an autonomous, dissident figure, in ambivalent relation to social order and authority. Its hero embodies mature, white male privilege while attacking white maleness in its corporate trappings. This ambivalence recalls the power dynamics of the western genre, in which (almost without exception) white male heroes mediate between the "savage" frontier and a feminized or feminizing civilization. In *Point Blank*, Walker's apparently natural combination of silent authority and visible defiance marks him as both a personification of traditional U.S. masculinity and a figure worthy of emulation by young members of the emerging counterculture (to use again the phrase coined by Theodore Roszak in 1968).[8] This latter appeal, like Eastwood's popularity among younger audiences, indicates an apparently contradictory celebration of middle-aged, aggressive masculinity as a legitimate alternative to "the system" of patriarchal capitalism.

Although Walker's stolidity and relentlessness make him a useful signpost for the viewer, such qualities do not lead to his ultimate triumph in narrative terms. Instead, in accord with the pessimistic worldview of 1940s and 1950s film noir, Walker's ascription to conventional tenets of masculinity leads only to the deaths of those he encounters. The real victor, the film suggests, is "the Organization," a diffuse body with a corporate structure and surroundings (the amorphous name of the "Multiplex Products Company," respectable offices in a downtown L.A. high-rise, limousines and private jets, and a vacation retreat for group meetings). Significantly, the film labels the modern corporation as the enemy—a familiar theme of late-1960s and early-1970s films, deployed to different effect in films such as *The President's Analyst* (1967), *Zabriskie Point* (1970), and *The Parallax View* (1974). *Point Blank* simultaneously imbues its protagonist with the same ethic of individual perseverance encouraged by corporate structure. Indeed, the film depicts the Organization's directors as self-interested and amoral, characteristics Walker possesses as well. The film legitimates Walker's pursuit of money by repeatedly emphasizing his personal and psychological motivation. Similarly, the film grants Walker a perverse set of ethics: the money in question belongs to him, viewers understand, because of his role in its theft. The film thus champions individual self-interest outside capitalism, designating such interest as a valid (if still extralegal) pursuit in a democratic society. Comparatively, the film identifies individual self-interest within capitalism—that is, the power plays among the Organization's leaders—as emblematic of greed and treachery. In this respect, the film again allows viewers to channel frustrations about "the system" while supporting capitalism's founding principles. The film's conflict between entrepreneurial capitalism, which Walker represents, and the Organization's unsavory organizational capitalism further denotes the absence of alternatives to the dominant economic system, both within the film and in the culture at large.

The opposition between the strong-willed individual and the decentralized Organization, like many of the film's oppositions, demonstrates a fundamental confusion about definitions of masculinity. The film defines Walker's masculinity as distinct from the duplicitous and mysterious world of corporations, technology, and women, yet his masculine behavior works only in relation to these other categories.[9] While iconographically he embodies the conventional role of the taciturn loner, visually and narratively the film connects him with other characters in virtually every scene. Even the rare moments in which he appears alone highlight his movement toward other characters (his ex-wife, his former friend, or the representatives of the Organization) with whom he must interact to achieve his goal. Moreover, even his monomaniacal goal requires the assistance of others—his wife's sister and his intermittently appearing benefactor, in particular—so he is repeatedly linked to other social agents. Sharon Willis, in her discussion of 1980s and 1990s action films, argues that "these contemporary representations have anxiously and unconsciously realized that masculinity never exists as such. Rather, it is constructed within relations of and to race, class, and sexuality. What these films put forward as the central figure of masculinity in crisis is really white heterosexual masculinity desperately seeking to reconstruct itself within a web of social differences."[10] Walker's crisis, betrayal by his wife and criminal partner, differs from that of the policemen protagonists of films such as *Die Hard* and *Lethal Weapon*, the subjects of Willis's study. Nonetheless, *Point Blank*'s construction of its central character similarly denotes the anxiety surrounding definitions of masculinity in a changing social world. The film defines Walker's masculinity through his ghostlike detachment, but his undead quality is itself a consequence of his involvement with other social agents. Lynn (Sharon Acker) and Reese (John Vernon), his wife and partner, conspire to kill Walker, so in the film's causal logic, they produce his masculinity. (Indeed, in flashbacks, Walker hugs Reese at a class reunion and cavorts playfully with Lynn on a beach, suggesting a different inflection of masculinity prior to his betrayal.) Thus, the film simultaneously regards masculinity as a fixed, determinate category and as a free-floating abstraction: Walker's apparent invulnerability, a mark of stability, removes him from contact with the social world, rendering him isolated and insubstantial.

The configuration of Walker's masculinity in *Point Blank* also indicates tensions between film noir's conventional schema of masculinity and the operations of masculinity in the social world. Film noir bears a long history of sepulchral protagonists, including protagonists who appear dead at the beginning of films such as *D.O.A.* (1949) and *Sunset Boulevard* (1950), and the gaunt, fatalistic characters often played by actors such as Humphrey Bogart and Richard Widmark. Whereas the dead female figure in noirs such as *Rebecca* (1940) and *Laura* (1944) operates as a locus for (usually male) obsession and objectification, the dead or deathlike male protagonist appears as a legitimate if terminal alternative to the traditional Western male hero. Principles such as world-weariness, nonconformity, and internalized violence develop in film noir as responses to hegemonic formations of idealized masculinity. In his study of classical noir, Frank Krutnik identifies these and other formations of conflicted masculinity: "Masochism, paranoia, psychosis, homosexuality, [and] various forms of 'corruptive' sexuality [are] some of the principal ways in which this crisis of confidence in the possibilities of masculine identity is articulated within the noir 'tough' thrillers."[11] Popular films sometimes channel such signifiers of troubled or oppositional masculinity into explicit physical violence. With great frequency, though, cinema figures contestatory manhood in terms of misogyny or misanthropy, akin to the "corruptive sexuality" that Krutnik notes. Character traits that originally signify opposition to prosocial forms of masculinity themselves become conventional attributes of iconoclastic loners, recognizable by their challenges to authority. In archetypal noir narratives, such figures appear wary of social connection and powerless to effect substantial changes in corporate or social institutions. Nevertheless, the personal style, charisma, and controlled sexuality of many film noir protagonists make them objects of male emulation (in terms of spectator response) and female desire (at least the desire of women characters, if not always that of women viewers).

Film noir constructs a putatively antiauthoritarian version of masculinity that appears no less "natural" than the prosocial or authoritarian male heroes who populate the western genre. In *Point Blank*, Walker's lack of human emotion somehow renders him both threatening and sensual. As part of his mission to retrieve his money, he enlists the aid of his wife's sister, Chris (Angie Dickinson). While her initial response to him is largely unemotional, his detachment later arouses her ire, and she futilely pounds him with her fists to elicit a reaction. Though he does not respond, Chris retains a sexual interest in him, and the pair eventually have sex, despite no manifestation of romantic interest on his part (the implied sex occurs off-screen, though the two appear kissing in bed). While the film shows little interest in conventional displays of love or romance, the inclusion of the sex episode within the narrative reminds viewers that Walker's masculinity includes a sort of deathless virility, a way to attract women without affection or emotions. The film thus offers viewers a fantasy of wholly autonomous male sexuality. Walker's distance from the social world leaves him without obligation, responsibility, or a need to compromise his aggressive nature. The figure of the surly male who somehow attracts women appears with some frequency in action films of the period, including *Prime Cut* (1972) and *The French Connection* (as well as *The Getaway* and *The Omega Man*, to be discussed later). While this figure implicitly rejects emerging countercultural imperatives of group solidarity and cheerfulness, he does cash in on the superficial promise of "free love" promoted in mainstream discourses about the counterculture.

Point Blank consciously imports the worldview and social relationships of 1940s and 1950s film noir into the tumultuous social climate of the late 1960s. Like much 1940s and 1950s film noir, *Point Blank* simultaneously represents women and capitalism as threats to its male protagonists. The post–World War II era and the Vietnam War era align somewhat in their perceptions of working women. Feminist demands for women's equality in the late 1960s paralleled the World War II era integration of women into the U.S. workplace. Correspondingly, just as women were dismissed from many public roles at the end of the War, 1960s feminists were widely demonized for their perceived antagonism to traditional social structures. Both eras' representations of diminished male power reflected anxieties about expanded women's roles in U.S. society. Though the business world of the late 1960s remained an overwhelmingly male province, both in sheer numbers and in preferred codes of behavior and style, postwar models of organizational capitalism encouraged a mode of interpersonal conduct in which traits long connoted as feminine replaced or stood alongside traditionally masculine attributes. Corporate management style promoted qualities such as cooperation and diplomacy—social attributes that, even in the late 1990s, are usually associated with women rather than men—over or in tandem with putatively masculine virtues such as individualism and aggression. Such a redefinition of normative gender roles under capitalism, coupled with the reduced utility of physical strength thanks to the growth of white-collar occupations, facilitates the conception of corporate institutions as inherently emasculating.

Point Blank, reviving a persistent theme of film noir, depicts its protagonist's ineffectualness in the face of monolithic, capitalistic institutions. The film represents the Organization as omnipresent and cryptic, led by quarreling, ambitious men yet filled with compromising, subservient (and thus inadequately masculine) aides. In the logic of *Point Blank*, the modern, capitalist world appears cold and mechanical as well as feminized. For example, when Walker visits the Organization's offices, he first encounters a female receptionist, who hampers his mission with business-world protocol. The receptionist occupies the traditional role of woman as emblem of corporate friendliness, acting both as a welcoming receiver of guests and as a gatekeeper, a boundary through which others must pass to reach the men who control the company. Walker asserts his physical dominance over women and weak men—the receptionist and a host of unarmed, unintimidating bureaucrats—but his presence does not substantially alter the practices of the institution he challenges. Walker repeatedly overpowers the Organization's underlings to gain entrance into homes and offices, yet no one in the Organization capitulates to his demands for money, and at the film's denouement, Walker learns that he has been unwittingly aiding one of the group's leaders throughout the film. The film contrasts Walker's futile attempts to exert control over his world with Chris's successful efforts in related areas. In a scene in which Chris expresses her frustration at Walker by turning on all the appliances, lights, and other mechanical devices in the Organization's meeting compound, she appears to have a near-magical control over capitalist consumer products. She leaves Walker's side for only a few seconds of screen time, after which all of the house's appliances begin to operate in noisy synchronicity. Like the presentation of the receptionist as corporate sentry, the cacophonous-appliance scene conflates female power and capitalist technology and presents both as challenges to secure masculinity.

Point Blank, like many other films of its era, offers masculine authority as a means to forestall the challenges posed by feminism and capitalism. Throughout the film, Walker appears at odds with the modern, urban world in which he operates: he refuses to die or to accept corporate doctrine, and he does not participate in the domestic or consumer economy. The film rarely shows Walker driving a car—in cinema, usually an essential accouterment of the contemporary, autonomous, mobile, virile man— and he never appears in an apartment of his own. He is usually transported in other peoples' cars or simply appears at his destinations, and he occupies only other peoples' houses or apartments (Lynn's, Chris's, Reese's, and the Organization's, in turn). Representationally, the film offers him as able and self-assured in these situations, not as passive or dispossessed; he is neither obliging guest nor compliant passenger. Unburdened by domesticity or material possessions, Walker acquires a timeless, ahistorical quality. Marvin's other roles in mid- to late-1960s films demonstrate a star persona that moves fluidly among historical periods: he appears in westerns such as *Cat Ballou* (1965) and *The Professionals* (1966), World War II films such as *The Dirty Dozen* (1967) and *Hell in the Pacific* (1968), and modern crime films such as *The Killers* (1964). Other "tough-guy" stars of the era, including McQueen, Eastwood, and Charles Bronson, played a similar range of roles. The relative portability of the tough-guy character suggests that such a figure operates with equal potency across generic and historical categories. Though *Point Blank* reveals the inefficacy of such a type through Walker's ultimate failure to achieve his goal, the film nevertheless presents Marvin's masculinity as a model worthy of emulation. Implicitly, then, feminism's and capitalism's common refusal to accommodate such masculinity distinguishes both systems as opponents rather than allies of aspiring men.[12]

At the level of visual style, *Point Blank* privileges Marvin's masculine comportment even as it depicts an unbalanced, disorienting physical world. The film includes many arresting and unconventional frame compositions, and the frequent violation of continuity-editing principles intensifies the effect of the film's visual irregularity. Despite this destabilization, Walker as a figure continues to provide viewers a stable reference point. The film's opening scene, against which the title credits appear, shows his apparent death, with him lying on a concrete floor in the shadows of a dingy prison cell. However, a sequence shortly after his "resurrection" puts him in long shot, striding purposefully and alone down a long airport corridor. A montage of other brief shots follows, with multiple cuts back to the walking sequence, in which Walker, now in a medium shot, gazes head-on into the camera. During this period of rapid crosscutting, Walker's continuing, metronomic footsteps dominate the soundtrack, granting him a presence even in shots in which he is not visible. The interruption of Walker's movements diminishes his visual authority: just as the film surrounds him with modern technology, it literally truncates his actions through editing. Still, the film continuously depicts Walker in dominant or aggressive positions. In a sequence late in the film, a low-angle shot shows Chris, frustrated by Walker's stoicism, pounding on his chest until she collapses at his feet. The film then cuts to a high-angle shot of Walker standing motionless over her crumpled body, calling to mind cinematic and classical-art images of statuesque conquerors towering over defenseless maidens (or in retrospect, similar views in artist Frank Frazetta's fantasy poster art of the 1970s and 1980s).

Earlier, in depicting Walker's attempt to gain revenge for his wife and friend's betrayal, the film demonstrates the sexual connotations of his aggression. Following the walking sequence, Walker drives to his wife's apartment, where he bursts through the front door with gun in hand, grabbing her violently and looking for his nemesis Reese. He then races to the bedroom, where he unloads a series of bullets into the empty bed. In the wake of this violent episode, Walker slumps into a living-room couch, where Lynn then calmly relates the story of her growing affection for Reese (leading into a flashback sequence that shows Walker romancing Lynn, then the couple interacting with Reese). Walker then falls asleep on the couch, and the film replays, in slow motion and with slightly varied camera placement, multiple shots of him entering the apartment and firing his gun. This flashback, representing Walker's interiority, shows the film's preoccupation with his actions. In another representation of this interiority, the film repeats parts of the opening scene, in which Reese shoots Walker. While these flashbacks establish the dominance of Walker's perspective in the film, they also reenact his failures. The repetition of Walker's bedroom attack underlines the failure of his aggression, which the film represents as a deficiency of the sexual component of his masculinity. His return to the bedroom, the literal site of his sexual failure, also proves fruitless. Walker discharges his revolver—which throughout the film functions almost as an extra limb, used both as a shooting weapon and to perform manual tasks such as pointing and bludgeoning—and harms only a mattress, in a display of ineffectually "spent" masculinity. To compound the futility of this effort, the damaged mattress is shortly replaced with a pristine one (the film does not show this exchange, performed apparently by unseen emissaries of the Organization), removing the evidence of Walker's visit. Meanwhile, Walker sleeps on the couch, denoting his ouster from the conjugal bed. In the same episode, Lynn dies from an overdose of pills, and her body then disappears, doubly indicating Walker's inability to perform the role of protective husband.

The film's simultaneous emphasis on the figure of the male hero and on his repeated failures coincides with classical film noir's interest in the embattled, desperate male hero. Visually, though, *Point Blank* presents a world far afield from the nocturnal chiaroscuro that characterizes the visual style of film noir. The film lacks film noir's signature emphasis on nighttime settings, instead focusing on outdoor scenes amid sterile, colorless Los Angeles commercial sprawl—apartment blocks, car dealerships, airports, and other unmythical, quotidian settings. In place of traditional film noir darkness and shadow, *Point Blank* presents a world of distorted, antirealist color. In contrast to the highly saturated color of contemporary thrillers, *Point Blank* deliberately employs a desaturation process that, according to Boorman, results in a nearly black-and-white effect.[13] Often eschewing primary colors and emphasizing instead a wide variety of midtones, the film offers a world lacking in absolutes. The scene of Walker's violent intrusion into Lynn's apartment, for example, occurs literally in a gray area. Though an invader, Walker, in a slate-gray suit, blends completely with the setting, which features couches, chairs, carpeting, and wallpaper all in virtually identical shades of gray. In another scene, set in an Organization office, all the characters—including Walker and an assortment of his adversaries—wear jackets, shirts, and ties in slightly different shades of green. Other elements of the scene's mise-en-scène—curtains, walls, decorative objects, a desk phone—also appear in shades of green.

The visual world thus appears both highly regularized and impossibly distorted. Walker's chromatic harmony with his enemies both underscores the warped order of his surroundings and identifies him as partially complicit with the systematic masculine world that bedevils him. Significantly, the film envisions women differently, particularly in its adornment of Angie Dickinson's character with clothing in shades of yellow, gold, and red, colors that also permeate the settings in which she appears.

Point Blank, like traditional film noir, depicts the damage done to human relationships by impersonal social forces and institutions. The film also recalls film noir's fusion of female sexuality and male violence. In films such as *Double Indemnity* (1944) and *Kiss Me Deadly* (1955), women's calculated or cynical choices of sexual partners provoke male-on-male violence. *Point Blank* emphasizes a similar causality by locating its betraying women amid scenes of male violence, often as the sexual prizes around which men orbit. To facilitate his entry into Reese's guarded penthouse apartment, Walker asks Chris to create a distraction by initiating a bedroom rendezvous with Reese. The scene accords with the conventional pattern (in film noir, the spy thriller, and later the action film) of offering women as sexual bait to snare a predatory male villain. In *Point Blank*, men then retaliate against the women they have forced into sexually compromised situations (*The Getaway*, considered next, follows the same trajectory). The film connotes Chris's behavior both as an act of selfless courage—she disparages Reese repeatedly in dialogue, and her facial expressions and body language during her feigned seduction convey further disgust—and as a display of women's facility with sexual activity. The film's objectification of Chris is modest in comparison with other films of the period: only her bare back is shown, while Reese, bare-chested and wrapped only in a bedsheet, appears far more sexually vulnerable in subsequent shots. Still, the film invites viewers to take pleasure in her brief tryst as it foregrounds her body as an erotic commodity. Once Walker arrives to menace Reese, Chris disappears from the frame of action. She returns minutes later, long after Reese has fallen, naked, to his death. The film makes Chris partially culpable for this death, though, as her action lures him into a vulnerable condition. In a scene that follows shortly thereafter, another Organization leader chides Reese's guards for allowing Chris into the penthouse, further indicating her responsibility for Reese's death. Walker's culpability is presented ambiguously, because while he manhandles and threatens the vulnerable Reese, the latter appears to stumble from his penthouse balcony without being pushed by Walker, who reaches out for his cuckolder as if trying to prevent his fall.

The film's emphasis on the influence of female sexuality corresponds to rising popular anxieties about waning male power. Second-wave feminism, alternate models of masculinity developed by the nascent hippie and student-activist movements, and U.S. men's continued, unsuccessful engagement in Vietnam all contributed to public apprehension about the utility of traditional male roles in the late 1960s. Films often manifest such apprehension through insistence on the efficacy of traditional sex roles as well as through displacement of blame for men's shortcomings onto women. In *Point Blank*, just as Chris's sexual performance precedes Reese's death, Lynn's earlier affair leads to Walker's apparent demise. In film noir and the gangster film, women—prostitutes, gun molls, gold-digging mistresses, and the like—repeatedly orchestrate betrayals of men. *Point Blank* updates the concept by giving women instrumental roles in the formerly homosocial criminal world. In the flashback sequence that encapsulates her role in the story, Lynn appears first as Walker's domestic companion, then as a partner to both Walker and Reese, then as a participant in the Alcatraz robbery in which Reese shoots Walker. Walker and Reese's friendship bridges the worlds of work and leisure: the film depicts them as old friends who meet at a reunion and subsequently plan a crime. The inclusion of a woman in the men's private and public worlds disrupts both spheres. Notably, the film also insists upon exaggerated male bonding as a precedent to betrayal. Walker's memories of Reese include repeated scenes of the two men embracing, while the film never shows Walker embracing his wife. One repeated shot from their reunion scene shows Walker and Reese lying on a floor in a drunken clinch, while a crowd of other men step over and around them. The shot highlights the incongruity between male camaraderie and public intimacy. In one interpretation of such a dynamic, the social autonomy that women gain during the 1960s precipitates the dissolution of traditional male relationships, giving way to enmity and distrust. The film does suggest that overdetermined male bonds, rather than explicit female manipulativeness, result in male discord. Men's volatile social relations with each other, however, correspond to women's rising autonomy, their presence in both private and public spheres. The film represents triangulated desire as a condition that inevitably leads to betrayal and violence, and women play an active, if unprofitable, role in this equation.

Women's infidelity initiates male-on-male conflict in many texts throughout history, from Homer's *Iliad* to Claude Chabrol's *La femme infidèle* (1960) and Truffaut's *Jules and Jim* (1961). In late-1960s and early-1970s films, female infidelity gives rise to particular anxieties about male social roles. The birth-control pill, approved by the U.S. Food and Drug Administration in 1960 and in wide usage by the mid-1960s, grants women a measure of control and safety in sexual relations, eliminating the high risk of pregnancy that multiple sexual encounters previously posed.

Nevertheless, the so-called sexual revolution of the 1960s weighed more heavily on women, who still face moral and social condemnation for choosing multiple sexual partners, than on men, for whom promiscuity remains a mark of virility rather than a stigma. In *The Getaway* as well as *Point Blank*, women who use sex to achieve particular goals face enduring stigmatization, even if they act out of allegiance to male protagonists rather than for personal gain. For men, though, breaching ethical codes through violence, or failing in their implicit roles as protectors of women, represents only a partial, impermanent blemish on the masculine character.

The Getaway: Cathartic Violence and the Resuscitation of Masculinity

Like *Point Blank*, *The Getaway* foregrounds issues of male protectiveness and female infidelity, placing these issues amid a generic bank-robbery narrative. *The Getaway* begins by depicting its protagonist's internment in a sterile, impersonal penal system. Following opening shots of animals grazing outside a prison, the film's first scenes depict prison life, in which mostly white men in their thirties and forties clad in clean white shirts and pants perform moderate labor (working in a machine shop and clearing brush). For the present-day viewer, such scenes connote tedium and sterility rather than grim repression. In 1972, though, many years before the public awareness of prisons as violent, nonrehabilitative detention facilities for young men of color, scenes of white men working listlessly at menial tasks could still convey distressing impressions of servitude. The opening scene visually emphasizes confinement, displaying the prison's multiple gates and bars, bare walls, and noninteracting inmates and guards. These images contrast with brief, intercut shots of the protagonist, Doc McCoy (Steve McQueen), in a tender embrace with a woman, who is soon identified as his wife, Carol (Ali MacGraw); but in the film's early moments these shots represent an unattainable freedom and intimacy. The extended opening sequence alternates chronological narratives in a montage fashion. Shots of Doc's parole-board hearing, routine prison labor, and the flashback sequence involving Doc and his wife provide overlapping areas of engagement for viewers. The disordered montage, however, disrupts viewers' integration into any discrete episode. As in *Point Blank*, self-conscious montage editing makes viewers aware of the film's technical operations, creates narrative enigmas, and distances viewers from screen characters. Also like *Point Blank*, *The Getaway* narratively presents social institutions such as the prison system and corporate capitalism as deeply estranging.

The Getaway follows Doc and Carol, who reunite when Doc leaves prison. Doc gains release upon two conditions: unbeknownst to him, Carol must have sex with corrupt businessman and parole-board member Benyon (Ben Johnson), and Doc must help perform a bank robbery that Benyon plans. The robbery takes place, but another participant betrays the group; Doc and Carol escape with the robbery money, and Carol kills Benyon. The film's third act depicts the couple's flight from their accomplices in the robbery, from Benyon's corrupt-businessmen associates, and from the police. Doc and Carol work together during the robbery and the subsequent pursuit, but his discovery that Carol has slept with Benyon strains their relationship. Ultimately, Doc accepts his wife's devotion, and the outlaw couple escapes to Mexico.

The film combines multiple car chases and gun battles with continuous narration of the couple's attempted reconciliation. Their marriage appears troubled even when the two first reunite, with Doc remaining aloof and Carol making small talk about a visit to the hairdresser. After an idyllic swim, the two return home, where they strip off their clothes, preparing for sex. To Doc's dismay, he is unable to become sexually aroused, as euphemistic dialogue informs us. The scene does not follow cinematic conventions for sex or seduction, even the perfunctory displays characteristic of the genre. Action films, both during the late 1960s–early 1970s period and the 1990s, tend to restrict sex episodes to brief sequences of disrobing and embracing, proving the male's sexual prowess but not diverting substantially from overarching narrative concerns or demonstrations of aggressive masculinity. (However, an action subgenre, the 1970s blaxploitation film, often devotes considerable screen time to the hero's sexual interludes.) Sex scenes in male-oriented genres such as the cop film or the crime film tend to emphasize the male participant's virility and also his tenderness (in contrast to the aggression he can display publicly), alongside the woman's desirability and willingness. *The Getaway*, however, highlights Doc's sexual dysfunction, and attributes his awkwardness to the dehumanizing—or specifically, demasculinizing—conditions of prison life. Doc explains his lack of arousal by stating, "It does something to you in there," and Carol, in turn, plays the role of a patient and accepting partner. This exchange in some ways reverses conventional patterns of gender representation and partially destabilizes the notion of effortless male sexuality. Still, the scene concludes with the suggestion of sexual fulfillment, as the two appear in a happy romantic embrace before the cut to the next scene occurs.

The Getaway presents male decisions and prerogatives as the primary determinants of the couple's relationship. Doc's discovery of his wife's extramarital encounter provides the principal stress on their relationship, a stress that adds to the difficulty of their extended getaway. As such, Doc's response—rather than Carol's act or her own response to it—becomes the standard by which the film judges their situation. While the film represents Carol consistently as a believer in the relationship, it implies that only Doc's forgiveness will restore the bond between the two. In terms of a sexual economy based on conquest, Carol ostensibly "wins" the sexual battle by gaining an additional sexual partner, Benyon. (Only in the most perverse sense is this true, of course; objectively, the rapacious Benyon wins.) Doc, the cuckolded husband and sexually inactive prison inmate, loses. At the bodily level, though, Carol loses by prostituting herself, giving up her body to an undesirable sexual partner who has the power to free her husband. Though the imprisoned Doc is powerless to gain his own release, he also faces no bodily risk. His own body remains untainted by nonconsensual sex. Instead, the terms of his release degrade Carol. Notably, the film depicts Doc as initially unaware of the sacrifice his wife will have to make. Following his failed parole-board hearing, he meets with Carol during a visiting period, where he instructs her curtly, "Get to Benyon. Tell him I'm for sale—his price. Do it now." The conversation appears to display Doc's directness, his angry capitulation to Benyon's unstated job offer. The viewer soon learns, however, that the barter includes Carol. In effect, Doc's brusque instructions to Carol transform her into a unit of exchange. In this respect, the film implicitly critiques notions of male self-sufficiency. Doc's selfish belief that only he will have to compromise himself for Benyon results in Carol's fall from marital grace. The film later refers back to Doc's oversight when Carol accuses him of initiating her meeting with Benyon. Except for the scene in which Carol shoots Benyon as he prepares to tell Doc of her infidelity, the film generally presents Carol's concerns about the encounter as secondary to Doc's wounded ego.

The film mirrors Doc and Carol's troubled relationship with its depiction of another sordid, triangulated affair. After the robbery, the other surviving participant, Rudy (Al Lettieri), whom Doc has wounded and left for dead, kidnaps a married couple and uses their car to pursue Doc. The film portrays this relationship in an unusually misogynist fashion, even in comparison to the explicit antipathy to women shown in other Peckinpah films such as *The Wild Bunch* and *Straw Dogs* and other well-regarded films of the period such as *Five Easy Pieces*. In *The Getaway*, the kidnapped wife, Fran (Sally Struthers), appears as a dim sex object bored with her straitlaced husband, Harold (Jack Dodson), and fascinated by the crude, aggressive Rudy. Fran begins an affair with Rudy, to which the cuckolded Harold responds by hanging himself. In this episode, unchecked female sexuality proves lethal for the inadequate husband. The grim parallels to Doc and Carol's own predicament make the two protagonists appear considerably more deserving of the viewer's sympathies. Fran acts impulsively, or at best, out of self-preservation. Her affair with Rudy, unlike Carol's encounter with Benyon, appears unmotivated by concern for her husband's safety. Similarly, Rudy's physical violence against Fran (he assaults her both before and after she flirts with him) contrasts substantially with Doc's treatment of Carol, in which abuse occurs principally at the verbal level. Moreover, the film permits Carol to respond to Doc with insults of her own, granting her a degree of agency unavailable to Fran.

Contrasts among the criminals similarly establish Doc's authoritative presence as a laudable model of masculinity. Between Doc's reunion with Carol and the execution of the bank robbery, a short but detailed planning sequence distinguishes Doc's professionalism from his cohorts' wholesale wickedness. In this sequence, Benyon introduces Doc to the two other participants in the robbery, Rudy and Frank (Bo Hopkins), and the assembled participants later meet in a storeroom to discuss the logistics of the operation. The film presents the two other men as seasoned, untrustworthy criminals. Meanwhile, Doc appears as an outsider, not aligned with his partners or with Benyon, and he operates as a professional, efficient manager during the storeroom conference. Doc wears a formfitting black sweater (a conventional, utilitarian uniform for a bank robber or safecracker) and glasses (indicating a cerebral nature that marks him as the ideal organizer of this group; he does not wear glasses in any other scene) as he pores over blueprints and timetables and gives orders to the other men. Rudy and Frank, in contrast, appear tackily dressed and poorly groomed, with long, unkempt hair and gaudy shirts and coats. (In short, they look like 1972 heist-film thugs, while McQueen takes on a more traditional style, of mid-1960s vintage.) The other men also appear inattentive, overconfident, and vain: Doc chides Frank for not paying attention while Frank casually runs a comb through his hair, and Rudy scornfully rebuffs Doc's suggestion that he wear a bulletproof vest. Consequently, while the film denotes Rudy and Frank as willing participants in Benyon's enterprise, the individualized Doc exhibits behavior most in accord with codes of managerial efficiency. As in *Point Blank*, the male iconoclast appears best suited for the work of organizational capitalism, the system he explicitly opposes.

Doc's management of the robbery anchors the film's narrative in real-world logistical minutiae: timetables, electrical and alarm systems, transportation, tools, and personnel. The complicated logistics bear only on the robbery itself and lose significance immediately thereafter. In the manner of contemporaneous films such as *The French Connection* and *Charley Varrick* (1973), the intricacies of police or criminal procedure provide viewers a measure of cerebral involvement, followed by the cathartic release of a spectacular chase or gun battle. Such details help to ground the film in conventional generic terrain. Whereas earlier sequences disrupt linear causality, the robbery planning returns viewers to the level generic ground of crime procedure. Once the narrative turns to the planning of the robbery, the film's editing assumes a consistent pattern of linear causality. With crosscutting among various characters' activities, the men and Carol visit the bank, meet to plan the crime, disperse to acquire supplies, rejoin for the robbery itself, split into pairs for the getaway, and finally, meet again to consolidate the stolen money. Doc supervises this series of activities either personally or by prior instruction until the getaway, when he crashes a getaway car, and Rudy, in another vehicle, shoots Frank. The shooting displays Rudy's insubordination, whereas Doc's crash provides the film's first incident of kinetic, chaotic spectacle. Rather than appearing as a failure of Doc's driving abilities, the crash grants viewers a moment of spectacular fulfillment. Slow-motion photography of the car crashing into a residential porch dilates the event and heightens its visual impact.

The robbery and subsequent escape represent a fantasy of managerial aptitude that occupies viewers cognitively and viscerally. The violent shooting and the crash transform the otherwise straightforward exercise of the robbery into an active, arresting display. The participants receive both financial reward and the danger and thrill of pursuit, a thrill viewers experience vicariously. Like other action narratives of the period, *The Getaway* uses technical and logistical elements to suspend resolution. In its depiction of the robbery planning, the film presents a limited number of variables that viewers can reasonably apprehend. The film thus constructs viewers as, like Doc, experts on the impending robbery. *The Getaway* rewards viewers' engagement in narrative complexities, and the final presentation of the nearly successful event satisfies viewers who have followed the intricate plan closely. Informed viewers can identify the mistakes made during the robbery and anticipate upcoming narrative developments. Similarly, crosscutting during the getaway includes shots both of narrative relevance and of principally visual interest. The film grants access to Doc and Carol's perspective through point-of-view shots of the getaway car's interior, and shots of Frank's killing appear from two angles, an inside-the-car shot and a long shot showing his dead body rolling from the car. The sequence returns repeatedly to shots of a burning building and car, reminding viewers of the destruction the robbery causes. As in other action narratives, such images foreground pyrotechnic spectacle rather than essential story information.

The entire robbery sequence follows a generic pattern that is also closely aligned with capitalist principles of organized, directed work: deliberation, planning, performance of a task, and resolution. Rudy's treachery partly undermines this efficient labor. A greater source of conflict, though, and a larger area of the film's investment, is Carol herself. Her sexuality, her mindset, and her mere presence—in short, her femininity—deform and reshape the male heist narrative. Doc performs his appointed tasks without error or delay, while women and less competent men make mistakes: Frank shoots a guard, and Carol stalls a getaway van. The film uses such errors as evidence of character predilections. The devious Rudy soon murders the unwitting Frank, and Carol later loses the robbery money to another thief, an event Doc disparagingly refers to as "the oldest con in the book." Displaying his partners' explicit failures, the film by default acclaims Doc's worldliness and skill. Carol herself participates in Doc's public, work life, implicitly as a subordinate, since he leads the operation. The film thus frames Doc's admonishment of Carol's mistakes as the justifiable prerogative of a demanding manager, though viewers might also regard it as the vindictive bullying of an insecure husband. The film provokes this second view later as well, when Doc slaps Carol repeatedly after learning of her liaison with Benyon. Even when Carol places the responsibility for her tryst on Doc, saying "You sent me to him, you know," Doc does not respond. By never requiring Doc to acknowledge his own guilt overtly, the film permits his character to remain virtuous, diminished only by Carol's actions and accusations. The film indicates Doc's contrition only through the gradual return of his affection for Carol, never obliging him to compromise his masculine ethic of silence and reproach. Instead, his ability to work through his internal crisis silently and invisibly codes him as, if anything, more masculinely self-possessed. The outward signs of Doc's masculinity—his stern expression, his conservatively stylish clothing, his aggressive driving—remain constant, as does his aptitude for violence. Unlike *Point Blank*, in which Walker's failed marriage leads to his physical vulnerability, *The Getaway* does not translate Doc's failings as a husband into a failure at aggression. Though cuckolded, and though he and Carol experience repeated setbacks in their attempts to escape their pursuers, Doc ultimately retains his wife's devotion and successfully eludes or overcomes his adversaries.

Although *The Getaway* presents Doc's stubbornness and anger as the basis for a predominant narrative conflict, ultimately the film validates a model of aggressive, emotionally suppressed masculinity. The psychological travails of the couple's relationship coincide with their physical distress. Carol loses the money during a period of physical and emotional vulnerability, just after Doc assaults her. Similarly, at the nadir of their relationship, the pair must leap into a passing garbage truck that deposits them at a large trash dump. By this point, the film's action plot has metaphorically bullied its romance elements into submission. Of course,

Hollywood films of many genres link action and romance narratives. By virtually fusing those two plotlines, though, *The Getaway* requires that the romance ascribe to the conventions of a male-oriented genre narrative. (Using a formulation from Steve Neale, we could say that the film is generically modeled as action, while it bears only the generic markings of a romantic melodrama.[14]) The couple's perseverance through action defines their relationship. Largely foregoing displays of intimacy between the couple, the film presents their mere togetherness as a sign of love and fealty, thus according with a familiar belief in a man's sheer physical presence as a sign of commitment. Inflections of femininity do not bear on the story's outcome. The couple's physical triumph over Rudy and Benyon's accomplices occurs through Doc's skill and good fortune, not Carol's own agency. The film's closing episode similarly views heterosexual relationships from an exclusively male perspective. Doc and Carol hitch a ride in the pickup truck of an elderly cowboy (Slim Pickens), who voices his approval of their marriage and the marital institution generally, although his own wife does not appear in the scene. By rewarding this cowboy with a portion of the stolen money, the film reinforces a traditional, patriarchal version of marriage in which women function as material support for male activity or hallowed but invisible objects of esteem.

The Omega Man: The Future of Embattled Manhood

Steve McQueen's dispassionate masculine presence accounts substantially for his enormous popularity in the 1960s and 1970s. In films such as *The Great Escape* (1963), *Bullitt*, and *The Towering Inferno* (1974), McQueen appears as a highly competent Everyman who exudes charisma despite lacking any particular verbal flair or captivating mannerisms. With McQueen, the introverted, undemonstrative man becomes a celebrated man of action. Aspects of his offscreen persona testify to the supposed authenticity of this masculinity: in addition to performing many of his own film stunts, he was an accomplished automobile and motorcycle racer.[15] McQueen's casual masculinity contrasts sharply with the more deliberate masculinity embodied by Charlton Heston, popular hero of mainstream religious epics such as *The Ten Commandments* (1956), *Ben-Hur* (1959), and *El Cid* (1961) as well as the more fantastic *Planet of the Apes*. Heston's epic, active masculinity serves as a prototype for the nearly invulnerable action heroes of the 1980s, including characters played by actors such as Sylvester Stallone and Arnold Schwarzenegger. In *The Omega Man*, Heston's bravura monologues, his air of unflagging self-assurance, and his ability to ward off a mob of assailants single-handedly all construct a form of heroic masculinity that films such as *Rambo* and *Commando* (1985) refine still further. As in the two 1980s films, *The Omega Man* presents militant masculinity as both the cause of and solution to international and local conflicts.

Compared to expensive, elaborately produced science-fiction films such as *Planet of the Apes* and *2001: A Space Odyssey* (1968), Warner Brothers's *The Omega Man* is a relatively modest affair, with special effects limited to small fires and explosions, brief car and motorcycle pursuits, stuntmen's acrobatics, and fanciful makeup. The film's premise, that a biological virus has killed most of Earth's population, results in a "less is more" approach toward visual spectacle. The film's opening scenes, for example, consist of shots of Heston's character, Robert Neville, driving around deserted downtown Los Angeles, and these shots achieve visual impact through the sheer absence of people and movement. Neville is an Army scientist trying to develop a vaccine to counteract the germ-warfare virus, which kills its victims or transforms them into nocturnal albinos. Neville faces an antitechnology cult of mutants led by the charismatic Matthias (Anthony Zerbe), who appears as a television newscaster in flashbacks to the pre-plague era. As the film progresses, Neville locates a hidden group of unharmed human survivors, romances one of their leaders, Lisa (Rosalind Cash), and ultimately dies a martyr after successfully concocting a serum that can defeat the virus. The film's fantastic, apocalyptic narrative uses conventional linear storytelling, diverging from linearity only for a few expository flashbacks presented as Neville's memories.

The Omega Man's fanciful narrative, inexpensive spectacle, and images of a shirtless Heston—forty-seven years old during the film's production, and looking no younger—patrolling Los Angeles can appear unintentionally humorous by contemporary standards. Nevertheless, its depiction of a super-heroic white man as the savior of humanity anticipates many later science-fiction and action narratives, including *Star Wars, Blade Runner* (1981), *The Terminator* (1984), and *Total Recall* (1990). *The Omega Man* defines Neville as global savior through multiple plot conceits: he develops the experimental vaccine, he tests the vaccine on himself (thus making his blood the source of antibodies), he uses a transfusion of his own blood to save a plague victim, and immediately prior to his death, he turns over a jar of his curative blood to another scientist. In addition, in presenting Neville as an Army scientist who abandons his military affiliation to save humanity, the film enters the familiar narrative territory of male redemption, albeit on a public and fantastic, rather than a personal, scale. The overdetermination of Heston's agency within the narrative testifies to the film's anxieties about masculinity (particularly white masculinity), anxieties that later films continue to manipulate profitably. *The Omega Man* further constructs Heston's character as a fantasy of autonomous masculinity through its attention to material possessions and sartorial style. Neville drives a series of sporty convertibles, alternates among various conventional hero outfits (a safari jacket, a zip-up track suit, and a military jumpsuit, with dark sunglasses accompanying each), and lives in a fortified brownstone filled with video monitors and museum-quality artworks. Heston's character thus embodies both a *Playboy* or James Bond lifestyle of bachelor luxury and a more retrograded male fantasy of violent self-preservation in a postapocalyptic setting.

By narrating the villains' repeated assaults on Neville's home, the film represents heroic, cultivated Western masculinity literally under siege. The film represents Neville not only as "the last man alive" (a slogan used in the film's advertising) but also as an amalgamation of masculine ideals. Neville is scientist, physician, mechanic (he operates numerous generators that he has installed around the city), scholar (at one point, he quotes T.S. Eliot), fine-art connoisseur (his apartment contains familiar paintings from the Renaissance to the twentieth century), athlete (during a reconnaissance dash around town, he proclaims in monologue that he has broken the world record for the mile run), and indefatigable warrior. The film implies that Neville's masculinity belongs to overlapping, universal categories that transcends history. His shifting wardrobe reflects his apparent embodiment of multiple historical paradigms of masculine bearing. In one of his many bizarre costumes, for example, Neville wears a vaguely Edwardian outfit of ruffled shirt and velvet coat. Similarly, he engages in both mass and elite cultural pursuits: muscle-car driving and art appreciation, marksmanship and chess, athletics and Scotch-drinking. Through his diverse activities, Neville appears as both a classical gentleman and a willing participant in popular recreational culture.

The Omega Man offers its protagonist as the standard-bearer of simultaneously conservative and progressive ideologies. Neville's material possessions and predilections link him to both traditional U.S. values and shifting youth-culture attitudes. His bachelor lifestyle and his use of a series of cars and motorcycles signify both youthful rebellion and conventional, masculine material power. Tipping the balance, his frequent use of guns and his ideology of self-preservation make him a model of libertarianism. To temper the presentation of Neville as an anachronistic conservative, the film shows him entering a movie theater to watch *Woodstock* (1970; conveniently, another Warner Brothers release), during which he recites the film's dialogue to give the impression that he has viewed it repeatedly. Apparently he seeks solace in the documentary's images of huge crowds of sun-drenched adolescents, a sharp contrast to *The Omega Man*'s repeated shots of barren urban areas. Hence the film suggests that, rather than reveling in his life as a solo supermale, Neville would prefer the hierarchy-free social utopia that *Woodstock* connotes. This sequence includes shots of Neville turning on a generator and operating the film projector, constructing him as the *deus ex machina* who preserves the film document of youth culture. The film presents this ideologically ironic gesture straightforwardly, making the traditional, conservative male responsible for the resuscitation of an exterminated counterculture.

Along with its protagonist who adheres to both progressive and conservative models of male behavior, the film presents a distorted and contradictory view of early-1970s race relations, framing racial conflict in terms of black characters' sympathy or antagonism toward the film's two white leaders. The film contrasts Neville's ostensible liberalism with a paranoid, racist nightmare of militant blacks who rise up to persecute a white hero. Characters appear both as advocates of racial equality and as simplistic, racialized types. While Neville visibly embraces white culture—in his clothing, artistic tastes, and scientific and military pursuits—he also appears as a friend or lover to the film's virtuous (i.e., trustworthy and compliant) black characters. For example, he seduces Lisa, a virtuous black character and the only woman in the film, and consummates the relationship immediately after killing a black male intruder. Heston's screen affair with Cash recalls similar pairings of aging white men with younger black women in 1970s films. As in Clint Eastwood's *Play Misty For Me* (1971) and *The Eiger Sanction* (1975), the introduction of a black woman as a sexual partner connotes the progressiveness of an otherwise conservative star persona. Lisa later succumbs to the virus herself, an incident the film codes as a betrayal, albeit a passive one (rather than taking action against Neville, she simply leaves his side, and when she later recovers from the virus, she is contrite). Neville also saves Lisa's teenage brother, Richie, from the plague through a blood transfusion, an act the boy repays by criticizing Neville's militancy, observing: "You're hostile—you just don't belong." Through this interaction, the film briefly interrogates Neville's characteristic white male isolation. His penchant for violent action locates him on the side of the antisocial, but ultimately, his altruistic tendencies threaten his own survival. Neville hastens his own death by granting autonomy to Lisa and her brother: Richie leaves to negotiate with Matthias, and Lisa's abandonment of Neville leads to his mortal wounding. While Neville's willingness to share his bodily fluids with black women and children apparently denotes his liberalism, the film uses the black characters' subsequent betrayals to remind viewers of the limitations of racial equality.

Furthering the film's confusion about race, the plague-ridden cult that persecutes Heston appears both outside racial categories and hyperconscious of such categories. The film's plague transforms its victims' skin into a uniform pale white. However, while most of the cult's white members remain hooded throughout the film, a key black lieutenant usually appears unhooded, showing off his bleached-white face and hair. Similarly, Lisa and Richie also appear in various stages of the disease, with their skin, hair, and eyes turning white. The film's makeup and costuming thus foreground the spectacle of transformed blackness. At the same time, the film presents a cartoonish version of racial solidarity. When Matthias's lieutenant decries Neville's home as a "honky paradise," Matthias chides him for recalling "the old ways" of racial antagonism. Nevertheless, the film codes the lieutenant as a subversive, violent militant—an angry black-power stereotype—despite his bleached complexion. Although a member of Matthias's antitechnology "Family," the lieutenant carries a hidden pistol, showing his lack of solidarity with the Family's agenda.[16] While *The Omega Man* includes heavy doses of gun violence and features many shots of a grinning Heston wielding a machine gun, the film still manages to present a black man's mere possession of a firearm as illegitimate. In the film's logic, the black lieutenant both betrays his associates and poses a threat to Neville. Through its depiction of Lisa, Richie, and the unnamed black lieutenant, the film presents assimilated blacks—in this case, blacks who are literally bleached white—as threats to legitimate white masculinity.

The film clouds the Family's racial associations through the group's articulation of an aggressive antitechnology stance. Rejecting the implications of black liberation's "by any means necessary" stance, the integrated group here pursues a primitive agenda of siege warfare. Unlike *Point Blank* and *The Getaway*, *The Omega Man* aligns its protagonist explicitly with contemporary technology (as well as with luxury and sophistication). In this film, critics of technology pose a threat to heroic masculinity. The Family battles Neville because he represents military uses of science and technology. In his hyperbolic rhetoric, Matthias refers to Neville as the "creature of the wheel," a "lord of the infernal engines," and so forth. Neville appears somewhat conflicted by his association with destructive institutions, as killing contradicts his mission to save humanity. The film implies that Neville kills only in self-defense, though his choice of exclusively lethal weaponry belies any humanitarian impulses. The Family's arsenal, by comparison, appears infantile and silly: they wield clubs, torches, and archaic siege machines such as flaming catapults. Their chosen Luddite stance, rather than aligning them with peace-loving or environmentalist sensibilities, codes them as more violent and destructive than the trigger-happy Neville. The film allows Matthias to articulate a fairly coherent antitechnology position, but his exaggerated rhetoric, his clear connotations as a grotesque villain, and the Family's barbarity and inhumanity render such a position entirely unsympathetic. Contrastingly, the film presents Neville's final act, the transfer of power to a fellow white male scientist, as unproblematic and socially beneficial.

Although Neville dies at the film's conclusion, a younger white male protagonist emerges to carry on Neville's patriarchal, scientific mission. Through this character, *The Omega Man* reconstructs science as counter-cultural and even revolutionary. At its midway point, the film introduces Dutch (Paul Koslo), a young ex–medical student who rides a motorcycle and dresses in worn-out jeans and leather jacket, with no shirt beneath. Dutch's outlaw-biker look, wild hair, and alternative lifestyle (he cares for a group of scruffy children in a commune-like outpost outside the city) identify him as a representative of the young counterculture. The film even presents Dutch as a critic of science; he blames scientists like Neville for the global cataclysm. At the same time, he idolizes Neville, reciting the title of one of Neville's medical-journal articles when they first meet. Similarly, visual cues present Dutch as a caring patriarch, as when he is shown repeatedly with a band of white children. Meanwhile, his ostensible partner Lisa never appears alongside this group in shot compositions. At the film's end, when Dutch receives the serum that will cure the plague, he becomes a new white hope, a man capable of thwarting Matthias's false revolution with a prosocial counterprogram. Just as the film transforms the era's real oppositional voices—including black militants and critics of science—into caricatures of intolerance, it reimagines hegemonic science as countercultural and hip. Feminism is absent altogether, with the possible exception of a brief scene in which Neville and Lisa share a laugh about the impracticality of birth-control products in a depopulated world. The doctrine of free love is ironically validated, but with its intent reversed. Through this moment of nostalgia, the film implies that conservative attitudes toward sex—the use of sex explicitly for procreation—offer security for an uncertain future. Conservative, masculine survival skills gain new relevance as well, as Neville's technical aptitude and physical endurance allow him to function unimpaired in the postapocalyptic world. The film's ultimate validation of male militancy and technology also sustains conservative conventions of the science-fiction film genre. Whereas the crime film and film noir show interest in criminal protagonists, men overtly at odds with traditional social institutions, science-fiction films' dystopian environments often result in the explicit affirmation of or nostalgic longing for traditional values and institutions. *The Omega Man* affirms the value of biological science, for example, even while admitting the dangers of misuse of scientific knowledge.

The film's recurrent connotations of Neville as a Christ-like martyr indicate the versatility of conservative notions of epic, heroic masculinity. Even excluding his religious epics, many of Heston's roles not only mythologize him but often feature explicitly Christian themes. In *The Naked Jungle* (1954), Heston plays a South American plantation owner who loses but perseveres, Job-like, in a protracted battle against a huge ant colony. *Planet of the Apes* offers Heston as a future Adam, ready to rekindle the fallen human race with a mute, sexually attractive consort. *The Omega Man* identifies Heston's character as a Christ figure both narratively and visually. In one scene, a young girl asks him, "Are you God?" a question to which he does not reply. Neville's persecution by the Family and its Pontius Pilate–like leader Matthias also recalls the travails of the biblical Christ. The film's most heavy-handed symbolism occurs in its closing shot, in which the dying Neville reclines against a cross-like column in a shallow pool reddened with his blood, his legs bent and arms floating outstretched in a crucifixion pose. The film ends with a solarized version of this shot, lending the conventional religious image a contemporary, vaguely psychedelic sheen. As we have seen, the film substantially overdetermines Neville's signification, presenting him simultaneously as a *GQ*-style super-bachelor, a rebel advocate of countercultural values, and finally a martyr of biblical proportions. Consequently, attacks on his swaggering masculinity represent assaults on an unimpeachable piety and devotion.

The adaptability of Heston's star persona to both religious epics and science-fiction films testifies to both genres' interest in forms of masculinity that transcend ordinary physical limitations and social conflicts. Frequent shots in both *The Omega Man* and *Planet of the Apes* show Heston bare-chested and glistening with sweat, recalling his similar appearance as Christian heroes in *Ben-Hur* and *El Cid*. While displays of the partially naked male body occur with great frequency in films that depict male physical prowess, the visual connection between Heston's religious and science-fiction roles indicates a preoccupation with classical, epic visions of masculinity. With biblical and gladiatorial epics out of favor in the late 1960s and early 1970s, Heston's characters advance classical and Christianity-based images of male power into future-oriented narratives. Conservative ideologies accompany such representations. *The Omega Man* conflates women's movements, antiwar sentiments, environmentalism, and critiques of corporate capitalism into a broad-based threat to heroic masculinity. Neville's exaggerated virtue and proficiency, which the film code as essential to the proper functioning of democratic society, counter these corrosive, dissenting perspectives.

The Omega Man's conflation of progressive ideologies into a mono-lithic threat to male autonomy accords with the representations of masculinity in *Point Blank* and *The Getaway*. All three films, whether overtly supportive of capitalism or not, offer male protagonists whose managerial efficiency and coolness under pressure identify them as ideal capitalist functionaries. Meanwhile, their antagonists take on aspects of capitalism in negative ways; *The Omega Man* depicts its villainous Family as an organized group that conducts meetings and trials and has a clear hierarchy of leadership and established headquarters. Characters that might otherwise appear as revolutionaries thus become unquestioning agents of a misguided authority figure, while the solitary, righteous hero's allegiances to the former state power go largely unexamined. Notably, all three films also portray male protagonists threatened by their sexual partners' encounters with other men. The heroes of *Point Blank* and *The Getaway* are explicitly cuckolded by their wives, and these affairs predicate violence against the wives and others. *The Omega Man* represents its heroine's betrayal metaphorically. When Lisa journeys alone for food and clothing, she hastily succumbs to the plague. Her physical transformation appears immediate rather than protracted (as for the other case shown), and thereafter, entranced by Matthias, she wears a mischievous smile and tells him, "I want you." Basically, then, Lisa willfully rejects Neville's human companionship to join Matthias's side, with the film coding her choice in terms of vacillating female desire. Like the two other films, *The Omega Man* shows interest in female transgression predominantly for its effects on male agency. In all three, men are undone or undermined by women's sexual weakness and untrustworthiness. Consequently, the women who stray from their rightful men receive punishment—physical assault or death—which the films depict as legitimate or at least unexceptional. Such a dynamic parallels prevailing Vietnam-era ideologies of male privilege: women still implicitly represent male property, and men's assertions of sovereignty ostensibly justify whatever treatment women receive.

In these three films, women enjoy more substantive roles than in the majority of action films of the 1980s, yet they exist on screen largely to illuminate issues in masculinity. In their attempts to address and reconcile threats to male power, the films offer the possibility of broad-based audience appeal but also risk fundamental damage to narrative or thematic coherence. *Point Blank* represents the vengeful loner as the ideal worker, tireless and goal-oriented. *The Getaway* depicts patriarchal oppression through an unjust penal system and rapacious villains but nonetheless withholds authority from its female protagonist. Finally, *The Omega Man* fuses conservative and countercultural tastes and behaviors. After the onset of the blockbuster era in the mid-1970s, studio films often fit into narrow genre categories and marginalized ongoing cultural conflicts. The superficial ideological coherence of 1980s action films occurs partly through the exscription of women or their assignment to largely ornamental roles. Overall, then, the cultural battles waged in male-oriented action films of the late 1960s and early 1970s end in stalemate, with unresolved issues set aside for reconsideration by later filmmakers and critics.

Mature male heroes are a fixture of the films discussed in this chapter, and later, by the end of the 1990s, action cinema again grants considerable attention to aging men. In the intervening years, such figures recede from view; action-based cinema of the late 1970s and 1980s makes little allowance for middle-aged male heroes. Corresponding with the period's blockbuster mentality, popular films in the late 1970s and early 1980s construct masculinity in ways meant to appeal to young viewers: in *Jaws*'s narrative of men who leave community ties behind to fight an exaggerated menace, in *First Blood*'s displays of Stallone's hypermuscular masculinity and solitary survival in the jungle-like terrain of the Pacific Northwest, and in *Star Wars*'s vision of boyish heroes mobilizing fantastic, toylike weaponry to save the universe. While these films make appeals to older viewers as well—through *Jaws*'s presentation of Robert Shaw as a conventional male avenger in the mold of Melville's Ahab, *First Blood*'s appeal to disenfranchised Vietnam veterans, and *Star Wars*'s resuscitation of 1930s and 1940s Flash Gordon and Buck Rogers serials—they move far afield from the putatively realist environments of previous male-centered films such as *Bullitt* and *The French Connection*. Still, the figure of the mature male hero in a contemporary, pseudorealist setting did not altogether disappear. Instead, he rose to exceptional prominence in popular novels, novels in which iconic presences such as Marvin, McQueen, and Heston loom large.

4

Airport Fiction: The Men of Mass-Market Literature

Before the 1980s and the so-called Reagan revolution, the globe-trotting military adventurer, popular for most of the twentieth century, appeared perhaps in decline in U.S. popular novels and films. In the late 1960s and early 1970s, the U.S. military's failures in Vietnam called into question the utility of the international-soldier model. Subsequent events during the Carter administration, most visibly the aborted hostage-rescue mission in Teheran in 1980, further eroded popular confidence in military institutions and military ideology. In popular U.S. cinema, the war film had all but disappeared. The war in Vietnam was portrayed most often from domestic perspectives, in films such as *Coming Home* and *The Deer Hunter* (both 1978), which highlight the debilitating psychological effects of warfare.[1] Film studios chose different settings for the representation of successful male conflict. These included the science-fiction battleground and western-genre allegiances of films such as *Star Wars* and its sequels. Here and in the *Star Trek* series (1979 and following), *Flash Gordon* (1980), and *Tron* (1982), military war and hand-to-hand or small-arms combat were transformed into family-friendly, live-action cartoons (a trend hugely revisited in the early years of the current decade). Another outlet appeared in what might be called working-class competition films, films such as *Smokey and the Bandit* (1977) and *Every Which Way but Loose* (1978), both among the top grossing films of their release years. The more realist underdog drama *Rocky* and its sequels also validated a form of aggressive masculinity, if in the confined realm of sports. Active men also moved from war zones to the urban frontier of police films such as *Fort Apache, the Bronx* (1981). Closest to the model of the war film was the crumbling-infrastructure milieu of disaster films such as *The Towering Inferno*. In that film, a military model of organization allows male (fire-) fighters to rally against a singular threat. The film's conflicts and alliances among men hearken back to the war film, but the setting is shifted to the contemporary urban United States. Meanwhile, in fiction, war novels such as Gustav Hasford's *The Short-Timers* (1979) portrayed the horrors of war rather than its glory, while espionage-fiction writers such as Robert Ludlum and Frederick Forsyth focused on the relatively bloodless realm of Cold War information gathering.

In the 1980s, however, resuscitated images of militant, male leaders and heroes in U.S. politics and popular culture supplanted the previous years' critiques of state-sanctioned global violence and its effects on the men who engage in it. Expanded U.S. military spending and the patriotic, militant rhetoric of the Reagan presidency produced a cultural climate in which traditional male heroism again could be endorsed unapologetically. In cinema, the early 1980s saw the return of Clint Eastwood's Dirty Harry character, absent since 1975, in *Sudden Impact* (1983), as well as the popularity of Sylvester Stallone's muscular Vietnam veteran John Rambo in *First Blood* (1982). In fiction, Tom Clancy's hugely successful *The Hunt for Red October* (1984) reasserted the primacy of U.S. intelligence and military power. Authors such as Stephen Coonts, Harold Coyle, and W.E.B. Griffith would also profitably exploit this newly prosocial attitude toward military and intelligence institutions.[2] Clancy's and Coonts's so-called techno-thrillers not only depict military conflict on a global scale but also extensively catalog the logistical underpinnings of such conflict. Clancy's novels in particular represent the activities of bureaucrats, administrators, and analysts alongside the exploits of military personnel of varying ranks and services. His fiction connects the bureaucratic and military worlds through exhaustive description of technical apparatuses and procedures: weapons, vehicles, communications equipment, medical operations, and engagement strategies.

Novels such as Clancy's privilege hierarchical activity in military and bureaucratic organizations over the spectacular feats of solitary heroes. These texts immerse readers in complicated and putatively realistic group activity. Rather than granting primacy to the visible attributes of male heroism, novels often rely on readers' psychological and experiential familiarity with protagonists' situations. The narratives of male-oriented popular novels often call for a mode of heroism that accords with readers' own presumed cerebral (and to a lesser extent, physical) capabilities. Similarly, they offer readers the experience of male mastery as a consequence of reading itself. With their interest in technical description and historical detail regarding military technology and weaponry, the novels promise to confer expert knowledge of these historically male disciplines. The enormously popular works of Clancy and fellow thriller writer Clive Cussler find their largest audiences among white, middle-aged, professional men.

These novels' protagonists exhibit cerebral qualities, managerial capacity, and conservative, prosocial values. Such traits closely align the central characters with the mindsets, experiences, and workplace duties of the books' principal readerships. These novels, many of which have been produced as major-studio films, appear as mature (by virtue of their graying or balding protagonists and most loyal audience) versions of Hollywood action films or thrillers. They combine domestic and international settings, male protagonists who think and act in conventionally heroic ways, and violent interpersonal and military conflict. They repeat and refine conventions of ritualized male conflict, earning enormous popularity and longevity in the process. Works such as Clancy's and Cussler's contribute substantially to the proliferation of normative models of active masculinity.

Clancy and Cussler remain among the most popular authors of contemporary fiction. Throughout the 1980s and 1990s, their novels routinely achieved high positions on national and international bestseller lists— Clancy was the most successful U.S. writer in any genre in the 1980s and 1990s—and their early-2000s works have been bestsellers as well. Along with horror writer Stephen King and legal-thriller writer John Grisham, Clancy is one of the most successful novelists of all time. As of the late 1990s, his novels had been translated into twenty-three languages and sold in forty countries.[3] His last 1990s novel, *Rainbow Six*, released in summer 1998, moved immediately to the top of the U.S. best-seller list, initially outselling the second-place title by a margin of seven to one.[4] In a five-year period, three of Clancy's novels were adapted into successful Hollywood films: *The Hunt for Red October* (1989), *Patriot Games* (1992), and *Clear and Present Danger* (1994). (A fourth successful adaptation, *The Sum of All Fears*, followed in 2002.) In addition to his many novels, Clancy authored or coauthored seven works of nonfiction by the end of the 1990s, the last being *Every Man a Tiger* (1999), an account of air combat in the Persian Gulf War cowritten with a retired Air Force general. Cussler, although not a household name to the degree that Clancy is, has commanded large audiences since the mid-1970s, and his last novel of the 1990s, *Atlantis Found* (1999), spent nearly ten weeks in the top ten of the *New York Times*'s list of best-selling hardcover fiction. Like Clancy, Cussler has forayed successfully into nonfiction, coauthoring *The Sea Hunters: True Adventures with Famous Shipwrecks* (1996), which appeared in paperback in 1997 with a one-million copy first printing.[5] Cussler, too, has had less success with cinematic adaptations than with novels: of his nearly two dozen best-sellers, only the 1976 novel *Raise the Titanic* was produced as a studio film in the twentieth century. The expensive film performed dismally at the box office in 1980, nearly bankrupting its British financiers and long hindering film adaptations of Cussler's novels. (His 1992 novel *Sahara* was adapted as a medium-budget action film in 2005.) Regardless of their successes as feature films, the novels of both Clancy and Cussler have achieved substantial cultural visibility worldwide. Both too have intriguingly refined genre-fiction conventions surrounding narratives of male agency.

Clancy's and Cussler's novels doggedly preserve constructions of heroic, idealized masculinity within the generic terrain of the spy thriller and the nautical thriller. While indebted to popular-fiction conventions, Clancy and Cussler repeatedly reference cinematic masculinity as well. Their novels call upon paradigms of masculinity developed in 1960s and 1970s films. Men who came of age with these films are no longer exclusively targeted as consumers of mainstream action films, but they do form the primary audience for popular military novels and thrillers. Lacking abundant representations of male activity in mainstream film, older men can find such representations instead in mass-market fiction (produced of course by similar media conglomerates). Marked declines in book reading among young adults have contributed as well to novels' courtship of more loyal, older readerships.[6]

The social reality of corporations and the military differs substantially from the streamlined, exaggerated worlds of genre texts. Clancy's and Cussler's fictions both traverse the landscape between these disparate spheres. Both writers' novels play out against a backdrop of international politics, global espionage agencies, and corporate and military conflict. Such narratives grant prominence to government agencies, the military, and the soldiers, bureaucrats, and managers who fill buildings and bases. These texts combine the generic world of action and intrigue with the narrow military or business world of ordered, ostensibly purposeful interactions. In Clancy's and Cussler's novels, the white-collar worker's narrow range of skills and experiences grants him access to a vast and alluring world of international intrigue. Problem-solving skills and managerial prowess substitute for previous signifiers of active masculinity such as physical strength and personal charisma. The novels advance a model of heroic masculinity that privileges competence and self-esteem (not coincidentally, two prominent components of business manifestos and self-help books) over physical toughness, agility, and facility with violence. Clancy's and Cussler's novels also present restraint as a necessary component of heroic masculinity. Restraint represents civilized masculinity and separates thoughtful, self-controlled heroes from reckless villains. Similarly, by validating restraint, the authors explicitly compensate for their middle-aged heroes' waning physical strength. In both men's novels, physical talents prove to be only intermittently useful. The novelists part ways in other areas, though. Clancy's novels feature extensive description of procedures both familiar and esoteric, from suburban traffic patterns and characters' deliberations over neckwear to condensed treatises on submarine propulsion. Clancy's novels promise descriptive if not psychological depth. Cussler works in a more fantastic, cartoonish mode. In his world, adults engage in conventional adolescent pleasures: car chases, gunplay, seafaring adventure (often in fanciful underwater craft), and brief sexual episodes. Clancy's novels include most of these elements as well, though he repeatedly uses rhetorical gestures to assert differences between the "real" world of his fictions and the artificial world of film westerns and television police dramas. Cussler's work rarely insists upon such a disjuncture, instead remaining faithful to popular fiction's illusionist conventions of character and action.

This chapter examines a range of 1980s and 1990s novels by each author (of Clancy's novels, I address mostly those featuring the technocrat hero Jack Ryan), with some concluding attention to their post-9/11 novels as well. Clancy's and Cussler's formative works illuminate the textual operations underway in popular fiction during the Reagan–Bush era of economic growth and military buildup. These novels show how political and economic factors shape fictional models of active masculinity. The novels' privileged traits, such as managerial skill and cerebral ability, could in principle be attributed to female as well as male characters. However, both writers identify their protagonists' domains as expressly and emphatically masculine. This gendering process occurs through configurations of plot, character, and narrative space. The novels also surround their protagonists with a palpable but often intangible masculine aura, revealed through dialogue among men, internal monologue (in Clancy's novels), described gestures, and invocations of male intuition. Both writers represent corporate, military, and government institutions bound together by masculinist codes of honor, brotherhood, and loyalty. In addition, both writers' male protagonists spend active and leisure time manipulating vehicles and apparatuses coded as masculine. The men interact with high-technology products such as nuclear weapons and computers and with modes of military transportation such as combat aircraft, helicopters, and submarines. Cussler's novels add classic automobiles to the mix, signifying male luxury, taste, power, and mechanical aptitude.

Both writers also define their narrative worlds through the exclusion or marginalization of women characters. In their novels, women appear principally as dutiful mates, sexual temptresses, or token figures against which male expertise can be judged. Women tend to weaken or inhibit male characters' homosocial relations with their male coworkers and off-duty associates. These supporting men are usually linked to the protagonists' work realms, as former military comrades or workplace associates with whom the protagonists maintain friendly relations. While women characters represent the social world the heroes are sworn to protect, they more frequently impede rather than aid the heroes' goals. At the same time, both Clancy's and Cussler's novels introduce the recurring figure of the exceptional woman, defined according to masculine categories such as candor and rationality and set apart from conventions of femininity such as domesticity and desire for romantic commitment. In her casual relations with men, the exceptional woman reduces male anxieties about interactions with women and legitimizes the otherwise exclusionary codes of male interpersonal conduct. This figure, usually the protagonist's sexual or romantic interest, functions as the ideal "man's woman." Her sober logic and lack of emotionality correspond to the male hero's militant, patriarchal worldview. Columnist Sean French disingenuously identifies Clancy as a "radical feminist" because of these strong female characters.[7] Generally, though, Clancy's figurations of women systematically justify the aggression and competitiveness of the male hero's world, a world to which most women are denied access. Both Clancy and Cussler present narrative worlds that women can enter safely only if they divest themselves of conventionally feminine traits. Even when the exceptional woman does participate in masculine activities, her heavily emphasized beauty—an unimpeachable radiance set against the male hero's more rugged, understated appearance—distinguishes her from the novels' male agents.

Clancy's and Cussler's novels link corporate and military divisions of labor and models of problem-solving, indicating that such models are best suited to resolve global crises. This worldview is all-encompassing; dissenters are ridiculed or simply excluded. (Cussler occasionally crafts a caricature of a liberal politician, and Clancy sometimes assails a powerful woman or a political activist.) The novels emphasize professional hierarchies, and they implicitly value the specialized labor of middle-class workers under capitalism. That labor serves as a bridge to a comprehensive world of suspense and action. In the novels, cinematic constructions of active, masculine space validate and embellish the routinized world of multinational capitalism. In a manner similar to action cinema's frequent conflation of private and public spaces, Clancy's and Cussler's novels largely erase categories of interiority and the private. The novels take place instead in a wholly public dimension that legitimates patriarchal constructions of identity. Men do not bring their problems home because they rarely go home.[8]

Economic developments in the United States in the 1980s and 1990s eroded public faith in the post–World War II model of organizational capitalism and corporate loyalty. These changes included the leveraged buyouts of the 1980s, ongoing corporate "downsizing," the recession of the late 1980s and early 1990s, the rise of corporate consultants and independent contractors, and the subsequent growth of the high-tech and information-technology economy. All contribute to a changing understanding of multinational corporations' relationship to their blue- and white-collar workers (groups that remain disproportionately male). Susan Faludi reports in *Stiffed* that General Motors, Chrysler, IBM, and AT&T together eliminated nearly one-half million jobs in the first half of the 1990s (60–61). Similarly, in a case study of laid-off aerospace workers in Southern California, Faludi notes a loss of one-half million jobs in Los Angeles County alone, including more than fifty percent of all aero- space jobs in the region and a total of one-quarter million manufacturing jobs (52). Throughout the 1980s and 1990s, though, Clancy's novels fetishized the organizational structures of traditional institutions. Such emphasis could reassure readers that venerable notions of corporate loyalty were not obsolete, and that qualities of white-collar labor remained fulfilling.

Clancy's and Cussler's novels depict successful, working fraternities of middle-aged men. Amid evolving business and economic conditions, their representations of traditional male solidarity offer paeans to a dying era of group loyalty while disavowing negative economic shifts. In a March 2000 essay, business writer Michael Lewis argued that the late-1990s U.S. labor shortage, the rise of corporate stock options, and the emergence of free- spending, high-technology startups together encouraged a decline in workers' loyalty to corporations and a general public skepticism about cor- porations' contributions to social good.[9] Lewis's argument intersects with Faludi's view of a 1990s crisis in male identity. She points to an eroding pact between men and the larger public world, a pact "forged through loy- alty, through a conviction that a man's 'word' meant something in the larger society, through a belief that faithfulness, dedication, and duty would be rewarded in kind, or at least appreciated in some meaningful way" (595). Clancy's and Cussler's novels thoroughly redeem archaic notions of loyalty and duty, and they passingly acknowledge ongoing eco- nomic and technological developments. However, they locate these devel- opments only within conventional representations of espionage and the military, institutions that still rely on the masculine compacts Faludi describes. In other words, these somewhat recession-proof institutions stand in for all others.

Triumph of the Technocrat

Tom Clancy's novels advance an explicitly conservative worldview. His fiction foregrounds patriarchal, militant characters and environments.

At the same time, it co-opts emotional rhetoric and superficially validates family and domestic concerns. At the narrative level, Clancy presents relatively fast-paced stories of international conflict focused around single themes or situations, such as Cold War political and military relations, terrorism, drug trafficking, and threats of nuclear war. Though particular heroes and villains receive prominent treatment, an ever-growing cast of supporting characters, along with extensive technical descriptions and strategic information, add complexity to the novels' principal conflicts. Ideologically, Clancy establishes connections among various spheres—political, military, business, academic, and domestic—both within and across national borders. He also labors to overcome the visible or implicit contradictions of specific intersections, for example, highlighting the relative sameness of marriage in the United States and Russia in *The Hunt for Red October,* or asserting similarities between corporate and military strategies in *Patriot Games.* Unlike the extensive category of British spy fiction, in which intelligence agents often work autonomously, with little relation to military actions or immediate political situations and with subdued nationalism, Clancy's novels also adopt an emphatically pro-U.S. stance. Clancy's recurring protagonists embody and explicitly defend U.S. social structures, economic practices, and military and intelligence activities. Although the Vietnam War altered both U.S. military policy and popular perceptions of the wartime capabilities and responsibilities of the United States, Clancy's novels expound the virtues of the (largely male) participants in national-security activities and the venerable institutions that support them. Clancy's novels reassert the primacy of U.S. military power after Vietnam (and after the end of the Cold War, though Russia and the Soviet Union figure prominently in many of his 1990s and early-2000s novels as well). They also provide moral and strategic lessons for the successful negotiation and deployment of that power.

An overwhelmingly male cast of characters implicitly connects the various realms—military, political, academic, and in passing, corporate—in which Clancy's narratives occur. In the novels, shared masculine codes of friendship, diplomacy, emotion, ethics, and action undergird the institutions in which power is held and exercised. The fundamental similarities among Clancy's narrative realms allow their protagonists—and more significantly, their readers—to shift smoothly among them, without disorientation. The composite status of Clancy's frequent protagonist, Jack Ryan, facilitates shifts among institutional codes and discourses. Ryan, as constructed by Clancy, is a former Marine lieutenant, then a stockbroker (a long-past career in the novels, used to show the character's familiarity with but ultimate rejection of "the rat race"), then a Naval Academy instructor (with a doctorate in naval history, identifying him as an academic), and finally, a CIA analyst (the position he occupies, at various ranks, in many of Clancy's novels). The breadth of Ryan's experience makes his character intermittently appealing to a range of white-collar readers whose own backgrounds intersect with the character's. Moreover, Ryan's successful heroics allow readers to share vicariously in his experiences and imagine them as their own. Despite Ryan's frequent declaration in the early novels that "I'm only a historian," he consistently plays an instrumental role, helping to foil political terrorists, drug traffickers, and foreign superpowers. Clancy validates characters' military affiliations above other categories. Still, many characters, military or otherwise, demonstrate the proper masculine bearing that grants them access to a similarly esteemed realm, that of male camaraderie.

My argument concerns Clancy's oeuvre as a whole, and this chapter includes textual analysis from a range of his 1980s and 1990s novels. For precision of analysis, though, I devote most attention to two of Clancy's 1980s novels, The Hunt for Red October, published in 1984, and Patriot Games, published in 1987. While relatively wide in scope, these novels are ultimately more contained than many of Clancy's later epics, such as the 900-page The Sum of All Fears (1991) and the 1,300-page Executive Orders (1996). The sheer heft of Clancy's later works partly accounts for their appeal—simply transporting a hardcover copy is a manly labor—but the shorter works offer compelling narrative operations that the sprawling structure of many of his later novels partly obscures. The Hunt for Red October, Clancy's first novel, narrates a Russian submarine commander's attempted defection to the West, along with U.S. and British efforts (crucially Ryan's) to assist him and gain possession of his technologically sophisticated vessel before opposing Soviet submarines can destroy it. (Clancy's second novel, Red Storm Rising 1986, presents another Cold War narrative, a scenario of a global war between the United States and the Soviet Union.) Patriot Games, Clancy's third novel, deals with an IRA splinter group's attempts to kill members of the British royal family as well as the family of Jack Ryan, who has foiled the assassination attempt that opens the book. Other Clancy novels, including in the 1990s Without Remorse (1993), Debt of Honor (1994), and Rainbow Six (1998), feature ex-Navy SEAL John Clark, a considerably more active and aggressive figure than the often deskbound Ryan, who in Executive Orders becomes U.S. president. (Ryan does appear in complementary roles in some of John Clark novels. Clear and Present Danger [1989] and Debt of Honor showcase them both, and Ryan makes cameos in others.)

Most critical work on Clancy deals with his novels' foreign-policy positions. Amid this interrogation, some critics have called attention to Clancy's figurations of masculinity and family.[10] These latter issues of representation are central to my analysis; in particular, I hope to demonstrate how the novels' constructions of gender, family, and characters' overall worldviews function alongside the books' complicated plots and nationalist overtones. Critics routinely find fault with Clancy's slender characterizations and simplified psychological conflicts, yet such elements provide a substantial foundation for the larger ideological projects of his texts. Reviews of Clancy's books repeatedly assert that the author describes technical operations and narrates action sequences well, but provides "cardboard" or otherwise inauthentic characters. Thus, plot elements and description fulfill criteria for genre fiction (i.e., thrillers should thrill, just as they should give access to some secretive institutional world such as the CIA's). Curiously, reviewers do not grant generic characters the same exceptions. Somehow the lack of psychological realism bedevils reviewers more than the many implausible plot contrivances (such as Ryan's or Clark's serendipitous involvement in countless events of global significance). Yet the highly conventionalized characters and formulaic narratives of novels such as Clancy's carry ideological and aesthetic weight precisely because of their generic qualities. By assessing only Clancy's characters in terms of their putative realism or lack thereof, critics acknowledge Clancy's broader milieu of male camaraderie, political intrigue, and military strength as a legitimate, authentic representation of social reality and distributions of power. Clancy's imagined social world legitimates its characters' patriarchal, militant, and nationalist codes of behavior. In Clancy's networks of subplots and minor but significant events, such codes appear indispensable. When individuals fail to abide by particular cultural and institutional codes, catastrophic consequences ensue for other members of the social world. In Clancy's world, human error appears principally as a moral failing or a lapse in professionalism. Conversely, characters adhering to the strictest moral and professional codes tend to succeed against all odds. While many of the novels' incidental passages—concerning popular tastes, parenting strategies, marital relations, and the like—bear only marginally on plot concerns, they provide the novels' connective tissue, presenting readers a coherent world of common experiences and attitudes.

Throughout Clancy's novels, shared interests in particular subjects, however rarefied or quotidian, connect male characters. Whether the subject is television sports or shipbuilding, though, the areas of interest remain implicitly male dominated. Women only rarely enter the equation, either as complement or impediment. In *Patriot Games*, for example, the common experience of military service engenders a friendship between Ryan and the Prince of Wales (who, like most heads of state in Clancy's novels, is not referred to by name). Clancy also notes in passing that Ryan's wife, Cathy, and the Princess share an interest in the violin, but he devotes no extensive dialogue to this subject. In this and other respects, Clancy constructs women's pursuits as greatly subordinate to those of men.

Repeatedly, promotion of male experience appears to take a back seat to promotion of broader social and economic conservatism—esteem of family, limited government, and support for existing class hierarchies. Yet even here, women matter only insofar as they are visible along continuums of male achievement, defined according to professional and economic criteria. In *Executive Orders*, for example, President Jack Ryan designates a friend, wealthy investment banker George Winston, as treasury secretary. Following his confirmation, Winston makes an impromptu speech against progressive taxation, singling out Ryan's wife, a highly paid surgeon and now First Lady, as a laudable example of "the marketplace at work" (574). In the rest of his speech, which continues for five pages of the novel and includes the unchallenged assertion that "[w]e don't *have* a class system in America" (576, italics in original), he names numerous professional athletes and politicians, all male. By leading with the example of Cathy Ryan, Winston's pontifications appear supportive of gender equality. Women who command six-figure salaries are the norm in Clancy's market meritocracy, but only because of the broader exclusion of other kinds of women. Clancy's Superwoman substitutes for all other women, leaving the bulk of the massive narrative free to depict the work of men. Notably, Winston's speech occurs immediately after a scene in which an evildoer canvasses the Ryan children's private school, planning a kidnapping. As in other Clancy novels, Cathy Ryan's professional work leaves her children unprotected, and ultimately it is Jack Ryan who is called upon to protect them. While validating exceptional mothers at one level, the novels implicitly scold them at another.

Discussions of sexual activity also reinforce male bonds at women's expense. Male characters often casually extol their own potency, yet corresponding dialogues about women's sexual experience do not occur. In *Patriot Games*, Ryan engages in much good-natured banter concerning his wife's pregnancy, which has occurred during an English vacation. Such dialogue presents Ryan as a standard-bearer of the traditional family, proudly attesting to the procreative value of marital sex. In another example, the following exchange from *The Hunt for Red October*, Ryan's close friend Skip Tyler regards marital sex in a manner that both trumpets his virility and supports conservative notions of family:

"Ha!" Dodge laughed. "Johnnie says you have a bunch of new kids."

"Number six is due at the end of February," Tyler said proudly.

"Six? You're not a Catholic or a Mormon, are you? What's with all this bird hatching?"

Tyler gave his former boss a wry look. He'd never understood that prejudice in the nuclear navy. It came from Rickover, who had invented the disparaging term *bird hatching* for fathering more than one child. What the hell was wrong with having kids?

"Admiral, since I'm not a nuc anymore, I have to do *something* on nights and weekends." Tyler arched his eyebrows lecherously. (176, italics in original)

Clancy offers Tyler's antiquated sexual beliefs as oppositional to implied institutional preferences. Repeated demonstrations of male potency, the passage suggests, challenge the careerist, anti-family principles of a military service branch. In reality, both options represent explicitly conservative understanding of work and family.

Men's interests can differ, Clancy suggests, because their superficial antagonisms testify to a more fundamental kinship. The small disagreement apparent in the previous exchange relies on the men's shared knowledge of an exclusive institutional discourse. In another episode in the novel, an examination of a sonar frequency grows into a minor dispute about musical taste. After his superior officer compliments his hearing, sonar operator Jones, a fan of Bach, unusually chides the officer for his less cultured preferences:

"You've got better ears."

"That's cause I listen to better music, sir. That rock stuff'll kill your ears."

Thompson knew he was right, but an Annapolis graduate doesn't need to hear that from an enlisted man. His vintage Janis Joplin tapes were his business. (74)

In this passage's economy of taste, either musical choice (Bach or Janis Joplin) appears to represent departures from predominant cultural beliefs. Thompson's unspoken defense of his tastes suggests a 1960s notion of rock music as countercultural. Even in the novel's mid-1980s setting, the idea of classic-rock music as unconventional seems quaint, though perhaps not to readers of Clancy firmly entrenched in the U.S. cultural mainstream. Clancy presents Jones's enjoyment of Bach as similarly exceptional, though the notion of classical-music appreciation as eccentric works only within the particular context of military experience. Ultimately, the noted disparity in rank between the two men—"Annapolis graduate" versus "enlisted man"—indicates the real issue at stake in the debate. Clancy applauds Jones's idiosyncrasies while paying tribute to the military's hierarchical structure. Similarly, he enshrines old-world power (military academies and the officers they produce) in populist trappings (classic-rock fandom).

Ideological sleight-of-hand—such as the construction of a large, traditional family as a challenge to U.S. institutions—abounds in Clancy's work. This craftiness is perhaps most notable in the presentation of the patriotic CIA functionary Ryan as an antiestablishment figure. In one scene in *Patriot Games*, Ryan ponders his and his wife's class situation during a reception at Buckingham Palace: "She'd been raised in a similar atmosphere, a big house in Westchester County, lots of parties where people told one another how important they all were. It was a life he'd rejected, and that she'd walked away from. They were both happy with what they had" (95). Clancy contrasts the royal family's opulent surroundings with Ryan's "$300,000 home on Peregrine Cliff" (85). Since working-class characters or representations of poverty are absent from Clancy's narrative world, his protagonist appears relatively austere. Indeed, Clancy repeatedly offers Ryan's "rejection" of a moneyed life as a sign of virtue. Importantly, though, Ryan's rejection of the business world occurs not because of a lack of aptitude, but simply because of apathy. Early in *The Hunt for Red October*, Clancy offers a brief biographical sketch of Ryan from the perspective of the character's CIA superior: "Ryan had made money on his own in four years as a stockbroker, betting his own money on high-risk issues and scoring big before leaving it all behind—because, he said, he hadn't wanted to press his luck. Greer didn't believe that. He thought Jack had been bored—bored with making money. He shook his head. The talent that had enabled him to pick winning stock Ryan now applied to the CIA" (55). Again, Clancy asserts the compatibility of business skills and military-intelligence interests. National service presumably offers Ryan the sense of fulfillment that materialism cannot. As this and later novels demonstrate, though, material success often comes easily to those most devoted to government service.

The comparison between business pursuits and national-security work offers readers further means of identification with Ryan's situation. Following the novels' logic, any reader's business activity hypothetically qualifies him for intelligence work. The strategy similarly absorbs virtually all capitalist enterprise, with stock trading at any level becoming an implicit training ground for CIA work. (Of course, in this system, the moral stock trader will abandon his vocation for the nobler calling of espionage.) The construction of the investment banker turned treasury secretary in *Executive Orders* follows a similar trajectory—who better to trust with a nation's fiscal health than a man whose profession is to make money? Notably, *Executive Orders* also echoes the middle-class virtues of the *Patriot Games*-era Ryan, as President Ryan finds the White House lacking the "intimacy" of an ordinary home (627). Made anxious by its excessive luxury, Ryan asks himself, *"Did real people really live that way?,"* and answers, "Not real people, just royalty, and the family sentenced to the presidency" (628, italics in original). Ryan's disavowal of the trappings of power connotes his simple humanity and effaces his own privilege and spectacular good fortune.

Ryan's disavowal of hero status further constructs him as a male ideal. He performs dutiful acts of national service yet shuns public accolades. Through Ryan, Clancy reminds readers of the value of anonymity and the perils of celebrity (perhaps disingenuously, given the author's own penchant for self-promotion). Clancy privileges a conservative model of masculinity in which worthy men avoid being the object of public spectacle. In Clancy's ideological realm, interest in appearances or acceptance of public merit indicates vanity, a marker of errant masculinity. Introducing Ryan's character in *The Hunt for Red October*, Clancy writes, "The only people Ryan needed to impress were those who knew him; he cared little for the rest. He had no ambition to celebrity" (46). In *Patriot Games*, Ryan foils an attempted assassination on the British royal family in the novel's opening pages, then repeatedly disclaims hero status for this act. However, each of the novel's central narrative threads—Ryan's relationship with the Windsors, Irish terrorists' pursuit of Ryan, and the climactic battle sequence staged at Ryan's home, where the royal family has come for dinner—follows directly from this initial event. While rhetorically validating anonymity over celebrity, Clancy depends upon the dynamism of public figures and events to propel his narrative. After the novel's opening terrorist attack, a wounded Ryan recovers in a British hospital, where U.S. and British intelligence agents, as well as members of the press, interrogate him:

> "The press wants to see you," Taylor said.
> "I'm thrilled." *Just what I need*, Ryan thought. "Could you hold them off a bit?"
> "Simple enough," Owens agreed. "Your medical condition does not permit it at the moment. But you should get used to the idea. You are now something of a public figure."
> "Like hell!" Ryan snorted. "I like being obscure." *Then you should have stayed behind the tree, dumbass! Just what have you gotten yourself into?* (38, italics in original)

In the logic of the story, Ryan's desire for anonymity stems both from his own modesty and from the need to avoid disclosure of his confidential CIA work. Clancy here presents public fanfare—in particular, mass-media attention—as a distraction from men's authentic, private activities. Association with the visible, public sphere requires attention to appearances, to surfaces; in short, to an illegitimate masculinity aligned with codes of femininity.

Paradoxically, public and press scrutiny contribute to the delegitimation of masculinity. For Ryan as well as for the CIA itself, public attention curtails clandestine activity. By the time of *Executive Orders*, Ryan, as president, is sufficiently visible to warrant an extensive plotline surrounding his vice president's efforts to discredit him, efforts that include secret meetings with gullible journalists.[11] In the earlier *Patriot Games*, Ryan withstands police and press inquiries about his past intelligence work with a CIA-devised cover story. He offers an airbrushed account of his past and later meditates on his statements. Readers might expect the character to feel guilty, as he effectively lies to the journalists and civil authorities of an allied nation. Instead, he responds with irritation, an irritation Clancy invites readers to share. Publicity compromises Ryan's autonomy and, later in the novel, his family's safety. Ryan comes to embody proper intelligence-agency conduct, as well as the roles of protective husband and father. Through cause-and-effect narration and emotional appeals, Clancy persuades readers that Ryan's heroic-parent status depends on obscurity and government-sanctioned obfuscation.

Just as Ryan prefers to work without public fanfare, so Clancy's novels promote a view of U.S. intelligence functioning behind the scenes, without public scrutiny of its actions. Ryan's dutiful, initially unheralded service implicitly validates the labor of readers, whose potentially unfulfilling jobs can be reimagined as vital to national economic and political interests. In her own analysis of Clancy's novels, Susan Jeffords argues that like the activities of the Reagan and Bush administrations surrounding the Iran/Contra conflict and the Persian Gulf War, Clancy's fictions attempt "to rationalize the coversion of U.S. public information systems and to present that rationalization *as a form of managerial necessity*."[12] Assessing Ryan's managerial capacity in *The Sum of All Fears*, Jeffords notes the novel's insistence that Ryan's intelligence-gathering requires the daily labor of countless "professionals" whose private or governmental service contributes immeasurably to national security. Jeffords argues that Clancy's novel offers a tacit promise to readers whose routine work goes unappreciated: " 'You will probably never know the real role your work plays in world events, but be assured that it will' " (551). Such a promise, she argues, "may serve as a productive panacea for many workers' increasing senses of alienation, anonymity, and displacement" (550).

By presenting workers' systematic alienation from the products of their labor as a positive attribute of the capitalist economy, Clancy also disconnects readers from responsibility for the acts of corporations, institutions, or military or governmental bodies of which they are a part. In *The Hunt for Red October*, Clancy presents such denial as a necessary component of Ryan's work: "He had little interest in field operations. Ryan was an analyst.

How the data came to his desk was not his concern, and he was careful to avoid finding out" (49). Ryan's enforced ignorance aligns with a spy-fiction tradition in which excessive knowledge of sensitive information proves lethal. At the same time, such a position distances him and readers from the moral and ethical consequences of global intelligence gathering. Clancy uses devotion to family and friends as a wholesale sign of characters' moral bearing. In his world, then, principles of ethics and compassion need not extend into the world of work. Such moral relativism appears consistent with the paradoxes of 1980s and early-1990s values. The Reagan/Bush veneration of the traditional, Christian family took place against a backdrop of hostile corporate takeovers, the savings-and-loan industry collapse, Wall Street junk-bond scandals, and revelations of U.S. government involvement in arms sales to Iran and support for Nicaraguan paramilitary groups.

The valorization of unscrutinized private life coincides with a conservative disdain for mass media, particularly news media. In Clancy's world, public knowledge of international events endangers national security and threatens individuals. In *Patriot Games*, publicity surrounding Ryan's antiterrorist escapade leads to an assassination attempt on his wife and daughter. *The Hunt for Red October* follows the actions of a renegade Soviet submarine crew and attempts by both Russian and allied U.S./British navies to retrieve it. Though the political leaders of the involved nations engage in tense political and military interactions, the crisis abates partly because of the absence of media attention. Clancy thus endorses the view that intelligence operations—and by extension, successful engagement with military foes—succeed through circumvention of public knowledge. In *Patriot Games*, Ryan must sidestep press inquiries about his past. His irritation at this scrutiny appears legitimate because such inquiries would merely edify the reading public, not benefit the CIA. (Indeed, as the novel's transitions between scenes indicate, media attention instead provides Ryan's terrorist enemies with information about him.) By contrast, Ryan willfully submits to interrogation by British police and intelligence agents, who, like him, appear simply as men dutifully serving their nation.[13]

Clancy takes care not to alienate readers by disdaining all mass-media products. Instead, he constructs a hierarchy of fictions that privileges his novels as the most authentic and reliable source of information about police and military procedure, in contrast to television or film representations. In *The Hunt for Red October*, Clancy contrasts Ryan's labor with the "glamour" of cinematic spies: "Analysts had none of the supposed glamour—a Hollywood-generated illusion—of a secret agent in a foreign land" (55). In *Patriot Games*, though, Ryan deflects reporters' suspicions of his intelligence work by commenting, "I'm not good-looking enough to be a spy" (64).

The ironic gesture to such an image subtly reinforces the "Hollywood-generated illusion" that Clancy disdains. The gesture also assures savvy readers that Ryan is enjoying a joke at reporters' expense. Elsewhere in *Patriot Games*, Clancy makes further appeals to readers who may engage with the popular media that Ryan derides. In a conversation with British police, Ryan observes: "Most of what I know about police procedures comes from watching TV, and I *know* that's wrong" (31, italics in original). Meanwhile, Secretary Winston observes during his antitaxation speech in *Executive Orders* that "[i]f there is an idle-rich class in America, I think the only place you find them is in the movies" (575). Through these characters, Clancy sanctions the consumption of popular entertainment while reassuring readers of their mastery over works ostensibly less authoritative than Clancy's own. Notably, another form of popular entertainment, televised sports, remains venerated, further aligning readers' presumable preferences with Ryan's. *The Sum of All Fears* features terrorists' detonation of a nuclear bomb at the Super Bowl, and disrupted television broadcasts alert faraway viewers to the disaster (and provide the opportunity for Clancy to describe the effects of a nuclear blast on satellite communications). In earlier works too, sports are offered as the one unimpeachable form of television programming. In a more modest episode in *The Hunt for Red October*, Clancy depicts Ryan as a stereotypically male football addict: "Ryan made the mistake of turning the TV on to the beginning of Monday Night Football. Cincinnati was playing San Francisco, the two best quarterbacks in the league pitted against one another. Football was something he missed living in England, and he managed to stay awake nearly three hours before fading out with the television on" (63). Ryan, characterized as sleep-deprived immediately prior to this episode, succumbs to the allure of the most mainstream of male pursuits. Again, the exclusive appeal to male pastimes implicitly disavows feminine pleasures while making Ryan's character sympathetic to a wide range of male readers.

In depictions of work and leisure pursuits, Clancy privileges an exclusionary, old-boy network of male camaraderie, veiling patriarchal power imbalances with the language of "tradition." Before a closed-door White House briefing in *The Hunt for Red October*, a general reassures the nervous Ryan that "[e]verybody in this damned cellar puts his pants on the same way as you" (100–101). With the formation of an exclusively male coalition through a simple rhetorical gesture, differences among individuals recede. Male cohesion thus ensures the successful execution of national-security doctrine. Similarly, Clancy advances a conservative notion of tradition as tacit justification for military policy. In *Patriot Games*, Ryan and his wife attend a private security ceremony at the Tower of London, during which a British tower sentry extemporizes about tradition:

> "Tradition is important," Evans said. "For a soldier, tradition is often the reason one carries on when there are so many reasons not to. It's more than just yourself, more than just your mates—but it's not just something for soldiers, is it? It is true—or should be true—of any professional community."
>
> "It is," Cathy said. "Any good medical school beats that into your head. Hopkins sure did."
>
> "So does the Corps," Jack agreed. "But we don't express it as well as you just did." (120)

Clancy offers the British tradition as a model for appropriate conduct by the younger United States, disregarding differences between the two nations' political and military systems. At the same time, the incorporation of other "professional communities" into the discourse of tradition normalizes contradictory belief systems. Ryan's wife, for example, swears allegiance to the "tradition" of a medical school that long denied admission to women, and Ryan's beloved military has similarly been forced to change its long-standing exclusionary policies. The British ceremony that Clancy describes, though, can be performed only by retired soldiers. Because women's integration into military ranks remains a relatively new phenomenon, the ceremony ensures male exclusivity for decades beyond Clancy's narrative.

Clancy presents networks of male friendships as an inevitable byproduct of inborn masculinity. The men praised in his novels radiate a natural charisma that gains them a wide circle of friends and earns them the admiration of women. Ryan and his close friends—predominantly military personnel or other government employees who Clancy depicts as upright family men—do not pursue power but instead acquire it almost incidentally. In *The Hunt for Red October*, Ryan convinces Navy officials to hire his old friend Skip Tyler for essential strategic-analysis work. From an outsider's perspective, such recruitment might represent a conflict of interest, but in the novel's schema, Tyler appears the logical choice because of his specialized expertise and his willingness to work tirelessly and without the administrative delays that performing the work through conventional channels would entail. Through this episode, Clancy presents another apparent contradiction: while his novels trumpet the value of teamwork and official routine, they also feature an assortment of superlative individuals without whom the conventional apparatuses of power would be ineffectual. Clancy resolves such a contradiction by promoting a paradoxical ideology in which organizational hierarchies are necessarily comprised—in democratic nations, at any rate—of exceptional individuals who transform their routine labor into a series of challenges that test their skills.

Skip Tyler's casual friendship with Ryan leads to Tyler's profitable engagement in a secretive submarine-tracking operation. Similarly, Ryan's own range of acquaintances converts him from chair-bound analyst to globe-trotting field operative. Ryan's list of social and business contacts extends to the most influential heads of state and military leaders. Ryan acknowledges one of these contacts in a briefing with the president in *The Hunt for Red October*:

> "The judge tells me you know the commander of that British task force."
>
> It was like a sandbag hitting his head. "Yes, sir. Admiral White. I've hunted with him, and our wives are good friends. They're close to the Royal Family."
>
> "Good. Somebody has to fly out to brief our fleet commander, then go on to talk to the Brits, if we get their carrier, as I expect we will. The judge says we ought to let Admiral Davenport go with you." (115)

Ryan's sphere of acquaintances in this passage alone includes a CIA chief and former Texas State Supreme Court judge, naval admirals on two continents, the British royal family, and the U.S. president. Such breadth of contacts justifies Ryan's presence on the novel's key military mission, a mission that otherwise would not appear to require the services of a mid-level CIA functionary. Ryan's desire to impress only "those who knew him" attests to his homespun character and his preference for close friendships over political connections. Conveniently, though, many of Ryan's close friends happen to be men of great influence. Ryan's friendships with statesmen and military leaders appear either as fortuitous coincidences or as the inevitable fruits of a model life and career.

Clancy facilitates his characters' many career-based interactions by presenting them as constantly at work. To cement bonds among his male characters and to separate exceptional men from unmotivated wage-earners, his novels repeatedly invoke the Protestant work ethic. When British police appear to question Ryan in *Patriot Games*, their fatigued condition signifies their devotion to duty: "Both senior detectives were well dressed, and both had the red-rimmed eyes that came from an uninterrupted night's work" (25). Ryan, too, makes frequent references to his long hours, which serve as a badge of honor rather than an indication of unreasonable working conditions. Nowhere in his novels do men in democratic countries long for early retirement or vacations. Russian sailors on the Red October daydream about a planned trip to Cuba's beaches, but readers may infer that the sailors' unrewarding toil under Communism justifies their desire for leisure time. For U.S. characters, leisure time serves principally to prepare men for further grueling service. In *The Hunt for Red October*, a diligent sonar operator receives an extra-long shower as a reward for his tireless labor: "Commander Mancuso was given to awarding this sensuous pastime in return for above-average performance. It gave people something tangible to work for. You couldn't spend extra money on a sub, and there was no beer or women" (259). The peculiar nature of submarine work conveniently neutralizes the issue of financial compensation, and by asserting women's absence, Clancy reinforces the notion of submarine service as an exclusively male domain.

The long working shifts that Clancy's men perform help to distance them from the traditionally female spheres of home and family life. Clancy insists upon his male characters' devotion to their wives and children, but men rarely appear at home with their families. The tour-of-duty nature of military service, particularly naval service, implicitly absolves men of regular responsibilities for domestic labor or child care. Conversely, because women are assigned to the domestic and familial spheres, military service or long working hours are not possible for them. While Clancy offers a discourse of paternal responsibility, men in his novels tend to serve their families best by working outside the home to keep their nations' defenses strong. Women, by contrast, usually appear as devoted wives and mothers without outside professions or interests. Cathy Ryan is the novels' sole positive representation of active femininity; women's activity elsewhere in Clancy's books dangerously encroaches on terrain that men successfully patrol. Periodically Clancy narrates the strains of men's efforts in the public sphere, as when Ryan's long hours prevent him from fulfilling a quota of fathering time:

> "I'm home!" Jack announced. Silence. That was odd. He went downstairs and found the kids in front of the TV. They were doing too damned much of that, but that was their father's fault. He'd change that too. He'd cut back on his hours. (*The Sum of All Fears*, 570)

Children's avowed bad habits are attributed to male neglect. Curiously, mothers have no discernible positive impact on their children. In this passage, the children's lack of interest in their father is a byproduct also of their mother's unease; she suspects Jack of adultery. Her suspicion disallows her positive agency within the family. Though Clancy represents her anxiety sympathetically, this anxiety inhibits her mothering. Cathy Ryan's suspicions abate in the wake of the novel's more explosive events, and Clancy later invokes family only in Jack Ryan's fears that his family might die in a nuclear blast.

Clancy's formation of virtuous masculinity includes the tendency to regard women, and the institutions of maternity and marriage that surround them, as sacrosanct. Villains, of course, do not enjoy marital bliss. In *The Sum of All Fears*, a scientist from the former East Germany, linked both to Communism and terrorism, reflects on his home life as he prepares for a last-minute trip: " 'What do I tell my wife?' Fromm asked, then wondered why he'd bothered. It wasn't as though his marriage was a happy one" (298–299). In the realm of virtue, Clancy uses Skip Tyler's love for his wife as a device through which to render the character's crippling brush with death:

> His most vivid memory was of waking up, eight days later he was to learn, to see his wife, Jean, holding his hand. His marriage up to that point had been a troubled one, not an uncommon problem for nuclear submarine officers. His first sight of her was not a complimentary one—her eyes were bloodshot, her hair was tousled—but she had never looked quite so good. He had never appreciated just how important she was. A lot more important than half a leg. (*The Hunt for Red October*, 173)

The passing reference to Tyler's "troubled" marriage normalizes marital problems within the military but assigns blame to the conditions of service rather than to the people involved. More significantly, the scene depicts male vulnerability as a necessary precondition for positive gender relations. In Tyler's case, the accident, a semicastration, only serves to make him more virile, as he and his wife go on to bear many children. Only through a traumatic event—a car accident in this case, but the stress of combat also suffices—do men learn of women's innate goodness and dependability. Such an equation might appear to privilege women's roles and to critique notions of rigid, aggressive masculinity. However, such events tend not to occur within the range of women's experiences. When terrorists attack Cathy Ryan and her daughter in *Patriot Games*, Clancy represents the incident in terms of her husband's reaction:

> He reflected that God had given him a wife he loved and a child he treasured more than his own life; that his first duty as husband and father was to protect them from an often hostile world; that he had failed; that, because of this, their lives were now in strangers' hands. All his knowledge, all his skills were useless now. It was worse than impotence. (278)

Unlike Tyler's accident, in which the victim realizes his devotion to his spouse, this event principally affects the party not involved. Though his wife has been hospitalized, his own physical symptoms—"worse than impotence"—demand the reader's attention more than Cathy's do.

The threat to Ryan's masculinity solidifies his enmity toward the terrorists rather than stirring Cathy's devotion to her husband, which never appears in question.

Clancy presents Cathy Ryan as the ideal female counterpart to Jack Ryan's technocrat hero. *The Hunt for Red October* pays tribute to her character mostly in passing, holding her as a worthy but nonvisible mate for Jack Ryan. In *Patriot Games*, though, she fulfills marital, maternal, and career obligations. She is a prominent eye surgeon, and the novel features an episode in which she performs emergency surgery on a child's wounded eye. To some extent, Clancy represents her presence in the traditionally male world of Western medicine as a matter of course; because of her dedication and professional skill, she has earned her place in this world. At the same time, though, this world appears particularly challenging for a woman, as when Clancy points to its disturbance of her beauty regimen: "A green cap was over her hair, and she wondered yet again why she bothered to brush it out every morning. By the time the procedure was finished, her hair would look like the snaky locks of the Medusa" (248–249). By evoking the mythological image of female monstrosity (an image repeated later in the same chapter), Clancy indicates that Cathy's work inevitably compromises women's otherwise hallowed appearances. The Medusa reference also hints that Cathy's power is dangerous to men.

Throughout *Patriot Games*, Clancy contains Cathy Ryan's power by associating it with traditionally feminine goals and occupations. Through her medical profession, she acquires a range of attributes that Clancy normally assigns to masculinity: manual precision, technical and scientific knowledge, demanding working hours. However, Clancy also emphasizes the maternal, nursing dimension of her work, a facet not apparent in representations of male doctors here or in *The Hunt for Red October*. As she prepares for the emergency surgery on the child, injured in a daytime accident, Cathy's maternal impulses contrast with male doctors' emotionless demeanors: "A new sound arrived, the high-pitched shrieks of a child in agony. The doctors moved into the OR. They watched dispassionately as two orderlies were strapping the child down. *Why weren't you in school?* Cathy asked him silently" (*Patriot Games*, 253, italics in original). The passage also links maternal concerns to a moralizing tendency, further prescribing a notion of women as socially conservative, despite the novel's occasional assertions of Cathy Ryan as a "liberated woman." In a scene later in the chapter, Clancy depicts Cathy as an aggressive driver, racing her sports car through rush-hour traffic. Again, though, Clancy links her ostensibly masculine behavior to traditionally female tasks: her "weaving through traffic like a race driver at Daytona" occurs just after she picks up her daughter from a day-care center, and she drives quickly so she can arrive home in time to prepare dinner for the family (262). Significantly, Clancy also constructs a privileged background for Cathy Ryan's character that explains her relative autonomy. Cathy's assertiveness and self-confidence, according to Clancy, derive from her upper-class upbringing: born into a moneyed family, she is accustomed to the trappings of wealth and the assurances it brings.

Cathy Ryan's superficial "liberation" allows Clancy to use her character as a conduit for antifeminist and misogynist rhetoric. In *Patriot Games*, the Ryans attend a reception in which they mingle with members of the English aristocracy. Customarily, Jack discusses political and military issues with the men of the gathering, while Cathy chats with the women. When the event initially occurs in the novel, Clancy narrates only Jack's activities. Many chapters later, a conversation between the couple recalls the episode:

> "Did I ever tell you what—no, I didn't. It was one of the ladies-in-waiting. I never did find out what they were waiting for. Anyway, this one countess . . . she was right out of *Gone With the Wind*," Cathy said with a chuckle. It was his wife's favorite epithet for useless women. "She asked me if I did needlepoint."
> *Not the sort of thing you ask my wife.* Jack grinned at the windows. (161, ellipses and italics in original)

By presenting Jack Ryan's thoughts immediately after Cathy's statement, Clancy reminds readers as to whose perspective guides the narrative. Similarly, just before the quoted exchange, Cathy twice refers to Jack as a "chauvinist pig" after he makes sarcastic comments about a Barbie doll they have purchased for their daughter. (Barbies also figure marginally in *The Hunt for Red October*, revealing the limited scope of Clancy's interest in children, or the limited interest he presumes of his readership.) Cathy's accusation, playfully delivered, indicates her as an easygoing woman, one for whom sexual slights represent only the harmless idiosyncrasies of a loved one, not systematic patriarchal inequities. Jack's "chauvinist" positions appear as a facet of his waggish charm. With Cathy Ryan, Clancy constructs an ostensibly strong-willed woman who responds sympathetically to her husband's masculinist pronouncements. Such a dynamic can appeal to middle-aged male readers of Clancy's novels, men who may find themselves uncomfortable in a social climate in which patriarchal privilege is intermittently questioned. By distilling the legacy of feminism to casual husband–wife banter, Clancy presents women's interests and desires as easily apprehensible and reassures women readers of the trifling nature of male sexism.

Rather than proffering a model of female power independent of or complementary to male strength, Clancy constructs an ideal woman who does not challenge male agency. Despite Cathy Ryan's apparent autonomy, her husband still fulfills the conventional male protector role. In addition to his feeling of impotence following the terrorist attack on her in *Patriot Games*, Jack rises in chivalric fashion to defend her from a verbal assault from her overbearing father. In contrast to the novel's levelheaded hero, Clancy describes Cathy's father as "a man who had not learned the limitations of his power" (308). Women's need for protection from such men stimulates the prosocial, defensive impulses of sympathetic men such as Jack Ryan. Occasional displays of masculine proficiency notwithstanding, Cathy Ryan's character exists principally to sanction displays of male power.

Clancy contains female strength by necessitating its dispersion into the domestic and maternal spheres. He represents female power not tethered to these spheres as illegitimate, as threatening to the established social order of the United States. In *Patriot Games*, the sole powerful female character aside from Cathy Ryan is a French assassin, represented only through surveillance photos. Jack Ryan conceives of her in ardently heterosexual terms: "She didn't look dangerous—she looked like every man's fantasy. 'Like we used to say in college, not the sort of girl you'd kick out of bed. Jesus, what sort of world do we live in, Marty?'" (339). Ryan appears incredulous at the prospect of an attractive female killer, notwithstanding the conventionality of such a figure in spy fiction and cinema, about which Clancy does not comment. Ryan's response suggests that unsanctioned female power betrays some commonly held code of global morality. Clancy's novels present male killers, however vilified, as commonplace figures (and notably, such men are not eroticized). Women who kill, however, even if on the side of justice, become targets for criticism. *The Hunt for Red October* includes a minor female character, Sissy Loomis, an FBI agent who apprehends a villainous senator's aide. A fellow FBI agent joins her to complete the arrest, after which Clancy presents the male character's views about his female coworker: "The inspector had been in the FBI for twenty years and had never even drawn his service revolver in anger, while Loomis had already shot and killed two men. He was old-time FBI, and couldn't help but wonder what Mr. Hoover would think of that, not to mention the new Jewish director" (315). Lacking the patriarchal tradition of the "old-time FBI," Loomis appears incapable of restraint, a quality Clancy consistently applauds in his male characters. Even her first name, Sissy, lends childlike connotations to her character, who wields irresponsibly the power granted to her. The anonymity of the accusing character, and the simultaneous invocation of Hoover and the "Jewish director" dissociates the male agent's attitude from a particular political affiliation. Through the nameless character's judgment, Clancy implies that the two presumably adversarial leadership styles—that of the ultraconservative Hoover and that of a Jewish director, whose religion stereotypes him as a liberal (or some other sort of antithesis of Hoover)—would both find fault with Loomis's actions. Clancy invokes a range of male authorities, real and fictional, to raise objections about the mobilization of female power.

The very existence of powerful women among Clancy's characters might suggest a willingness to evaluate positively women's gradual advancements in pubic and professional life since the 1960s. However, the vigor with which Clancy regulates such characters bespeaks an antiprogressive impulse. The novels' putatively strong women prompt male characters to reclaim their traditional power. As noted previously, Sean French argues, somewhat facetiously, that "by traditional standards, Tom Clancy is a radical feminist. There are no docile women in his fiction" (34). More to the point, women are altogether in short supply in Clancy's novels. French disregards the novels' small contingent of unnamed secretaries and doting wives, not to mention the overwhelmingly male constitution of Clancy's military and political worlds. French continues, "Women fly planes, shoot missiles, kill on behalf of America, alongside the men. Uncomfortable but true, and revealing perhaps of a huge social change. If Tom Clancy is saying it, then ordinary people must believe it" (34). One would be mistaken to regard Clancy's fiction as a wholesale approximation of popular beliefs. His novels expound viewpoints by turns more extreme and more craftily manipulative than the views held by the bulk of his mainstream readers. French's noted discomfort suggests instead a plausible narrative motivation for Clancy's occasional insertion of women characters into dangerous situations. Women's presence accentuates the danger of narrative events; threats to women simply produce stronger emotional reactions than do those to men. Correspondingly, the presence of women transforms the male protector role from an abstraction—with men facing danger to protect women and children who are removed from the action—into a palpable necessity. In *The Hunt for Red October*, after U.S. pilots win a strategic victory over a wayward Soviet warplane, they tease the enemy pilot and provoke a crude sexual threat:

> "Thank you, 106," the voice acknowledged. "You see, we have some trainee operators aboard. Two of them are women, and we don't want them to get rattled their first time out." Suddenly it was too much. Shavrov thumbed the radio switch on his stick.
>
> "Shall I tell you what you can do with your women, Yankee?" (212)

Clancy presents the U.S. men's observations about women's lack of combat-readiness as jocular, while the Russian's angry retort indicates incontestable misogyny. Just as Jack Ryan's sexist barbs are softened by his wife's unperturbed reception of them, here the Russian pilot's stereotypical remark supplants the latent sexism of the American speaker's observation about women's delicacy. In this exchange, male U.S. military personnel become chivalric defenders of female virtue. Later, an overanxious Russian pilot does fire a missile at a U.S. plane, making good on the earlier rhetorical threat. Fortunately, a supercompetent man pilots the targeted aircraft and manages to escape; Clancy withholds the spectacle of female soldiers dying in warfare.

Clancy further secures the masculine terrain of his novels against female intervention through a co-optation of emotional responses and sentimental rhetoric. Clancy's hierarchy of male behavior esteems men who are both professional and capable of sentiment and disparages those who are unprofessional, unrestrained, or unsentimental. Clancy represents such base men, such as the Irish terrorists of *Patriot Games*, as barbaric or inhuman. When Ryan first encounters the terrorist leader Sean Miller in a London courtroom, he appraises the Irishman in characteristically analytical fashion:

> Then he looked at Miller's eyes. He looked for . . . something, a spark of life, humanity—something that would say that this was indeed another human being. It could only have been two seconds, but for Ryan the moment seemed to linger into minutes as he looked into those pale gray eyes and saw . . .
> *Nothing.* Nothing at all. And Jack began to understand a little. (100, ellipses and italics in original)

Antisocial behavior, Clancy implies, arises from a failure to exhibit "humanity," which for Clancy entails a particular constellation of beliefs, including patriotism, a sense of duty, and special esteem for women and children. Clancy's books abound with men who lack humanity, whether ruthless terrorists or unscrupulous lawyers or politicians. Contrastingly, women typically appear as sentimental or emotional by nature, so departures from such behavior—as in the unrestrained FBI agent Sissy Loomis or the female French assassin—represent an affront to social order. The capacity for heartfelt statements or emotional displays, Clancy suggests, separates good men from villains and makes virtuous men appealing to women.

Clancy's validation of male sentiment obviates the need for attention to women. Through homosocial networks of military and political camaraderie, Clancy's male characters share profound emotions with each other. Clancy does not include women characters amid such exchanges: his novels appear incapable of rendering male–female relationships based on friendship or professional interaction. Instead, women characters serve often as witnesses to men's romantic, explicitly heterosexual sentiments. Aside from intermittent assertions about the sanctity of motherhood, women's emotional displays rarely appear. Such displays might invalidate men's own hard-won empathetic faculties and restraint. In *Patriot Games*, Jack Ryan's presents an expensive necklace to his wife, initiating a display of affection between the two:

> "It's wonderful. Oh, Jack!" Both her arms darted around his neck, and he kissed the base of hers.
> "Thanks, babe. Thanks for being my wife. Thanks for having my kids. Thanks for letting me love you."
> Cathy blinked away a tear or two. They gave her blue eyes a gleam that made him happier than any man on earth. *Let me count the ways . . .*
> "Just something I saw," he explained casually, lying. It was something he'd seen after looking for nine hours, through several stores in three shopping malls. "And it just said to me, 'I was made for her.' "
> "Jack, I didn't get you anything like—"
> "Shut up. Every morning I wake up, and I see you next to me, I get the best present there is."
> "You are a sentimental jerk right out of some book—but I don't mind."
> (162–163, italics and ellipsis in original)

The self-reflexive reference to literary fiction offers an ironic defense against male self-consciousness. However strong-minded women (or men) are, Clancy suggests, they still desire the normative pleasures of a bourgeois lifestyle and a heterosexual, nuclear family. The passage also represents female emotions from a male perspective, a recurring strategy in Clancy's work. Cathy's tears trigger Jack's own response and substitute for her own interiority. Notably, even this tender moment advances Clancy's discourse of professionalism and rigor, as he describes Jack's shopping experience in terms of hours spent and labor invested. Jack's admonition to his wife to "Shut up"—even with its ostensibly playful tone—further betrays the power relations operating in the episode.

Men can subsume traditionally female emotions in Clancy's world, but such behavior does not ultimately feminize them or impair their masculinity. Instead, men compartmentalize sentiment, laying it aside when purely active, masculine capabilities must be mobilized. In *Patriot Games*, Jack Ryan must divorce himself from emotion when his terrorist foes invade his home and mistreat his family: "He could hear his little girl whimpering anyway. Jack had to ignore it. There wasn't room in his consciousness for anger or pity now" (473). While softhearted sentiment guarantees Ryan a moral victory over his opponents, Clancy represents it as burdensome in situations that call for strategy and physical action. In such situations, for which Clancy's male characters constantly prepare themselves even as they disavow heroism, masculine capabilities of clear thinking and swift action take precedence. For Ryan, conflict revives a deeply internalized military persona and transforms him into a machine-like warrior: "Ryan was proceeding on some sort of automatic control that the Marine Corps had programmed into him ten years before. It was a combat situation, and all the lectures and field exercises were flooding back into his consciousness" (471). Whatever warm tendencies Ryan displays to his wife, he never abandons the connection to military discipline that defines his masculinity.

The "flood" of combat-ready lucidity that overcomes Ryan as his family is threatened also galvanizes the reader for climactic action, a relatively precious commodity amid Clancy's network of technical operations and detailed military procedures. Overall, attention to characters' routine activities far surpasses narration of violent action. While the novels regularly manifest the characteristics of technical manuals or military training guides, they also construct characters as familiar, sympathetic types to maintain readers' personal investments. Characters serve as readers' guides to the unknown, the indecipherable, and the exceedingly technical. Clancy's novels feature disparate settings and situations unfamiliar to many of his readers. Counterbalancing these situations, the Ryans' concerns about sub-urban traffic, parking spaces, clothing choices, child-rearing, and enter-taining mirror the quotidian activities of the novels' middle-class, middle-aged readers. The novels' relatively narrow range of experiences fulfills a normative function. Whether depicting heads of state or low-level bureaucrats, Russian military commanders or Irish terrorists, Clancy pres-ents characters whose behavior does not stray far from the mainstream of white, middle-class U.S. life. Family and interpersonal relations, financial concerns, and daily labors dominate characters' lives.

Conversely, Clancy represents transgression through inadequate or overabundant attention to bourgeois concerns. In *Patriot Games*, for exam-ple, a black American man who works with the Irish terrorists is coded as money-hungry. Greed helps to define him as a traitor to U.S. beliefs regarding legitimate financial aspirations and transnational affiliations (meanwhile, he is disarmed of a political motivation, as his skin color con-notes him, however misguidedly, as not of Irish ancestry). Similarly, in *The Hunt for Red October*, Clancy briefly narrates the actions of a bumbling, drunken Soviet surgeon, making a point of the character's disregard for the codes of professional conduct and skill that U.S. readers presumably hold dear. Clancy offers professional incompetence and greed as clear indices of moral decrepitude. Other controversial social realities are wholly absent. Walter L. Hixson, in an analysis of Clancy's novels in relation to 1980s Cold War discourse, argues that "[m]uch like the Reagan administration itself, Clancy's characters dealt with poverty and racial inequality by acting as if they did not exist."[14] Clancy's narrative world thoroughly excises sexual transgression, drug use, and other social behavior deemed marginal in mainstream U.S. cultural discourses. Clancy's novels presume to offer readers sweeping depictions of global events and institutional cultures. The books delineate narrow social and experiential boundaries, yet somehow a limited perspective affords total knowledge. Consequently, the world's social, political, and cultural differences are easily apprehensible, not to mention capable of resolution within a finite span of pages. The difficulty of this operation may suggest why Clancy's novels from the 1980s to the present have ballooned from a length of four or five hundred pages to double or triple that length.

A measure of the popular appeal of Clancy's novels derives from the author's visible public persona, which established him as a flesh-and-blood brand in the mold of Martha Stewart or Michael Jordan. Throughout the 1980s and 1990s, he maintained a higher profile than similar best-selling authors, meeting with Republican presidents, purchasing large stakes in professional-sports franchises, and lending his name to series of books, computer games, and television series.[15] Magazine profiles of Clancy frequently call attention to the traditionally masculine elements of his lifestyle, mirroring many elements of his fiction: his advocacy of firearms, his network of acquaintances in politics and the military, and notably, the implicitly masculine process of his own writing.[16] A 1989 *Time* magazine article on Clancy describes his writing process in physical terms: "Clancy has been at loose ends since he came down from the adrenaline rush of completing [*Clear and Present Danger*] (he wrote the final 45 manuscript pages in a single day to meet his May 1 deadline)."[17] Though hasty writing does not regularly connote artistic achievement, the article earlier distinguishes Clancy's work from that of other popular novelists: "In fairness, he should not be dismissed as merely another book-biz commodity, the action-adventure counterpart to Danielle Steel or Sidney Sheldon. For one thing, Clancy's narrative prose rarely descends to the all too familiar level of 'I'm dictating as fast as I can' " (67). The two statements explicitly contradict one another, with rapid writing signifying either rigor or laziness. The verbal act of dictation is attributed to the female romance novelist Steel and the male romance and horror writer Sheldon, though, while the physical "adrenaline rush" accompanies the writing of military thrillers. The comparison endows Clancy's novels with an aura of masculine labor. Such intensity of effort has been attributed to many respected male writers since World War II, including Jack Kerouac, Hunter Thompson, and William Vollmann. This rigor has not been similarly linked to multimillionaire authors of mass-market best-sellers. Moreover, the profile argues that "to measure Clancy's output solely in terms of bookstore Q-ratings and royalty statements would be to distort the moral seriousness that undergirds his fiction" (67). The combination of vigorous effort and moral weight, then, distinguishes Clancy's novels from the putatively lazy, amoral, not-virile work of other authors. The positioning of the author as a man of vigor defines his novels as embodiments of this vigor. Transitively, Clancy's persona reassures readers that the time commitment and mental efforts of reading will carry corresponding moral—and perhaps even aerobic—rewards.

Like many writers of popular fiction, Clancy frequently connects narrative situations to his readers' physical environments. In particular, the physical situations of air travel and sedentary office work are present in Clancy's thrillers. By association, the act of reading a Clancy novel guarantees analytical rigor, tireless and worthy effort, and the execution of a prosocial masculinity. Clancy's writing style, occasionally strident but mostly devoid of literary pretensions or artful affectations, allows for the experience of reading in otherwise distracting environments. His novels, like much other mass-market fiction, are mainstays of airplane cabins and airport lounges. Though his novels are too lengthy to be read in full during a single airplane flight, their terse dialogue and frequent shifts in location accommodate the interrupted reading practiced by business travelers. In *Patriot Games*, following the novel's explosive opening episode and its aftermath, Clancy asks readers to settle into the act of reading by putting his protagonist in a similar circumstance, seeking diversion on a long airplane flight. The invocation of air travel works as an intervention, an attempt to elevate the experience of reading Clancy. More than eight pages of the novel describe the Ryans' transatlantic plane flight, with narration of Jack Ryan's discomfort in air travel interspersed with what amounts to an encyclopedia entry on the physics of flight. Shortly after the flight begins, Ryan's situation mirrors that of the presumed reader's: "He fished the paperback out of his pocket and started reading. This was his one sure escape from flying" (128). After thus extolling the utility of the reading act, Clancy describes in detail Ryan's reading posture, then comments, "[h]e'd selected well for the flight, one of Alistair Horne's books on the Franco-German conflicts" (128). The passage partly informs the reader that he or she is not the esteemed scholar that Ryan is. While readers immerse themselves in Clancy's popular novel, Clancy's hero reads a serious work of military history. At the same time, invoking real authors and real wars, Clancy makes implicit claims for his own work, positioning it as popular history and identifying his readers as amateur historians. Clancy incorporates civilian air travel as well in the final paragraph of *The Hunt for Red October*, closing the novel with a scene in which the exhausted Jack Ryan falls asleep on a plane flight. The brief episode both ends the narrative on a tranquil note and serves as a cue to readers who, having finally completed the thick novel, can be permitted to doze off themselves. The rigorous (by virtue of its relatively high page count and its many exhaustive technical descriptions) novel finally authorizes readers' own rewarding slumber.

Just as Clancy presents information about jet propulsion and airplane construction as irrefutable fact, he invites readers to situate the novel's ideological conceits in the realm of historical truth as well. In a 1998 interview, Clancy says of his readers: "They're people who want to know how the world really works. My covenant with my readers is that I tell them the way things really are. If I say it, it's real."[18] In a scathing counterpoint to Clancy's assertions of truth, though, *Washington Monthly* editor (and former naval intelligence officer) Scott Shuger details the myriad falsifications and exaggerations surrounding military technology and procedure in Clancy's 1980s novels. Noting the then President George Bush, Sr., and Vice President Dan Quayle's public accolades for Clancy (Quayle's during a Senate speech given while still a congressman), Shuger argues that Clancy's novels generate unjustified public support for seriously flawed national-defense programs.[19] Apart from delivering conservative polemics in narrative form to readers worldwide, then, Clancy's novels can serve also to distort legislators' understanding of pressing foreign-policy issues. Clancy's repeated claims to authenticity help him disavow the novels' generic situation. In Clancy's generic world, a narrowly conservative worldview enables a low-level government bureaucrat to ascend the ladder of success, helping save the world repeatedly, and finally becoming president. Is this "the way things really are?" The broader effect of Clancy's work is the normalization of a peculiar model of semi-active, compassionately conservative masculinity.

Big Boy Toys: Arrested Adolescent Saves World, Gets Girl

However successfully they immerse readers in their thick, fictional worlds, Tom Clancy's novels unmistakably bear the imprint of the persona "Tom Clancy." Most of his novels include multiple dedications, introductory author's notes asserting the validity of technical information, and sometimes a short postscript relating his fictional scenarios to real military operations. His presence brackets his novels, and within the narratives, Clancy uses his protagonists and his readers as conduits for his convictions.

Clive Cussler situates himself differently in relation to his fictions. His novels' frequently antirealist plot conceits—such as the secret moon colony in *Cyclops* (1986)—necessarily limit the clarity of the political positions articulated in his works. Correspondingly, Cussler wisely eschews rhetorical devices such as solemn author notes (some of the books begin with heartfelt or patriotic dedications, while *Deep Six* is dedicated to four defunct taverns). Instead, he offers whimsically self-referential gestures within the narratives themselves. His 1990 novel *Dragon* includes a sequence in which the globe-trotting adventurer Dirk Pitt, a vintage-automobile enthusiast, engages in a classic-car race in which "Clive Cussler" appears as a competing driver who thoroughly tests Pitt's mettle. Cussler's literal insertion of himself into his own fictional world attests to his novels' sense of play with literary conventions, to his readers' presumed amusement with such a conceit, and perhaps to his own inflated self-regard. Cussler does not lend his own character any defining features, aside from an assumed interest in classic automobiles.[20] Instead, he aims for dry humor through the uncanny juxtaposition of author and character:

> When the Hispano-Suiza pulled alongside, Pitt walked over and introduced himself as the driver stepped from behind the wheel to recheck his hood latches.
>   "I guess we'll be competing against each other. My name is Dirk Pitt."
>   The driver of the Hispano, a big man with graying hair, a white beard, and blue–green eyes, stuck out a hand. "Clive Cussler."
>   Pitt looked at him strangely. "Do we know each other?"
>   "It's possible," replied Cussler, smiling. "Your name is familiar, but I can't place your face."
>   "Perhaps we met at a party or a car club meet."
>   "Perhaps."
>   "Good luck," Pitt wished him graciously.
>   Cussler beamed back. "The same to you." (224–225)

In the ensuing race, Pitt narrowly overtakes Cussler. He subsequently becomes engaged in a more dangerous car chase, as Japanese criminals kidnap his romantic interest, a pro-trade congresswoman. The playfulness of the classic-car race—a contest of relatively slow-moving vehicles in which only pride and showmanship are at stake—serves as a contrast to the next chapter's chase, in which characters' lives are endangered. The departure of the Cussler character after the classic-car race alerts readers to the gravity of the following episode. The later chase is the domain of Pitt's character, not Cussler's, and so the novel's promise of purely fictive excitement is reasserted.

The different ways Clancy and Cussler signal their own works' fictional qualities suggest how readers might most contentedly engage with the worlds the novels devise. Clancy's novels construct putatively realistic narratives of military action and political conflict, albeit with a dose of sensation (as when a vengeful Japanese pilot crashes a plane into the U.S. Capitol in *Debt of Honor*, killing the president, most of his administration, and the entire Congress and Supreme Court). In comparison, Cussler borrows from earlier models of fantastic, adventure fiction such as Jules Verne's *Journey to the Center of the Earth* (1864) and Stevenson's *Treasure Island*. Cussler presents the hero of most of his novels, Dirk Pitt, as a physical and cerebral ideal, a handsome, restless adventurer gregarious among men and irresistible to women. In contrast to Clancy's dense realization of technical and strategic information, Cussler provides readers with the travel-guide thrills of myriad exotic locations, recurring cliffhangers, and countless permutations on the formulae of narrow escapes and last-second rescues.

Recurring elements in Cussler's novels include nautical settings and action, evil conspiracies bent on world domination, and searches for lost historical treasure—as the very titles of *Raise the Titanic* (1976), *Inca Gold* (1994), and most unequivocally, *Treasure* (1988), attest. *Treasure* combines a search for a fourth-century library of art and jewels with a battle against a powerful group of international anarchists. *Dragon* includes a Nazi treasure horde amid its narrative of a Japanese businessman's plot to blackmail Western nations. *Deep Six* also features an Asian cartel that plunders merchant vessels and plans to overthrow the U.S. government. In each case, Dirk Pitt, a more rugged American variant on the James Bond type, uses his matchless ingenuity and endurance to restore global order and U.S. hegemony. In addition to their similarities to Ian Fleming's Bond novels of the 1950s and 1960s and the novels' subsequent film adaptations, Cussler's novels borrow conventions from existing popular-literature and film genres geared principally toward men and boys. The novels' nautical settings, narratives of male fraternity, and casts of lawless, seafaring smugglers and killers recall popular English and U.S. narratives of pirates and adventures. Cussler's predecessors include the nineteenth-century novels of Verne and Stevenson as well as twentieth-century series such as Edward Stratemeyer's 1920s Hardy Boys children's mystery novels. Cussler's terse, stylized prose also borrows from the conventions of 1930s and 1940s pulp storytellers such as Kenneth Robeson (author of the *Doc Savage* and *The Avenger* series), Robert E. Howard (creator of the mythological hero Conan), and Edgar Rice Burroughs (author of the *Tarzan* series). Distancing his novels from such fantastic fare, Cussler uses contemporary settings rather than historical or mythological ones. Similarly, he draws upon current political and cultural anxieties, usually surrounding fanatical challenges to the military and economic domination of the United States. (Cussler also incorporates environmental threats, particularly to oceans, and manmade biological viruses.) Also distinct from the mostly male worlds of pulp adventure fiction, Cussler supplies romantic interests for his heroes. In their generally conservative ideological positions as well as their interest in the work of political and government agents, Cussler's novels also overlap with the techno-thrillers and spy thrillers of Clancy, Ludlum, and Coonts. Still, Cussler's rapidly paced narratives and fantastic plots locate his fiction in a less cerebral category than that of his peers on the best-seller lists. Where the other writers at least fabricate a recognizably adult world, Cussler unabashedly imagines a playground of protracted adolescence.

Still, Cussler's adolescent fantasies involve, and are read by, mostly adults. They also figure adult worlds of politics and capitalism in significant ways. Cussler's novels are preoccupied with searches for historical treasure, stolen cargo, and weapons that pose threats to democratic nations. Amid their discourse of the fantastic, the novels recurringly invoke history: Incan society in *Inca Gold*, ancient Greece and Egypt in *Treasure*; *Raise the Titanic*'s sunken ocean liner; and in *Sahara*, ancient Egypt, the Civil War, and a vanished Amelia Earhart–like 1930s pilot. Many of the novels feature prologues set in the distant past. Cussler mobilizes history to legitimate his hero's adolescent-style activity. Borrowing from pulp tradition, his novels reconceive historical events and cultures as sites of vigorous present-day activity. If Clancy's novels partly transform dry technical manuals into quick-paced narratives, Cussler's do the same for middle-school history texts.

Cussler's narrative alchemy reproduces other contemporary discourses as well. Through the objects of his searches, Cussler's hero pursues a fantasy of entrepreneurial capitalism in the relatively autonomous space of the world's oceans. Pitt searches for *Raise the Titanic*'s familiar passenger liner, *Treasure*'s library of antiquity, and *Inca Gold*'s cultural artifacts. These objects bear both market and historical value, making Pitt's adventures exercises in both cultural preservation and personal financial gain. Pitt enjoys the moral rewards of government service and by implication, the more tangible rewards of commercial enterprise (Pitt works for a government agency, yet Cussler suggests through the characters' material possessions that the character profits substantially from his treasure searches). Moreover, his efforts cross institutional lines: just as Jack Ryan works simultaneously as white-collar analyst and hardboiled field agent, Dirk Pitt effectively undertakes military operations alongside historical salvage work (unlike in Clancy's novels, though, no rhetorical maneuvers explain the conflation of the apparently incompatible spheres). Cussler also presents Pitt's seagoing skills as amenable to explicitly prosocial ends, as when Pitt deploys his talents in *Dragon* to halt a madman armed with nuclear weapons. Throughout Cussler's novels, the search for treasure coincides with the need to overcome a violent threat to the United States and its allies. Pitt begins *Sahara*, for example, on a search for sunken Egyptian riverboats, and is soon recruited to thwart a deadly plague, a slavery operation, and both regional and global tyrants. Even *Dragon*, amid its host of menaces, includes a trove of valuable art held by villains. Cussler thus regularly conflates Pitt's entrepreneurial ventures with prosocial missions and cultural stewardship.

In their representation of heroic masculinity, Cussler's novels transport an adolescent ideal into a putatively adult world of political intrigue and conflict rooted in capitalist and nationalist enterprises. The very name "Dirk Pitt," with its phallic connotations, monosyllables, and harsh consonants, represents an adolescent fantasy of adult male virility and activity. Like Clancy, Cussler links his hero's missions to topical political and economic situations, often involving international-trade disputes, which allow Dirk Pitt to employ his seafaring skills. Cussler also provides intermittent technical description, though not in the exhaustive manner of Clancy. Cussler principally describes exotic weapons or scientific devices. *Deep Six*, for example, explains a particularly lethal chemical-warfare compound and a fantastic brain-implanted computer chip. Cussler also describes maritime vessels, diving procedures, and other apparatuses central to narrative action. Clancy's elaborate technical descriptions frequently suspend narrative development, demonstrating instead the novels' avowed utility as information sources and their characters' cerebral capacities (and, by extension, readers' brainpower as well). Comparatively, Cussler's relatively brief descriptions work as a narrative shorthand through which readers quickly apprehend Pitt's ingenuity and the dangers he must overcome. Clancy's novels construct a largely deskbound, technocrat hero who inevitably finds himself at the site of action. In contrast, while Cussler's hero is a friend and colleague of politicians, bureaucrats, and administrators, he is also a restless figure who refuses routine and bureaucracy. In *Deep Six*, Pitt discusses his attitude briefly with his recurrent romantic interest, Congresswoman Loren Smith:

> He nodded at the briefcase clamped in her left hand. "Your crutch. You'd be lost without it."
> "I've noticed you never carry one."
> "Not the type."
> "Afraid you might be taken for a business executive?"
> "This is Washington; you mean bureaucrat."
> "You are one, you know. The government pays your salary, same as me."
> Pitt laughed. "We all carry a curse." (234)

Through this passage, Cussler attempts to reconcile Pitt's explicitly prosocial endeavors with the character's rebel-hero persona. Cussler implies an organizational structure flexible enough to accommodate Pitt, who acts according to interdependent codes of personal interest (a virile desire for adventure, frequently combined with a revenge or rescue motivation) and national service.

Cussler, like Clancy, presents individualism and professionalism as complementary rather than contradictory value systems. For both authors, it is men who embody these values. In another episode in *Deep Six*, Pitt receives orders from Admiral Sandecker, his superior and close friend, before embarking on an undersea venture. In the interest of national security, Sandecker tells him little, giving only the tersest instructions: " 'If you dive on it,' Sandecker said coldly, 'you're not to enter. Our job is strictly to discover and identify, nothing else' " (183). At the end of the conversation, Sandecker anticipates that Pitt will not follow orders: "Almost as the words came out, Sandecker knew he'd waved a flag in front of a bull elephant. Once Pitt dropped beneath the river's surface, the thin leash of command was broken" (184). Pitt's situational rejection of authority appears as a positive trait, a sign of the hero's innate curiosity and his willingness to court danger. Moreover, he is like a "bull elephant," operating on a biological imperative to seek and act. In the novel's logic of professional conduct, Pitt's superiors accept his insubordination because he consistently achieves his goals. As in Clancy's novels, the most esteemed professionals subordinate themselves in the name of duty but simultaneously act as autonomous individuals, guaranteeing action.

Cussler's novels usually play out on the world's seas and oceans, and often on the remote ocean floor. These settings afford opportunities for action and interpersonal contact unburdened by shifting social values. In these settings, Cussler and his characters can also ignore contemporary social conditions such as economic inequality, class prejudice, and social injustice. These locales of course figure not only in Cussler's novels but in countless other literary and cinematic narratives of male testing. The unclaimed, unpoliced oceans provide settings for apparently boundless male action. As in the best-selling "man versus the elements" worlds of *Into Thin Air* and *The Perfect Storm*, Cussler imagines a world in which physically capable white men can prove their mettle without bureaucratic intrusion or concessions to women or other potential opponents. But these are not liminal spaces in which identities shift and social boundaries dissolve. Instead, the "high seas" settings of Cussler's fiction retain Western hierarchies of race, gender, and social power. Men are predominantly brave and resourceful, women are capable but willing, and foreigners and nonwhites plot to subvert democratic values and institutions. The novels' thematic preoccupations, then, are largely ahistorical: like their adaptable hero, the novels surface periodically to take stock of world conditions, then return to the deep, where male activity reigns. The absence of a controlling authority for such locations makes sea and ocean travelers susceptible to an array of human and elemental threats. In the face of such threats, Cussler's novels suggest, only an anachronistic man of action such as Dirk Pitt can offer protection.

Just as many of Clancy's novels filter a wide range of political, military, and technical situations through the perspective of a lone bureaucrat-hero, Cussler makes diplomatic and military conflicts legible by representing one man's management and resolution of them. Dirk Pitt engages closely with a relatively limited cast of characters, but those characters' influence and connections extend the boundaries of Pitt's world into all the novels' significant spheres of power. Cussler gifts Pitt with a congresswoman (Smith) for a lover, a retired senator for a father, and an eminent admiral (Sandecker) for a friend and superior, all of whom grant Pitt access to the highest ranks of U.S. political power. Congresswoman Smith's involvement in trade legislation routinely puts her in close contact with the novels' adversaries. Villains kidnap her in both *Deep Six* and *Dragon*, following the venerable adventure-narrative convention through which public and private agendas are conflated. Pitt's world is quite orderly: characters fulfill precise functions (or, as in the case of Smith, dual functions that help link plots and subplots), and all significant conflicts are satisfactorily resolved at the end of each novel. Readers gain an easily negotiable narrative world, in which putatively real mechanisms of power and physical laws exist alongside the hero's idealized persona of fantastic physical and mental aptitude. Distinct from science-fiction, fantasy, or historical-fiction genres, Cussler's present-day novels deliver readers into a heightened version of the world they already inhabit. Appealing to readers who feel they lack control of their own surroundings, Cussler's novels present a manageable and compact world. Vast conspiracies can be identified through the presence of a limited number of supporting characters, and individual acts of heroism produce a domino effect that restores political and economic conditions favorable to U.S. interests. Cussler uses time-honored genre-fiction strategies for the negotiation of real-world complexities. The novels owe the durability of their worldview predominantly to the iconic hero Dirk Pitt.

Cussler represents Pitt's masculinity as inextricable from capitalism and elite consumption. The author similarly links these economic systems to prosocial concerns such as national defense and historical preservation. Cussler's hero represents a fictional government agency, the National Underwater and Marine Agency, or NUMA. Pitt's investigation of offland crimes and performance of historical salvage operations make his work a

virtually unassailable component of national interests. The NUMA designa-
tion also dissociates him from the ethically compromised activities of other
government bodies. Cussler and Pitt need not apologize for FBI surveillance,
CIA insurgency, or the acts of aggression and environmental pollution undertaken by the military service branches. In addition, Pitt's efforts to defeat
rogue capitalists such as the villains of both *Deep Six* and *Dragon* tacitly
endorse the pursuits of other, nondeviant capitalists. Like the commodity-
conscious super-spy James Bond, Pitt himself venerates the products of capitalism. He lives in a converted airplane hanger that "had the look of a
transportation museum. The polished concrete floor held four long orderly
rows of antique and classic automobiles. Most gleamed as elegantly as the day
their coachmakers added the finishing touch. A few were in various stages of
restoration" (*Dragon*, 147). Pitt's reverence for "classic" vehicles indicates his
commitment to U.S. and Western European capitalism (he owns British and
Italian cars as well as American ones). This devotion also transforms capitalist commodities into sacred objects worthy of museum-quality display (but
crucially, private rather than public display; Pitt is neither showoff nor phi-
lanthropist). Cussler converts the traditionally masculine preoccupation with
automobiles from a conventional display of male ego into a mark of cultural
stewardship. Indeed, Cussler makes Pitt's relationship with cars at least as
meaningful as the hero's relationships with women. He is deeply saddened
after damaging one of his classic cars as part of a high-speed pursuit to rescue
congresswoman Smith in *Dragon*, and in *Deep Six*, the destruction of another
car furthers his desire for retribution. As in the representation of profound
companionship between a cowboy and his faithful horse in film, television,
and literary westerns, cars in Cussler's work serve as a male accessory that
mediates or supersedes men's social relationships.

In Cussler's novels, women exist to serve men's needs and to define the
parameters of ideal masculinity. Most of the novels' women function as
barely relevant aides to government officials, as helpless victims of cruel
villains, or as outlets for Pitt's magnetic sexuality. Rather than depicting
Pitt as a roving Casanova, though, Cussler typically shows women first
expressing sexual desire for Pitt, with his own attentions generally focused
on the mission at hand. Unlike Clancy's novels, in which marriage serves as
an index of men's humanity, Cussler offers an arrested-adolescent vision of
marriage as a threat to male autonomy. In *Dragon*, after Loren believes Pitt
to be dead, she meets for lunch with another woman whom Cussler has
presented as also worthy of the hero's affections:

> "Was marriage ever considered?" asked Stacy.
> Loren gave a brief shake of her head. "The subject never came up. Dirk
> wasn't the kind of man who could be possessed. His mistress was the sea,
> and I had my career in Congress."

"You were lucky. His smile was devastating, and those green eyes—God, they'd make any woman melt." (531)

Loren's career merits a passing mention, but the passage focuses on the absent Pitt, whose allure derives partly from his resistance to commitment. Similarly, Cussler presents Pitt's apparent indifference to women generally— "his mistress was the sea"—as a quality that earns women's respect. When he does engage romantically with women, his lack of concession raises his status further. In *Sahara*, Pitt kills a pair of men who assault a sunbathing scientist, Eva Rojas, whom he later takes to dinner. Following Pitt's spearheading of the dinner plans, Cussler observes, "[l]ike most women, Eva liked a take-charge man" (67). Loren Smith relishes Pitt's brusqueness as well. Meeting her for lunch in *Deep Six*, he compliments her beauty by saying, " 'Damn, you look ugly today.' " In the ensuing discussion, Smith comments, " 'I do give you credit, though. You're the only man I know who doesn't kiss my fanny' " (194). Her response validates male discourtesy, transforming it into a sign of truthfulness. Politeness, by contrast, appears a sign not of civility but of artifice, which is anathema to the plainspoken Pitt.

In addition to her wholesale acceptance of Pitt's rough-edged individualism, the hero's ideal woman combines a masculine ability to exercise social power with a requisite amount of feminine vanity. In *Dragon*, Cussler introduces Congresswoman Smith in her working environment but quickly turns the description toward her romantic pursuits:

> Tight-packed with energy, she was as elegant as a lynx and as daring as a tomboy. Respected for her political cunning, she carried a great degree of clout in the house [*sic*].
>
> Many powerful men in Washington had tried to win her favors on and off the House floor, but she was a private person and dated only men who had nothing to do with business and politics. She carried on a loose secret affair with a man she deeply admired, and was comfortable with the thought that they could never live together as intimate friends or as husband and wife. They both went their separate ways, meeting only when it was convenient. (180–181)

Cussler does not explicitly identify Smith as Pitt's lover, indicating their relationship instead through their obviously compatible characteristics. Smith's masculine attributes—"energy," "cunning," "clout," and her "tomboy" nature—demonstrate that she shares Pitt's values. Most importantly, her own uninterest in commitment supports the fantasy of autonomous bachelorhood that Pitt represents. Her avoidance of romantic partners who share her career similarly accords with Pitt's antibureaucrat stance.

Of course, Pitt's stated values indicate that he logically would not romance a politician, a contradiction Cussler does not fully resolve. However, Smith's "private" nature codes her to some degree as an outsider, one who endures Washington's atmosphere principally because of her dedication as a public servant. In a capsule description of Pitt, Cussler identifies the hero's casual nature as a quality that allows him to transcend social and attitudinal divisions: "He was a smooth article who moved easily among the rich and powerful, but who preferred the company of men and women who drank their liquor straight up and liked to get their hands dirty" (*Treasure*, 47). Pitt's "smoothness" contrasts with Smith's "cunning," locating him at a higher position in the novels' moral hierarchy. Cunning serves here as a floating signifier. It is first a conventional quality of politicians, a disproportionately male group. At the same time, it aligns with a broad cultural formulation of feminine duplicity and artifice.

The boundaries of Congresswoman Smith's body also distinguish her from her virile mate while connoting her suitability as a romantic partner. In a rare moment of female interiority in *Deep Six*, Cussler represents Smith alone, examining her body:

> She struck an exaggerated model's pose in front of a full-length mirror. The body was holding up quite well, considering thirty-seven years of use. Jogging and ballet classes four hours a week kept the centrifugal forces at bay. She pinched her tummy and sadly noted that slightly more than an inch of flesh protruded between her thumb and forefinger. [. . .] She steeled her mind to lay off the alcohol and desserts. (267–268)

The passage's insistently manly language—the use of words and phrases such as "struck," "kept at bay," and "steeled"—typifies Cussler's prose style and suggests its unsuitability to representation of women's psychological lives. Cussler consistently represents Pitt, whose age is close to Smith's, as one who is in the prime of his life. In comparison, "thirty-seven years of use" of a woman's body suggests a waning physical beauty. Smith's "exaggerated model's pose" underscores the impetus of the episode. The act of posing, with an implied but absent male gazer, reminds readers that Smith's beauty works principally to define Pitt's tastes, not to indicate her own self-fulfillment. Her body, too, requires scheduled maintenance— jogging, ballet, and dietary restrictions. This restrictive notion of female beauty applies to other women in Cussler's novels. In *Sahara*, he describes a NUMA scientist, Muriel Hoag, as "quite tall and built like a starving fashion model" (272).

Contrastingly, Cussler represents Pitt's physique as a natural byproduct of his vigorous lifestyle: "His main exercise was diving; he seldom crossed the threshold of a gym. [. . .] He was constantly busy, physically moving about, walking up to five miles a day in the course of his job" (*Dragon*, 65–66). Cussler thus privileges a working-class ideal in which routine labor produces physical strength. Introducing Pitt in *Treasure*, Cussler similarly discredits a bourgeois model of fitness by design: "Pitt was a lean, firm-muscled man in prime physical shape for someone who didn't run ten miles every day or look upon the exertion and sweat of bodybuilding as a celestial tonic against old age. His face wore the tanned, leathered skin of an outdoorsman who preferred the sun to the fluorescent lighting of an office" (47). Pitt's natural physique requires no extraneous activity; "crossing the threshold of a gym" represents, in Cussler's universe, an act of weakness or submission rather than a legitimate pursuit of self-mastery. Pitt's ability to maintain fitness in the course of his work situates him above white-collar workers in a hierarchy of male virtue. His casually maintained, ostensibly natural physical form easily surpasses his female counterpart's conscientiously shaped figure. Smith's sedentary career does not contribute to her physical fitness, and she finds herself pinching unwanted fat despite her exercise regimen.

Periodically, women who fall outside the novels' narrow parameters for acceptable female behavior appear. Some represent a femininity incompatible with Pitt's worldview, such as a waitress who cannot comprehend his grief over the loss of a car. Others represent inappropriate, unsanctioned female power. The sinister leading villain of *Deep Six* is an aged, wheelchair-bound Korean shipping magnate, Madame Bougainville. Forced into prostitution as a child, she has gained status after marriage to a prosperous Frenchman. Cussler depicts her as reclusive and disdainful of worldly pleasures, attentive only to her criminal enterprises. Because of her late husband's business success, she herself acquires power in the male-dominated industry of international trade. Her physical weakness requires that her son and other male functionaries perform the physical duties of the enterprise; in short, a monstrous foreign woman directs male servants to perform acts of violence and destruction. In addition to describing her ruthless activities and temperament, Cussler defines her villainy through her advanced age and infirmity, her Asian ethnicity, and her femininity. Bougainville's physical decrepitude indicates the abnegation of her expected role as a woman; her disabled body cannot serve or accommodate men. Similarly, her psychological ruthlessness represents her betrayal of conventional principles of female compassion. She exhibits no remorse, for example, when recalling an act of piracy that has caused many deaths. Racial difference further signifies the villainess's errant femininity, with the stereotype of the inscrutable Asian compounding readers' estrangement from her. Cussler regularly serves up nonwhite villains, using racial difference as shorthand for anti-Americanism. These racial constructions, like those of gender, further normalize the beliefs and activities of the novels' conservative, white, economically privileged characters.

Male Fantasies and the Real World

Given the shifting roles of the U.S. military and government in world affairs, as well as the changes in gender roles and responsibilities since World War II, Clancy's and Cussler's formulations of male heroism can appear hopelessly anachronistic, but their durability is inarguable. At the end of the 1990s, Clancy began positioning his works to appeal to younger generations of male audiences. The first in a series of paperback *Net Force* novels bearing his name as coauthor appeared in early 1999, coinciding with an ABC television miniseries of the same title.[21] Similarly, Clancy's multimedia corporation, Red Storm Entertainment, released a computer-game version of the novel *Rainbow Six* simultaneous with the book's release, further asserting the author's presence among those consumers who might not otherwise pay attention to his work. Somewhat later, his first work set after the 9/11 attacks, *The Teeth of the Tiger* (2003), showcased a younger group of protagonists, in particular Ryan's son, Jack Jr. At a trifling four hundred and thirty pages in hardcover, it is Clancy's shortest novel, another factor helping market it to younger readers. Meanwhile, Cussler's novels continue to sell in large numbers, and abridged versions have also been produced for younger audiences.[22] Narratives of lone, white, middle-aged heroes' triumphs over global threats and preservation of democratic-capitalist values still attract substantial portions of the U.S. reading public. In the post-9/11 world, the representation in both men's novels of a smoothly functioning national-security apparatus offers new reassurances. Throughout their work, both Clancy and Cussler transform the complicated networks and institutions of military power and multinational capitalism into coherent, relatively concise systems directly linked to the concerns of a small group of heroic individuals, principally men. Both novelists offer narrative stability and closure as an alternative to local and global trans-formations in political-military power, corporate ownership, gender roles, race relations, and family structure.

Cussler's work in particular offers a bulwark against real-world changes in male and female social roles. In a 1996 interview, Cussler called his novels "just plain, old-fashioned adventure."[23] "Old-fashioned" is perhaps the most significant term in his formulation, since his novels present a world in which male chauvinism is consistently rewarded and rarely dis-puted by female characters. Cussler offers the unimpeachable male icon

Dirk Pitt as an object for male readers' vicarious identification and female readers' mobilized desire. Cussler observes further, "I think, deep down, women still like the big, strong, mysterious guy to pick them up, carry them off, and save them from disaster" (16). Cussler's women characters illustrate his belief that women's fulfillment occurs principally through male agency. Women in his novels display strength and independence, but they appear lonely and discontented without Pitt's affection and protection. Comparatively, Cussler presents Pitt's own discontent as a sign of masculine restlessness and desire for adventure. Women serve principally as rewards for successful activity, on the same order of importance as a fine wine or a sumptuous meal, rather than as essential or complementary companions.

Clancy's novels, unlike Cussler's, present marriage and family as the motivation for male physical activity and mental effort. Clancy promotes a staunchly conservative marital and familial structure. However, he also represents communities of men and women working together—albeit in unequal roles, as with his portrayals of race—toward shared, socially constructive goals. Cussler, by contrast, depicts male heroism as self-fulfilling but principally reactive, accomplishing only immediate goals of averting some sudden threat. For all their conservatism, Clancy's Jack Ryan and his compatriots do possess a historical awareness. They recognize, for better or worse, their national and ethnic heritages. They also look toward a more peaceful future, in political and military terms if not social ones. Cussler offers his unrepentantly individualistic hero as a universal figure, but Pitt's lack of historical consciousness—aside from a veneration of antiquated military and transportation hardware—renders him unsuitable for social membership in any era. Pitt's longtime individualism liberates him from the patriotic and familial drumbeating germane to Clancy's novels. Still, such freedom does not align him with marginal social groups or discourses, nor does it link him to more progressive masculinities conceived in the wake of the women's movements of the 1960s, 1970s, and 1980s. Pitt exemplifies the paradox of the mass-market hero: he is a prosocial outsider, setting himself apart from the political and economic system under which he thrives. Clancy's Jack Ryan, on the other hand, repeatedly asserts his connections to family, friends, and nation, but these connections blind him to the differences that exist outside his narrow parameters of social value.

Superficially, Clancy's and Cussler's novels offer simple, unconflicted notions of male social roles. Yet both writers carefully negotiate opposition to their heroes' masculinities. Both rhetorically link men to military activity and capitalist enterprise even while disavowing aspects of both systems (e.g., violence and greed). Both too construct a managerial masculinity adaptable to countless situations, and both introduce superwoman figures to show their male heroes' tacit support of feminism's broadest principles. Their strategic configurations of contemporary masculinity differ in many ways as well. Cussler celebrates male physical activity and posits cerebral skills as a component of innate male resourcefulness. Clancy represents mental acuity and analytical skills as the product of rigorous training, as indicative of a professional orientation closely aligned with masculine agency. Cussler's protagonist manages his physical environment through force of will. Clancy's hero manages psychological space as well, exercising restraint and maintaining his humanity in all but the most stressful situations. Clancy's emphasis on restraint and humaneness allows his protagonists to manifest a sentimental streak that in Cussler's novels would connote weakness or femininity. Dirk Pitt is a caricature of traditional masculinity that succeeds in part through its very brazenness. Jack Ryan represents a slightly more nuanced model of manhood, contradictory yet versatile. For Clancy, male sentiment provides a reserve of psychological strength that elevates worthy men above their cold, amoral adversaries. Cussler's protagonist, on the other hand, draws from a well of cruelty and hardness to accomplish his fantastic deeds. Both writers, though, privilege militant, prosocial formations of masculinity that successfully accommodate the prevailing U.S. political, economic, and social order. Cussler uses his protagonist to proclaim the ahistorical quality of U.S. values. Clancy's Ryan, who venerates work and family while demonstrating individualism and proficiency in armed combat, serves as a standard-bearer of contemporary U.S. conservatism.

In their most recent novels, both Clancy and Cussler shrewdly reshape their milieus for the emerging world order of terrorist threats and global economic realignment. Significantly, both novelists rely on a legacy of masculinity transmitted through paternity as a means for renewal and retrenchment. With Jack Ryan Jr. and two of his cousins as its protagonists, Clancy's *The Teeth of the Tiger* constructs a younger man's world of covert intelligence activity. The codes of mature masculinity inform the narrative, but the faces are younger, the bodies more agile, and the crosscutting among plots more rapid than in previous Clancy works. Cussler, meanwhile, favorably complicates Dirk Pitt's world with the surprise introduction of two adult, fraternal-twin children—Summer and Dirk Jr.—in the final pages of the 2001 novel *Valhalla Rising*. Their mother is revealed as the disappeared love of Pitt's life, who had survived a catastrophic underwater earthquake but been horribly disfigured, given birth to Pitt's children, never contacted him again, and finally died (so Cussler rescues his hero from potential deadbeat-dad status). The children, both marine scientists (and the son a virtual clone of his father), aid Dirk Sr. in Cussler's following novel, *Trojan Odyssey* (2003). At the surreal end of that novel, set in 2006, Dirk Pitt marries Loren Smith, and Pitt again encounters the author Cussler. (The death of Cussler's own wife in the interim between the two novels may have contributed to the presentation of a happily married Dirk Pitt.) Whatever motivates Clancy's and Cussler's narrative decisions, both writers engage the post-9/11 world through heroic families—for Clancy, the nuclear unit of the Ryans, with the parents in the background; for Cussler, the patchwork family of Pitt, Smith, and the autonomous twins. The generational narrative celebrates the male lineage in particular. In both novelists' work, paternal influence strongly overrules that of maternity. Moreover, the fathers' examples prove exceedingly useful. Both Jack Ryan Jr. and Dirk Pitt Jr. take up their fathers' professions and contribute to international security. Meanwhile, Cussler explicitly extols the male role in marriage and parenting, simultaneously crippling and killing off the mother of Pitt's children. Even *Trojan Odyssey*'s marriage is balanced by Pitt's preceding defeat of the novel's villain (a megalomaniac industrialist), ostensibly a 400-pound man but climactically revealed as a slim, beautiful woman in an elaborate disguise. The image of this monstrous female masquerade ushers in Pitt's wedding; he patrols against a simultaneously aberrant masculinity *and* femininity before conceding to a conventional social arrangement.

In the 1990s, major film studios produced numerous successful films in the cinematic subgenre that might be termed the mature thriller. In addition to the film adaptations of Clancy's novels, films such as *In the Line of Fire, Air Force One, The General's Daughter* (1999), and *The Rules of Engagement* (2000) featured middle-aged male protagonists who alternately support and challenge the beliefs of the political, military, and intelligence institutions they represent.[24] These films, like Clancy's novels and those of other thriller writers who narrate the exploits of men beyond their physical prime, offer visual spectacle principally through atmospheric tension rather than representations of excessive violence or destruction. Moody, low-key lighting, displays of small-scale military and surveillance technology, and close-up views of actors' solemn, grizzled faces predominate. (*Air Force One* does feature fistfights and explosions, but these elements do not motor the narrative as they do in action spectaculars such as *The Rock* and *Armageddon*.) In these films, as in Clancy's novels—and to a lesser extent, Cussler's as well—male protagonists engage in physical violence only after exhausting other means of conflict resolution. In contrast to spectacle-centered action films, mature thrillers grant their protagonists moral and intellectual victories over their adversaries, much like the genre's novelistic counterparts. In the crudest terms, action films (of the not-mature variety) often present their heroes as supremely unreflective, while novelists such as Clancy offer their protagonist's interior monologues as a barometer for the character's actions. Both strategies renew and complicate conservative versions of male heroism.

While Clancy's and Cussler's novels reaffirm the validity of archaic or fantastic formations of masculinity, they also participate in a larger ideological project. The novels' representations of heroic masculinity, like those of cinema's mature thrillers, demonstrate the intransigence—and the corresponding versatility—of patriarchal beliefs. In Cussler's world, men best earn women's respect and affection when they resolutely refuse to modify their actions and beliefs to accommodate women's desires. Clancy provides a similar if more detailed model of gender interaction. He champions heterosexual institutions of marriage and family while depicting women as extrinsic to the male world of action, diplomacy, and physical and mental labor. Cathy Ryan's character functions primarily to affirm her husband's lifestyle, beliefs, and charisma. Clancy refers frequently to Cathy Ryan's good looks, but her husband's ordinary appearance does not diminish his physical appeal in her eyes. It is not important that an influential man be handsome, but it is essential that his wife be beautiful. These novels and mature thrillers partially counter the blockbuster action film's pervasive images of youthful, indestructible, emotionless masculinity. At the same time, they suggest that ideal middle-aged men are for the most part slightly warmer, less spry variations on their younger counterparts. Films featuring such aging heroes as Clint Eastwood and Harrison Ford— for example, the Eastwood of *Unforgiven* (1992) and *Absolute Power* (1997) and Ford in *Air Force One* and *Six Days, Seven Nights* (1998)—call viewers' attention to the actors' younger personas while providing assurances of the older men's continued physical and sexual capabilities. *Unforgiven* reminds viewers of Eastwood's past roles as a matchless gunfighter, while *Air Force One* assures viewers that the U.S. president can handle himself aboard a flying craft, because he was Han Solo in a previous incarnation. In popular novels and films featuring middle-aged male protagonists, physical strength figures centrally in definitions of masculinity. Even when writers and filmmakers represent a hero's physical strength as diminished from some earlier peak, the character's mental acuity and tactical skills tend to compensate for potential imbalances, enabling his physical triumphs. Constructions of mature masculinity depend on wisdom and professionalism as well, particularly since women characters rarely possess these attributes. The popular thrillers studied here judiciously manipulate the social roles their male heroes play, reconfiguring traditional masculinities in response to a changing social order.

5

Restaging Heroic Masculinity: Jackie Chan and the Hong Kong Action Film

Aside from the massive, long-term popularity of a certain Austrian bodybuilder and the notable but far lesser success of one Belgian karate champion, American action cinema has showcased principally actors born in the United States or in other English-speaking countries. The marketing of Asian stars in the United States has been particularly difficult, given the limited—and often derogatory or patronizing—connotations of Asianness in U.S. culture. Moreover, North American cultural stereotypes about Asians typically fail to distinguish among nationalities or ethnic groups, corralling Japanese, Chinese, Koreans, Vietnamese, and other groups into an undifferentiated, exotic mass. In Hollywood cinema since the 1930s, Asian male stars have appeared in a narrow range of roles, all circulating around a similar code of honor, tradition, and family obligation: for example, Toshiro Mifune's brooding patriarchs in *Grand Prix* (1966) and *The Challenge* (1982), and Bruce Lee's earnest kung-fu master in *Enter the Dragon* (1973). Performance, film form, and reception complicate these roles but do not upset the overall reductive typage. Because of restrictive cultural and generic conventions with regard to Asianness (and nonwhiteness generally), Hollywood studios produced virtually no films with Asian leads between 1973, when *Enter the Dragon* appeared, and 1998, when Hong Kong stars Chow Yun-Fat and Jackie Chan made their respective English-language debuts in *The Replacement Killers* and *Rush Hour*. Not surprisingly, all three of these films feature briskly paced action narratives geared to young and urban audiences. Also in the late 1990s, Hollywood studios granted supporting action roles to Hong Kong stars, including Michelle Yeoh in the James Bond adventure *Tomorrow Never Dies* (1997) and Jet Li in *Lethal Weapon 4* (1998).

Given the substantial changes in the U.S. film industry since the early 1970s, both in terms of corporate ownership of studios and in film production, distribution, and advertising, the success of Jackie Chan's films in a high-production, special-effects-dominated film genre merits careful consideration. This chapter examines Jackie Chan's star persona as it has developed over the course of his prolific and ongoing film career in Hong Kong and Hollywood productions, particularly as U.S. viewers interpret and respond to that persona. Compared with U.S. film conventions for male action heroes, Chan's persona offers a progressive version of masculinity that combines skillful but playful physical dexterity with comic self-effacement. Historically, the martial-arts genre, with which Chan and other Asian stars are often associated, has been only marginally successful in the United States, and pure martial-arts narratives rarely appear in theatrical release.[1] Consequently, white martial-arts stars such as Steven Seagal and Jean-Claude Van Damme have, in their more profitable films, appeared in straightforward action narratives involving gunfights, car chases, and a limited amount of acrobatics and hand-to-hand combat, rather than swordplay or martial-arts kicks and punches.[2] Moreover, in the 1990s, the appeal of professionally trained fighters such as Seagal and Van Damme was overshadowed by films relying on expensive pyrotechnics and digital effects rather than on scenes of hand-to-hand combat. Distinguishing him from the stylized American action-hero persona, advertising and promotion for Chan's successful U.S. releases—particularly *Rumble in the Bronx* (1996), *Supercop* (1996), and the *Rush Hour* series— has foregrounded his acrobatic and combat skills. Chan's characters also provide both the source and target of physical comedy. Contrasting too the stoic aggression and ironic detachment characteristic of U.S. icons of active masculinity, Chan's films foreground his characters' earnestness and emotional vulnerability.

Challenging the notion that Western models of masculinity reflect a monolithic global ideal, Chan's characters and his films' narratives rely on alternative modes of male heroism, modes scarcely evident in U.S. popular culture. Debuting as a child performer in low-budget Hong Kong martial-arts films, Jackie Chan appeared in more than fifty films by the end of the 1990s. He was Hong Kong's, indeed all of East Asia's, largest box-office draw from the mid-1980s to the late 1990s, serving as actor and often also as director, stunt choreographer, and screenwriter of films that blend furiously paced action sequences and stunts with whimsical comedy. Chan's star persona, developed over a broad range of films produced in Hong Kong and the United States, combines acrobatics, hand-to-hand combat skills, self-deprecating wit, and psychological and physical vulnerability. Until the mid-1990s, Chan's films relied principally on Asian audiences for their revenues. Though his Hollywood films rein in his antic persona to some degree, his roles for decades have displayed striking contrasts to U.S. cinema's archetypes of heroic masculinity.

Chan's star persona and his successful penetration of the U.S. action-film market in the 1990s represent a significant development for film action heroes. In their visions of heroic masculinity since the 1960s, film and popular literature have responded to pressures surrounding male cultural roles variously through violence, spectacle, exaggeration, and fantastic resolution of narrative conflicts linked to real social problems. In the vast majority of the formations of heroic masculinity this book has studied, the utility of conservative, often anachronistic models of male agency is repeatedly reasserted through form and narrative. Chan's films, in comparison, redirect the action films' narrative and visual energies toward progressive ends. Chan's many films with international settings and characters of different nationalities emphasize cross-cultural understanding. His historical martial-arts narratives as well as films with present-day settings show openness to modernity and cultural change. Finally, in contrast to U.S. films' frequently gratuitous, unmotivated violence, Chan's films redefine violent combat as both consequential and as a source of broad-based pleasure for viewers as well as screen performers. Chan's films often privilege reverence for and loyalty to governmental institutions, family, and Chinese culture. However, they simultaneously validate youthfulness, dynamism, and nontraditional roles for women. The progressive racial and gender politics of Chan's work, particularly when circulated among U.S. viewers and in other global film markets, offer an encouraging alternative to the cultural hegemony of Hollywood films that feature conventional, white male agency and violence.

Chan's persona both emphasizes the performer's physical mastery and situates him as a comic underdog. This persona challenges Western—and to some extent, global—definitions of heroic masculinity, suggesting the tenuousness of many historical models of male agency and control.[3] Physically, Chan incorporates into action-oriented narratives the burlesque body fundamental to comedy. His body's continuous motion emphasizes his vulnerability and thus calls into question conceptions of the ideal male body. Chan appears simultaneously active and vulnerable, in contrast to the archetypal action hero, whose physical presence paradoxically relies upon a literal inactivity or passivity. Chan's films further avoid the erotic, and often homoerotic, treatments of the male body common in U.S. action films. By U.S. standards of representation, Chan's costumes and bearing do not exude sex appeal, nor does his body attain object status through displays of flexed muscles or through the slow, deliberate movements that U.S. action films use to connote manly self-assurance and control. (Poking fun at the display of male vanity, *Rumble in the Bronx* features a brief comic interlude of Chan flexing his muscles at a store in front of a two-way mirror, unaware that others can see him.) Moreover, the comedy in Chan's films stems not merely from the actor himself, but from the actions of other characters and from the convergence of narrative circumstances upon the hero. Comedy often places Chan's characters in submissive, masochistic positions, destabilizing their control over the films' humor, if not their action.

Genre and the Development of the Comic Action Hero

Since the early 1980s, the action film has been Hollywood's principal money-making genre in international markets. Largely geared toward young, male audiences, both within the United States and abroad, action films through the late 1990s typically foregrounded solitary male heroes. As we have seen, the action hero's character traits largely accord with traditional Western definitions of idealized masculinity: physical size, strength, charisma, pronounced facial features, aggressive behavior, and the ability to generate action. The presumed "naturalness" of this combination of traits disguises the construction of male gender identity, an identity normalized in countless Western cultural pursuits, institutions, and media. As Chan's films demonstrate, however, Hollywood's typology of the action hero does not reign worldwide.

To contextualize Chan's films, attention to the dynamics of U.S. comic action cinema is in order. The muscular, athletic, skilled-with-weaponry male hero was conventionalized in films such as Douglas Fairbanks's silent 1920s adventure films, including *Robin Hood* (1922) and *The Black Pirate* (1926). Fairbanks's characters already showcased a comic high-spiritedness, grinning exuberantly during fight sequences and other scenes in which they command the attention of other men. Subsequent decades saw the refinement of the gun-toting, aggressive-by-nature offshoot of this figure. By the late 1980s, action stars such as Willis, Schwarzenegger, and Eddie Murphy added comic decorations to increasingly familiar conventions of plot, character, and the representation of violence. Late-1990s Hollywood action films routinely kept genre conventions in play through other forms of parody. Action-comedies such as *Grosse Pointe Blank* (1997) and *The Big Hit* (1998) introduced self-conscious characters and plot devices that lampooned the genre's fundamentally absurd approximation of historical reality. In the former, an assassin phones his therapist as he stalks a target; in the latter, a character in a gunfight also carries on an argument with his fiancée and her family.

Hollywood films that mix action and comedy usually subordinate conventions of one genre to the requirements of the other. As Steve Neale and Frank Krutnik observe, the broad range of possible comic situations permits comedy to work well as a hybrid genre (as does its lack of a specific iconography or setting). Neale and Krutnik argue that while other genres also combine into hybrid forms, comedy "seems especially suited for hybridization, in large part because the local forms responsible for the deliberate generation of laughter can be inserted at some point into most other generic contexts without disturbing their conventions."[4] Though audiences accustomed to action-film conventions often abide humor amid scenes of spectacular violence and destruction, comedic elements tend to be decorative rather than fundamental to narrative pacing or viewer enjoyment. Hollywood genre films usually structure the action/comedy mixture through "fish out of water" themes, either by drawing on elements of a specific star persona or building such themes into a story. For example, Eddie Murphy's streetwise, sarcastic persona clashes with conventional police procedures in the *Beverly Hills Cop* films (1984, 1987, 1993). Similarly, Dennis Hopper's manic persona lends humorous connotations to his villain roles in *Speed* and *Waterworld* (1995). Arnold Schwarzenegger's comic vehicles such as *Twins* (1988), *Kindergarten Cop* (1990), and *Junior* (1995) gain their primary comedic value from placing the action star in situations that deny his trademark physique the opportunity to fend off enemy hordes. This formula was revived in *The Pacifier* (2005), where the hard-bodied Vin Diesel plays a Navy SEAL who must babysit a scientist's children. In each of these examples, the foundations of the original genres—action or comedy—remain intact. While they contain some action, none of the Schwarzenegger comedies include action-film staples such as torture, mass destruction, or protracted gunplay. Conversely, the *Die Hard* series (1988, 1990, 1995) never strays into slapstick, which might threaten the integrity and suspense of the dominant action narrative.

Generic prescriptions have historically limited the interplay between action films and comedies. Comedy's inversion of social hierarchies potentially places the male hero's dominant gender position in distress, a transformation that poses serious structural problems for the action cinema. For action films to affirm their protagonists' traditional male role, comedic material must resonate outward from him; he must control the humor. If an action narrative makes the protagonist a comedic foil, he relinquishes some narrative or visual power, diminishing his apparent heroism and his ensuing generic credibility. In contrast, a wisecracking man who lives through beatings, gunshot wounds, and explosions can represent a traditional hero whose fortitude and self-assurance are so absolute that he can laugh in the face of danger. The successful action-comedy *Men in Black*, for example, stabilizes its protagonists' gender identities by isolating them from the fantastic world in which they operate. As they corral shape-shifting aliens and fend off a threat to the planet, they behave largely like protagonists in a conventional buddy-cop film. The heroes' dark sunglasses and black suits, for example, set them apart from the film's spectacular, cartoonish aliens, as well as from their fellow humans, most of whom they encounter only fleetingly. At the same time, the film limits the signification of its black protagonist's (Will Smith's) racial identity through his own removal from the film's social world. He exists in an institutional utopia where conventional racism is apparently absent (although grotesque exaggerations of immigrant aliens abound). Similarly, Smith's character becomes a comic foil only after demonstrating his abilities as a heroic policeman. Rather than critiquing or refiguring male identity, decorative comic elements here refine the reigning model, giving it the semblance of flexibility and renewing its appeal. In comparison, Chan's films, rather than using comedy to reinforce conventional signifiers of self-assured male power, mobilize comedy as an intrinsic component of the star's masculinity. Comedy provides Chan's male heroes with a source of strength and autonomy. It simultaneously motivates viewers to respond to his protagonists' vulnerability and self-effacement.

At the end of the twentieth century, the Hong Kong film industry remained the world's third largest national cinema, trailing only those of the United States and India.[5] Like other national cinemas, it produces mostly genre films, in both locally specific and globally popular genres. Hong Kong films long offered viewers either sentimental romances or crime and action dramas, broad frameworks allowing a wide range of narrative, stylistic, and tonal choices. Within these frameworks, elements from other forms such as musicals, comedies, fantasy, and historical epics often combine in a single narrative. In the 1990s, independent U.S. directors began to appropriate elements of Hong Kong cinema in their own films. Quentin Tarantino transformed Ringo Lam's *City on Fire* (1987) into *Reservoir Dogs* (1992); his later *Kill Bill* series (2003, 2004) mixes U.S., Hong Kong, Japanese, and other action-cinema traditions. Mexican American director Robert Rodriguez incorporated elements of John Woo's *The Killer* and *Hard Boiled* (1992) into his Hollywood debut, *Desperado* (1995). Conversely, many Hong Kong actors and directors in the 1980s and 1990s—most prominently Jackie Chan and John Woo—often consciously referred to the plots of existing Hollywood films.

The Westernization of Jackie Chan

Chan's films since the late 1970s set box-office records in Hong Kong and elsewhere in Asia, but until the mid-1990s he remained largely unknown to American audiences. Before New Line Cinema (controlled by Time Warner) and Dimension Films (a Miramax subsidiary) contracted for distribution rights to some of Chan's films, most of his Hong Kong productions received only limited release in the West, and his early English-language films fared poorly in the American market. He appeared as a comic supporting character in *The Cannonball Run* (1982) and its sequel and played the lead in *The Big Brawl* (1980) and *The Protector* (1985), both unremarkable B-grade action pictures noteworthy only for Chan's unusual stuntwork. In *The Big Brawl*, Chan's performance includes some comedy. In one mischievous fight sequence Chan's character, adhering to his father's dictate that he refrain from fighting, adopts a passive combat style, ducking or sidestepping his opponents' blows so that they collide with each other or with brick walls. Mostly, though, he appears in the film as a sincere and serious fighter in the Bruce Lee mold. In *The Protector*, as a sidekick to Danny Aiello's tough-talking cop, Chan plays a one-dimensional Asian Other, and his character traits include, almost exclusively, honor and solemnity.

The success of *Rumble in the Bronx* and *Rush Hour* raised Chan's profile considerably in the United States and western Europe. *Rush Hour* was among the top ten films in U.S. box-office receipts in 1998, a year dominated by the action blockbusters *Armageddon*, *Deep Impact*, *Godzilla*, and the late-1997 release *Titanic*.[6] While most Hong Kong films exported to the United States still play only in art houses or in Chinese American neighborhood theaters, Chan's first major-market U.S. release, *Rumble in the Bronx*, received widespread American distribution, complete with a high-visibility print and television advertising campaign. The film earned $9.8 million in its opening weekend in the United States and more than $30 million during its initial theatrical run, making it a great success for a modest-budget film produced outside the United States.[7] Traditionally, Hong Kong films' budgets are minuscule by Hollywood standards. Through the end of the twentieth century, Hong Kong films' production values and special effects were visibly inferior to those of Hollywood films. To counter this limitation, *Rumble in the Bronx*'s advertising highlighted Chan's performance of his own stunts and fight sequences. Similar emphases appeared in advertising for the rerelease the same year of *Supercop* (a film that originally appeared in Hong Kong in 1992 as *Police Story 3* and, retitled, played briefly in the United States in 1993). To broaden the films' appeal to American audiences, they were also dubbed into English, reedited to emphasize action sequences and comedy over character development, and provided with new rock and rap soundtracks, and in the case of *Supercop*, a glossier set of opening credits.[8] Though *Rumble*'s profits suggested that films with non-Western heroes could lure

U.S. viewers, U.S. studios remained reluctant to finance such ventures. Chan's first five films to gain wide release in the United States were produced in Hong Kong, with Hollywood-studio contributions limited to the above changes and to the films' marketing.

Chan's success in the United States has occurred partly because of the performer's comic persona, which distinguishes him from other action stars such as Schwarzenegger and Stallone. Relatedly, in the 1990s Chan gradually redefined himself as an action star rather than a martial-arts star. The more restrictive "martial arts" category limited Chan and other performers to low-budget productions with marginal viewerships, while the broader action category granted access to blockbuster fare with elaborate special effects and saving-the-world narratives. Perhaps paradoxically, the comic treatment of martial arts enabled Chan to broaden his appeal. While his flips, leaps, and kicks appear comically anachronistic in contemporary, firepower-heavy action narratives, his success with these historical combat forms mark him as a triumphant comic underdog, not an out-of-touch kung fu practitioner. The progressive ironization of the US action genre since the mid-1980s—with films such as the relatively humorless *Rambo* giving way to the more self-reflexive *Terminator 2*—produced by the mid-1990s a climate of audience awareness and expectations favorable to the broadly comic tone of Chan's films. The wisecracking action hero remained a staple of the genre in subsequent years, even in otherwise straightforward action films: Will Smith's characters, for example, emphasize comic exasperation in not only the *Men in Black* series but also the relatively serious *Independence Day* (1996) and *I, Robot* (2004). To integrate Chan's skills into this cinematic environment, most of his 1990s films include action sequences involving chases and acrobatics—particularly jumps, flips, and falls from high places—rather than the hand-to-hand combat sequences that dominate his 1980s releases. When hand-to-hand combat does appear in films such as *Rumble in the Bronx* and *Supercop*, fight choreography emphasizes the comically dancelike rhythms of Chan's movements over their practical combat value.

Before 1996, Chan and his films achieved only limited, primarily subcultural, recognition in the United States and other Western countries. He earned recognition among martial-arts fans, who helped form audiences for the films of performers such as Bruce Lee, Chuck Norris, and Steven Seagal. Relatedly, Chan's Hong Kong films were released intermittently in the United States throughout the 1990s for repertory theaters' "Hong Kong festivals" in collegiate and urban locations, drawing college students, Asians and Asian Americans, and cinephiles. Finally, Chan's films, like those of other Hong Kong stars such as Chow Yun-Fat and Jet Li, played in Chinese-language theaters in major cities' urban Chinatown neighborhoods.

These fan groups and theatrical venues accounted for a recognizable audience base but hardly constituted mainstream recognition of Chan and his films.

To achieve recognition and financial success in the United States and elsewhere in the West, Chan's films had to overcome linguistic, cultural, and generic obstacles. Since major studios, particularly in the United States, are loath to distribute subtitled foreign-language films, Chan's first four releases in the West—*Rumble in the Bronx, Supercop, Jackie Chan's First Strike* (1997), and *Operation Condor* (1997)—appeared with English dubbing. *Mr. Nice Guy* (1998, aka *A Nice Guy*), shot in Australia, was filmed in English, as was *Rush Hour*, his first Hollywood-studio production. Similarly, Chan's films widely distributed in Western markets have been those perceived as most accessible to non-Asian audiences, specifically those with plots or situations familiar to audiences of Hollywood thrillers and action films. *Supercop, Jackie Chan's First Strike*, and *Operation Condor* all feature Chan as a spy or adventurer, in the model of James Bond or Indiana Jones, who faces drug smugglers, global terrorists, or war profiteers. These films include sequences in many different international locations (Australia, Thailand, and North Africa, as well as Hong Kong) and rely on conventional action plots, masking the cultural differences apparent in many of Chan's other films. In contrast, films set in China's or Hong Kong's historical past or those featuring traditional martial-arts plots, such as *Project A, Part 2* (1987) and *Drunken Master 2* (1994), although enormously popular in Asia, were long withheld from rerelease in the West because of their apparent cultural specificity. (The latter film was eventually released theatrically in 2000, with English dubbing and some scenes deleted, as *The Legend of Drunken Master*.) In Chan's films with plots focusing on international espionage, the prescriptions of the action genre help to create relatively homogenous narratives that downplay their cultural origins.

The dubbing and reediting of Chan's films for English-speaking audiences also changes their comic meanings. In particular, the films' original Cantonese dialogue often includes reference to Hong Kong and Chinese cultural and historical situations. Even in its dubbed version, *Supercop* comically contrasts urbane Hong Kong residents and rural mainland Chinese, contrasts that Western audiences may fail to discern. Similarly, many of Chan's films, including *Supercop*, make direct or implied references to Hong Kong's return to Chinese rule in 1997, the implications of which may be lost on Western viewers. Perhaps more significantly, *Rush Hour* introduces elements of cultural confusion into Chan's persona, casting him in the mold of a misunderstood Chinese traveler—in accord with the familiar U.S. stereotype of the quizzical Asian tourist—who must prove his mettle to his American associates. These changes or differences notwithstanding, much of the global appeal of Chan's films lies in the actor's physical comedy, which carries a broad, comic meaning across specific cultures.

Promotional materials for Chan's U.S. releases downplay the films' possible cultural differences or reduce those differences to high-concept images and slogans. Promotional posters and print advertisements for *Supercop*, for example, depict Chan suspended in midair from a rope ladder, muscles flexed and teeth clenched, surrounded by attack helicopters and the flames of an explosion. The film itself includes no scene of this magnitude, though in a climactic stunt Chan does cling to a rope ladder attached to a helicopter. The poster's images of explosions and advanced military hardware correspond to Hollywood action-film conventions, as does Chan's pictured attire of black T-shirt, black jeans, and black sneakers, a costume that does not appear in the film either. Cultural differences also serve as a basis for marketing Chan's films. For example, *Rush Hour*'s advertising slogan, "The fastest hands in the East versus the biggest mouth in the West," reduces Chan's star persona to a single, easily apprehended idea. Similarly, the film itself relies on a monolithic conception of Asianness, introducing Chan's character and other Hong Kong or Chinese elements with stereotypical "Oriental" music (sounds of high-pitched strings and flute), and at one point surrounding its protagonists with a busload of camera-toting Asian tourists.

Rush Hour, Race, and Nationalism

Rush Hour, Chan's first major success in the West (its sequel performed even better), repeatedly enforces the notion of Chan and other Asian characters as tourists, as aliens in a Western cultural world. Unlike Chan's previous films, altered for U.S. distribution to obscure their Chinese heritage, *Rush Hour* explicitly emphasizes the foreignness of its Asian star. The film follows a Los Angeles police officer, Carter (Chris Tucker), investigating the kidnapping of a Chinese diplomat's young daughter. Carter receives unwanted assistance from the diplomat's close friend, Hong Kong policeman Lee (Chan). As the African American protagonist and his Hong Kong Chinese counterpart overcome their ethnic and cultural differences, they defeat the Chinese American gang led by a white Hong Kong crime lord (the British actor Tom Wilkinson). The film introduces Chan's character by showing him getting off a plane, highlighting his outsider status. He appears on planes twice more in the film, reemphasizing his tourist situation. Similarly, Lee appears throughout the film in locations around

Los Angeles where Asians might be expected to congregate: at Mann's Chinese Theater, in Chinatown, at the Chinese Consulate, and at an exhibition of Chinese artifacts. Lee's integration into the American cultural world is limited and turbulent, as when he accidentally starts a brawl in an African American pool hall. Lee's only contact with whites is through the film's FBI agents, who are depicted as unfriendly bureaucrats. The film's displayed lack of solidarity between whites and Asians reflects the legacy of anti-Asian sentiment in the United States. Significantly, the film also withholds the possibility of racial reconciliation. Instead, it portrays blacks and Asians as victims of the white power structure's misguided leadership. Meanwhile, the film's white characters appear as conventional supporting players who do not face the consequences of their inappropriate actions.[9] Notably, the film presents a white Englishman as the mastermind behind its Asian criminal organization, simultaneously applying imperialist stereotypes of Asians as nefarious criminals and of white Europeans as habitually corrupt but still innately qualified to lead groups of nonwhites.

Outside the sphere of its white characters, *Rush Hour* establishes connections between blacks and Asians, both at the narrative level and through the film's marketing. Just as Bruce Lee's films performed well among black audiences in the 1970s, Chan's U.S. releases have attracted large nonwhite audiences, particularly Asians and blacks.[10] While Asian viewers constitute a small fraction of U.S. film audiences, African Americans represent a reliable filmgoing demographic, and Hollywood studios in the 1990s shrewdly cast black actors to broaden films' appeal. *Rush Hour* characterizes its stars along racial lines: Chris Tucker's streetwise, trash-talking, sexually forward black man (the trademark persona of this comic star) counterposes Chan's modest, honor- and family-oriented Asian. During the film, racial and cultural ignorance, presented narratively through Carter's disdain for Chinese food and Lee's halting rendition of Edwin Starr's soul hit "War," give way to cultural solidarity. In a key scene (albeit one with little narrative function), Carter and Lee stake out the villains' headquarters, and Lee buys Chinese food for the pair from a street vendor. While Carter initially complains about the food, he soon begins eating it with relish. Carter then asks Lee to instruct him in disarming an opponent (a skill Carter will utilize in a later scene), and in turn, Carter shows Lee how to perform a serpentine dance move. The scene ends with the two characters dancing in rough synchronicity on the sidewalk. The film thus connects Tucker's physical fluidity, a principal component of his star image, with Chan's trademark poise and agility. Because of the scene's relative insignificance to the film's overall plot, it draws particular attention to the characters' cultural differences.

Through its foregrounding of Chan's racial and cultural difference, *Rush Hour* reshapes the version of masculinity that Chan's previous films develop. Chan appears here less as a heroic underdog than as an introverted, misunderstood "child" of Asia who requires coddling and protection from U.S. authorities and from U.S. cultural rituals generally. For example, Chan's first battle in the film, a poolroom brawl, results from his own linguistic blunder (attempting to mimic the slang of another bar patron, he addresses the black bartender as "my nigger," and a fight ensues). Only the tutelage of Tucker's character, the film suggests, can prevent such incidents. The comic elements of Chan's actions derive not entirely from the intrinsic qualities of the actions themselves—in another scene, he escapes from atop a moving bus by clinging to an overhanging street sign—but from reactions built into the narrative itself. The film repeatedly shows Carter staring at Lee in wild-eyed disbelief, adding an element of redundancy that Chan's Hong Kong films typically eschew. While such a reaction renders Tucker's character the comic straight man in a narrative sense, Tucker provides the visible source of humor, contrasting with the serious or distressed expressions that Chan's character often assumes.

Rush Hour's framing of male conflict and its insistence on cultural difference define the film as the product of a U.S. rather than a Hong Kong sensibility. Unlike the majority of Chan's films, which depict his characters' simultaneous allegiance and challenges to Hong Kong Chinese values and beliefs, *Rush Hour* identifies Chan's character as a staunch defender of Chinese cultural tradition. His clashes with the film's FBI agents appear less as conflicts among men than as diplomatic struggles stemming from cultural differences, specifically from Westerners' unwillingness to permit Chan's character to fulfill his duty to his countryman, Consul Han. To accommodate Western viewers, the film also limits Chan's challenges to Western notions of masculinity. His performance—as an actor, fighter, and stuntman—is fairly restrained in comparison to his earlier films, with most acrobatic or fight sequences lasting no more than a few seconds. Conditions of the film's production to some extent dictate this restraint. Owing presumably to insurance requirements, most of Chan's fights and stunts in the film are relatively unspectacular, and he wore a safety wire for the filming of a climactic stunt in which he falls from a great height onto a hanging tapestry. Overall, his character appears controlled and efficient, while the more flamboyant and excessive displays—including a dance after a car explodes in the film's opening scene, and much stylized mimicry of kung fu moves—are reserved for Tucker's character.

The construction of Chan as a conventional, if highly mobile, hero and Tucker as a comic prima donna reduces the overall signification of Chan's character. Since Chan already appears culturally and racially distinct from most of the film's characters (and its eventual viewers), the narrative stabilizes him by downplaying his otherwise comic persona. At the same time, the film limits the visible evidence of Chan's physical strength. While both *Rumble in the Bronx* and *Supercop* intermittently picture Chan in T-shirts or muscle-Ts that display his physique, throughout *Rush Hour* he wears a loose-fitting suit in which he does not appear physically powerful. Such costuming helps define the film as comedy- rather than action-oriented. By understating the physical presence of its strongest representative of East Asia, though, the film also reassures viewers who may be wary of the economic and military power Asian nations possess. The film similarly follows the Hollywood tradition of depicting Asian men as entirely without sexuality. While Chan's Hong Kong films tend to present romance and sexuality through entirely wholesome gestures—hugs between characters, or childlike pecks on the cheek—*Rush Hour* denies Chan's character even this connection to women. (Instead, the film reinforces the convention of the hypersexual black man, making a running joke of Carter's desire to have sex with a fellow police officer, played by Elizabeth Peña.) *Rush Hour* completes its neutralization of Asian masculinity through the defeat of the Chinese gang members at the film's climax. Studios' willingness to bankroll Chan's performances—New Line and Dimension with Chan's redistributed productions, New Line for the *Rush Hour* series, and Disney for the expensive martial-arts western *Shanghai Noon* (2000), its sequel, and others—clearly represents a step forward in terms of Hollywood's racial and cultural representation. Still, the U.S. film industry contains the culturally significant aspects of Asian male stars within particular narrative frameworks, reconstructing Chan as naïve, "fish out of water" tourist and taking the same approach for Jet Li's first lead role in a U.S. film, *Romeo Must Die* (2000).

Active Masculinity and Mobility

Physical movements, or the lack thereof, contribute substantially to Hollywood action cinema's conceptions of idealized masculinity. In action films through the end of the 1990s, audience identification depends on the construction of a powerful and charismatic protagonist, in accord with traditional Western formulations of heroic masculinity. As noted earlier, these archetypes emphasize connotations of physical presence: prominent body musculature; Nordic or Greco-Roman features, meant to indicate an imposing nobility; rigid posture and a fixed gaze, connoting authority; and a bearing that suggests self-confidence. Western action films have long fetishized the male body, relating it to classical statuary's static images of power. Displays of flexing muscles or tense postures (similar to soldiers at attention or athletes awaiting a starting gun) suggest bodies ready for action, if not in action.

In male-oriented U.S. film genres throughout the twentieth century, male protagonists paradoxically assert their agency and control over narrative events through physical stasis. The suggestion of male invulnerability demands physical inertness. Physical and linguistic signifiers of hardness or density—the chiseled faces of Schwarzenegger, Charlton Heston, or Kirk Douglas, with their square jaws and accentuated cheekbones; the deep voices and measured delivery of John Wayne and Sylvester Stallone; even suggestive names such as "Brick" or "Rocky"—connote indomitable power. The slow, deliberate movements of protagonists of westerns, notwithstanding the occasional quick draw or punch, suggest that motion itself is a travail. Wayne's unhurried actions in *Red River* (1948) and *The Searchers* (1956), Henry Fonda's self-control in *Warlock* (1959), and Charles Bronson's relaxed movements throughout *Once Upon a Time in the West* (1968) all denote their characters' tenacity and self-assurance.

The more Western heroes move, the more their masculinity is subject to redefinition. In genres such as the action film or spy film, character movements and body language frequently mimic the behavior of prowling beasts of prey. Inevitably, such representations intersect with androgynous images of motion. Arnold Schwarzenegger moves with "catlike" stalking motions in *Commando* and *Predator* (1987), among other films. Sylvester Stallone displays the boxer's "floating like a butterfly" poise in fight sequences in the *Rocky* films. Often the male hero moves with an eroticized sleekness or fluidity that parallels the visual allure of female runway models; witness Jean-Claude Van Damme in *Timecop* (1994) or Wesley Snipes in *Blade* (1998). In these instances, the male body in motion suggests an erotic display to be appraised by male or female viewers, yet codes of action negotiate these displays. Van Damme appears in his underwear for one action sequence in *Timecop*; costume and exposed skin notwithstanding, the film narratively defines him as being under threat and in action. Similarly, Snipes wears leather pants and vest for much of *Blade*; though attired like a bondage-club patron, he engages in extensive, bloody violence as well.

Numerous feminist theorists have called attention to the traditional organization of narrative around the male protagonist, producing an opposition between man as the determinant of action and woman as the facilitator or place-marker of male activity. Laura Mulvey argues in "Visual Pleasure and Narrative Cinema" that "the male protagonist is free to command the stage, a stage of spatial illusion in which he articulates the look and creates the action."[11] In an extension of Mulvey's project, Teresa de Lauretis observes that in the male-controlled space of narrative, "the female character may be all along, throughout the film, representing and literally marking out the place (to) which the hero will cross."[12] Given this structure, narrative generally favors active, mobile men and passive, inert women. The male action hero, however, demonstrates power most comprehensively through a lack of motion. Once in motion he appears vulnerable, active but also acted-upon. At a film's end, the return to physical stasis marks his ultimate success.

In cinema, male immobility often carries paradoxical meanings. The male body on the run often signifies escape or retreat. Films often use such behavior to comic effect, as in *Running Scared* (1986) and *Midnight Run* (1988), and certainly in Buster Keaton and Charlie Chaplin's films. Only when the protagonist "stands his ground" does he embody uncompromised male dominance.[13] The spectacle of the posturing male, fundamental to bodybuilding competitions and to other popular images such as movie posters and rock album covers, calls attention not only to the exhibition of male power, but also to the "to-be-looked-at-ness" of the male body. In their survey of film masculinity, Pat Kirkham and Janet Thumim note "the contradiction between the vulnerable passivity arguably implicit in the state of being-looked-at, and the dominance and control which patriarchal order expects its male subjects to exhibit."[14] However, they do not address the ways the mobile male body undermines the exhibition of dominance. Spectator sports, for example, represent the interplay of domination and vulnerability. Football running backs and receivers are usually chased, despite being positioned on "offense," and boxers move around the ring to dodge blows. In each case, other powerful males do the chasing or punching. Nevertheless, a successful escape or feint appears consistent with notions of male mastery over events, but only to a point. A satisfactory display of Western male power demands that the male eventually cease flight, and stand and attack.

Cinematic escapes and dodges generate meaning according to their generic contexts. In virtually all of his films, Chan uses flight as a survival strategy. The tactic appears incongruous with the "stand and fight" style of Hollywood action films, a style that depends upon a fundamental paradox: the inactive body of the action hero. Only in the limited context of what might be called the "escape film"—films such as *The Defiant Ones* (1958), *The Warriors* (1979), *The Running Man* (1987), *The Fugitive* (1993), *U.S. Marshals* (1998), and *Enemy of the State* (1998), in which a hero or group of heroes rushes from one perilous situation to another, pursued by policemen or villainous gangs—does flight adhere to the ideology of active male power. These films, built around the teleology of men's escapes, risk demasculinizing their protagonists with such a narrative device. Even in situations in which flight appears admirable or heroic, heroes are motivated not by a masculine logic of power and conquest but by a more ambivalent survival ethic. *The Fugitive* literally imperils the masculinity of Harrison Ford's protagonist. He is at the mercy of patriarchal institutions, the imprecise legal system that accuses him of murder and the law-enforcement apparatus mobilized to pursue him. In addition, he does not visibly embody conventional, active masculinity: he does not carry a weapon or display bulging muscles, and he cries several times. Meanwhile, the pursuing marshal played by Tommy Lee Jones assumes the more stable masculine role of the respected, canny authority figure. One source of Ford's credibility and appeal in the film is precisely this inability to occupy the active male role, which makes him an object of empathy rather than idolization. In most escape films, the protagonist's flight is made to appear sensible because his pursuers are more numerous or better armed, and often the hero's masculinity is proven at the climactic point at which he single-handedly overcomes his foes, as evident in *The Running Man* and *First Blood*. Even *The Fugitive* hedges its bets by concluding with a teeth-baring fight sequence. Within the action genre, then, the pursued can reassert their masculine identity by triumphing over overwhelming odds or superhuman representations of masculinity.

Comedy in Motion

While conventional U.S. action films consistently avoid locating their protagonists as targets of comedy or in other demasculinizing situations, Chan's films rely on comic treatments of escape that redefine his characters' male identities while reducing his antagonists to caricatures of "serious" masculinity. Chan's stunts resemble those of his predecessors Keaton and Harold Lloyd, but Chan's stunts and comedy operate in a significantly different generic context than those of the silent-film comedians. Keaton's and Lloyd's small sizes and lean physiques, for example, visually distinguish them as comic performers rather than as suitable protagonists for 1920s action and adventure films. Chan's similar agility, grace, and underdog persona translate effectively to the contemporary action genre, particularly because his comedy and acrobatics invariably coincide with displays of prowess in hand-to-hand combat. His onscreen victories ultimately demonstrate his manhood. At the same time, Chan's films import the pratfalls and deflating situations of comedy, adding a broader source of appeal to the predominantly male-centered identification that his fighting skill encourages. When Chan's films give precedence to his comic temperament, his opponents typically fail to overpower him. These men—criminal henchmen, gang members, and other fighters who use either martial arts or cruder fisticuffs—usually wear serious expressions and comport themselves rigidly, tactics shown as unsuited to victory over a comic hero. Resituated within conventions of comedy, Chan's adversaries play the role of straight men or comic buffoons instead of representing imposing physical threats to the protagonist. Comedy thus shifts the emphasis of Chan's films away from the action film's masculine schema of mastery and control. Nevertheless, his films, like Keaton's and Lloyd's, call attention to the physical mastery required to execute dangerous stunts. Notably, *Rush Hour* circumvents the representational problem of demasculinization (i.e., how to define a figure who grins youthfully and runs from his opponents as a worthy male hero) by depicting Chris Tucker's character as a fast-talking braggart who performs badly in combat or sheepishly avoids it. Compared to the hypercomic Tucker, Chan's character appears more conventionally heroic—and thus more ideally masculine—by default. Chan's previous films, though, foreground the star's reluctant-hero persona, renegotiating the action cinema's terms of idealized masculinity.

Chan's persona relies heavily on uninterrupted movement as a signifier of limitless maneuverability. His films usually include multiple martial-arts combat sequences, applying a trademark style that fight choreographer Craig Reid identifies as the "Perpetual Motion Technique." Its premise, Reid observes, "is the maintenance of continuous body motion throughout the entire fight sequence to give the impression of nonstop action."[15] In *Drunken Master 2*, for example, Chan battles scores of ax-wielding assassins for nearly five minutes of screen time, remaining out of his attackers' reach by leaping, punching, and kicking his way around a spacious teahouse. Fight sequences in his films typically occur amid elaborate sets, and combat covers a great deal of space, the result of Chan's traversal of horizontal and vertical distances. Chan's stuntwork directs viewers' attention to his physical interaction with surrounding architecture: his movements around indoor furniture and other obstacles, up and over walls, along the outsides of tall buildings, and clinging to moving vehicles. Such interaction makes viewers aware of the real spatial dimensions and structural properties of the objects displayed. In Hollywood action films, by comparison, the protagonist tends to dominate the spectacle no matter how disproportionately large the backdrop of action might be, and many objects function only to prove the protagonists' destructive capabilities. In an iconic scene in *Rambo*, for instance, Stallone's Rambo, after engaging in an explosive battle that levels a village of thatch huts, appears in medium shot while a massive fireball erupts behind him. Camera perspective allows Rambo and the fireball to appear roughly the same size, making the hero appear larger than life to the viewing eye. Rambo, bare-chested and sweating, runs toward the camera in slow motion, making his body a spectacle of dominance as well as an object for erotic contemplation (though the violent iconography partly challenges this appeal).

Jackie Chan's characters rarely, if ever, receive erotic or epic-hero treatment in his films. Though he engages in hand-to-hand combat throughout his films, he rarely appears shirtless or in the conventional action garb of a torn T-shirt or other revealing or form-fitting clothing.[16] Camera angles do not denote his character as an object: close-ups, conspicuously absent in his early starring roles, later highlight his comic facial expressions, eschewing "tough-guy" reaction shots and fragmentary shots of isolated limbs or muscles. When in motion, he appears most often in medium or long shots, so his body does not dominate scenographic space, and the camera does not devote attention to his body's proportions. The camera frames him primarily to capture him in action, to show his performance of acrobatic feats. (Chan's 1980s and 1990s Hong Kong productions particularly demonstrate these formal strategies. Later U.S. films such as *The Tuxedo* [2002] subordinate his speed and physical fluidity to close shots and the rhythms of rapid editing, so viewers see few uninterrupted movements.) Similarly, Chan's films typically include stunts and sets that dwarf his character. In *Project A, Part 2*, the lengthy final fight sequence occurs in an open-air market and concludes atop a multileveled bamboo tower, which Chan appears to cover from top to bottom (and vice versa). Throughout the sequence, Chan acts on the defensive, evading attackers and throwing obstacles in his pursuers' paths. He delivers his blows in transit and moves toward new ground from which to attack or ward off foes. The instinct for self-preservation takes precedence over dramatic, static "ready for action" poses.

Chan's perpetual-motion style not only showcases the actor's combat skills but also serves as a primary component of his comic persona. His acrobatic feats parallel those of a circus performer and align him with silent-film comedians such as Keaton, Chaplin, and Lloyd. Gerald Mast observes of early screen comedies, "[t]he essential comic object was the human body, and its most interesting movements were running, jumping, riding, colliding, falling, staggering, leaping, twirling, and flying."[17] As Jackie Chan gained popularity and assumed directorial control of his Hong Kong productions, the films' action gradually shifted from an emphasis on kung fu to a preoccupation with stuntwork and nonviolent acrobatic feats. Nearly every article about Chan written for a general-interest U.S. publication during his mid- to late-1990s rise to Hollywood stardom cites his interpretations of famous scenes from Keaton's and Lloyd's films, as if to remind readers that Chan was worthy of attention not merely as a foreign matinee idol but as an international performer drawing from a venerated film-historical tradition. In *Project A, Part 2*, Chan choreographs the spectacular fall of a huge decorative wall, updating Keaton's falling-house stunt from *Steamboat Bill, Jr.* (1924). In the first *Project A* (1983), Chan revisits the image from *Safety Last* (1923) of Lloyd dangling from a clock tower arm, placing himself atop a clock tower in a similarly perilous position. Differentiating his version from Lloyd's, and in accord with the sometimes masochistic appeal of his films, Chan, handcuffed, plummets to the ground.

Neither Lloyd's nor Chan's comic scenario fits the Hollywood paradigm of male action. Both men's stunts, like Keaton's, subordinate the heroic individual—represented visually by spectacular images such as that of Rambo noted above—to the discernible proportions of character and massive objects. Such a relationship aligns Chan again with silent-film comedians rather than with contemporary U.S. action stars. Writing on the history of film comedy, Tom Gunning notes Keaton's temporary help-lessness amid machinery. The comedian becomes "a projectile in thrall to the laws of mechanics."[18] Mechanical devices in Chan's films, like those in Keaton's, work as comic props, affording characters the opportunity to engage in humorous struggles. With few exceptions, the Hollywood action film uses encounters with objects or machinery for dramatic spectacle, not for slapstick. Hollywood action films put individual characters at the center of large-scale action, magnifying the protagonist to mythic propor-tions. In comparison, Chan's films, like those of the silent comedians, depict large events in relation to human dimensions. Again, the generic context provides the crucial difference: conventions of the action genre supplant viewers' everyday anxieties through fantasies of omnipotence, while comedy conventions engage directly with viewers' sense of social powerlessness and physical limitation. Most Hollywood action heroes embody fantasies of domination over natural and artificial worlds, while Chan's films establish putatively real relations with those domains. The lack of special effects in Chan's films and the regular-guy persona he typically adopts further contribute to this aura of authenticity.

Carnivalesque Space and the Grotesque Body

The action style and narrative settings of Chan's films incorporate sub-stantial elements of the carnivalesque and the grotesque. Through their use of the distinctively low cultural form of kung fu and through the mod-est class status of the films' sympathetic characters, Chan's films resemble a form of carnivalesque ritual. Mikhail Bakhtin's theorization of the carni-val world corresponds closely to the narrative terrain of Chan's films. Bakhtin defines the carnivalesque realm as a liminal and ambivalent space, a festive terrain that breaks down boundaries between performers and audience, celebrates transgression, and simultaneously mocks and affirms traditional institutions. Chan's films regularly transform scenes of violent action into displays of jubilant comedy. The films also close gaps between screen performers and viewers through Chan's ordinary-guy persona, his use of not only large- but also small-scale settings for action (e.g., homes, apartment buildings, and other familiar or indoor settings), and the provision of outtakes showing the films' production. The films typically challenge the utility of conventionally male forms of expression such as serious demeanor, anger, and brute physical force. Similarly, they satirize historical traditions and authoritarian institutions while ultimately affirming prosocial codes of behavior and cultural heritage. Action in Chan's films also parallels Bakhtin's theorization of the grotesque body. The kicks and leaps germane to kung fu correspond with the grotesque's focus on the lower body stratum, and Chan's thematized vulnerability further inverts the male action-hero persona. Bakhtin also argues that "if we consider the grotesque body in its extreme aspects, it never presents an individual body."[19] The grotesque body, he contends, is porous and connected to other bodies. Such fluidity is apparent in the numerous scenes in Chan's films in which he battles multiple opponents simultaneously. Both Chan and his foes move as a single choreographed unit, making repeated contact with one another. They also sweat visibly, another process Bakhtin associates with the grotesque.[20] The overall exaggeration and excess of the action sequences in Chan's films contributes as well to their grotesqueness.

Grotesque elements account substantially for the comic appeal and accessibility of Chan's films and for the challenge they pose to authoritarian aspects of masculinity. Through exaggeration and excess, the films transport the well-meaning underdog into a realm that degrades elite institutions and rituals, affirming folk values and ingenuity. Chan typically plays working-class characters (police officers, young peasants, or wandering adventurers), and while they often contend with authority or bureaucracy, their fighting prowess removes them to a differently ordered world where bodily displays determine status. Chan's working-class characters display apparently limitless dexterity and fighting skills, showing that a comic, acrobatic persona can achieve respect or renown in a wide range of situations, racial and class origins notwithstanding. Chan thus becomes a global ambassador for a revaluation of Asian masculinity.

The issue of body size is central to an understanding of Chan's star persona, particularly in reference to Western archetypes of masculinity. His body does not ascribe to the traditional iconography of classical, idealized maleness. Viewed by Asian audiences, Chan's height and body proportions appear average, if not ideal. In absolute terms, his small stature becomes evident in many of his films when he squares off against a much larger opponent. Chan's unexceptional size functions as a component of his star image. His films present his body in its natural scale, without embellishments of camera position or complementary casting that would reconstruct him as a proportionally dominant male. Chan's treatment bears comparison to Hollywood's long-standing tradition of using cinematic illusions to make its male heroes, from Alan Ladd to Sylvester Stallone, appear taller than they really are. Among U.S. action stars, for example, Stallone and Jean-Claude Van Damme, both men of less-than-average height, tend to appear alongside diminutive female costars or nearer the foreground of the picture plane relative to taller male costars, to create the impression of conventional, towering masculinity.

Many of Chan's stunts literally distort the traditional male form for comic effect. Early in *Armour of God* (1986), Chan curls up his body behind a round shield and rolls away from a band of spear-wielding foes, then uses the shield as a sled to ride down a grassy mountainside. (In this scene, his pursuers become objects of comic spectacle as well when they follow Chan en masse, riding their own shields.) In *Police Story* (1985), Chan uses an umbrella to hook himself to the lower rear, then to an upper side window, of a double-decker bus that escaping criminals have commandeered. Clinging to the vehicle like a tenacious insect, Chan twists his exposed body to avoid collisions with passing cars and to evade his assailants' attempts to knock him off the bus. In *Twin Dragons* (1992), Chan leaps feet-first into the back seat of a parked car during a chase, wriggling his body through the narrow aperture of the open window. In each of these scenes, Chan's body language again recalls Keaton's performance style: a man with a small but athletic, flexible body struggles with objects and contorts his body into comic, defensive shapes. Chan's visually amusing contortions of the body, like Keaton's, conflict with idealized male images. The erect or fully extended body represents the normalized view of the male physique, as a glance at any survey of Western figure art indicates. Consider, for example, Michelangelo's David, Donatello's fifteenth-century St. George, and American and European monumental sculpture and heroic painting generally, which represent erect posture or the standing, extended body as a signifier of available male energy.

Through demonstrations of the modestly proportioned body's access to confined spaces and the contortions necessary to dodge larger physical barriers, Chan implicitly critiques the Western action hero's characteristic hardness and rigidity. Chan's malleable physical form also emblematizes the social and geographic body's potential for mobility. Such a metaphor resonates strongly in Hong Kong, where, as Esther Yau argues in an essay on the colony's 1980s cinema, "the public's preoccupations are survival and upward mobility."[21] Hong Kong has long combined the cultural heritage of mainland, Communist China—emphasizing family ties and other Chinese historical traditions—with capitalism's emphasis on economic wealth and consumption. Chan's domestic popularity stems in part from his evocation of multiple facets of Hong Kong society and culture. Audiences can read his characters as loyal tools of the state or anticorruption reformers, persecuted underdogs or charismatic heroes, dashing adventurers or humble Everymen.

The narratives of Chan's films similarly provoke multiple readings, sometimes earnest and prosocial, sometimes jesting and antiauthoritarian. As Neale and Krutnik argue, comedians' "disruptiveness tends to be contained, and therefore motivated by a (culturally conventional) opposition between eccentricity and social conformity" (106). Chan's own ambiguous persona negotiates this volatile terrain. In *Armour of God*, he portrays an avaricious treasure hunter, ostensibly unconcerned with the plight of his companions. In the film's final sequence, though, concern for his friends' safety takes precedence over his own well-being. Moreover, the film concludes with the destruction of the antagonists' lair and treasure horde, a catastrophe Chan inadvertently sets in motion. To reconstitute his character as a happy-go-lucky adventurer, Chan finally shows no apparent remorse at his loss of fortune. Chan's character offers a simultaneously whimsical and searing critique of authority in *Project A, Part 2*, in which he plays a naval officer assigned to root out police corruption. Over the course of his investigation, he discovers both comic and sinister malfeasance among law-enforcement and government officials, and finds his most trustworthy allies among a group of revolutionaries. By the film's end, the members of the navy, the virtuous police officers, the revolutionaries, and even a band of motley pirates all rally around Chan's character. Class conflict drives the narrative of *Twin Dragons*, where Chan portrays both a working-class auto mechanic, Boomer, and his twin brother John Ma, a refined concert pianist. The film's comic situations and double-entendres rely on class disparities, but in the end, a double wedding equalizes Chan's characters and their respective mates. In these cases, and throughout his films, Chan serves as the locus for a negotiation of Hong Kong's class dynamics.

Masculinity Dismantled

Chan's kung fu fights also use comedy to exaggerate conventional trials of manhood. In one of his earlier kung fu comedies, *Fantasy Mission Force* (1982), Chan first appears as a contestant in a rural "fighting champion" tournament. Before combat, he engages in a game of psychological one-upmanship that revolves around oral fixations: his opponent smokes a cigarette, so Chan smokes a thicker cigarette. His opponent counters by smoking a cigar, and Chan responds with a larger cigar. Finally his opponent lights a pipe, and Chan follows by puffing on a comically oversized pipe, filling the screen space with smoke. Intimations of sexual insecurity and male performativity inform the scene's visual comedy. In the ensuing fighting match, Chan's blows do no apparent damage to his far larger opponent, exposing the preceding phallic showdown as a poor litmus test for male power.

Chan adopts the mannerisms and static posture of the invincible male only to expose those characteristics as ridiculous and laughably artificial. At the conclusion of the bus chase in *Police Story*, Chan assumes a stance that suggests the mythical qualities of the Western action hero. Standing alone on an open highway as the bus bears down on him, he patiently loads bullets into his revolver, then aims it at the onrushing vehicle. The driver, in a panic, brakes quickly, sending passengers flying through the front windows as the bus grinds to a halt directly in front of Chan's unflinching body. A shot of Chan standing rigid, gun pointed at an enormous bus, along with the scene's editing tempo and sound effects such as the villains' stupefied cries, code the event as comedy. With minor variations in editing and music, the scene would appear convincing in a Hollywood action narrative. Presented here, though, it self-consciously parodies the conventions of Western male heroism.

When Chan steps briefly into the boastful male-hero role, a villain or a female foil quickly deflates his attempt to assume a position of dominant masculinity. *Police Story* features numerous comedy sequences in which Chan churns out self-mocking double-entendres to which he appears entirely oblivious. During one sequence, Chan tries to impress a female friend with anecdotes about his dominant status in a relationship, unaware that his girlfriend can hear every inflated word. He wears only a towel during this scene, further connoting a male vulnerability that contradicts his braggadocio. His sweetheart reveals her presence by mashing a birthday cake into his face. The incorporation of this vaudeville trope suggests the artificiality of his adopted "ladies' man" demeanor. Later in the film, a female criminal informer whom Chan guards tape-records a conversation in which his words imply a clumsy sexual coupling. Chan, who plays a police detective, utters phrases such as "Watch what you're doing," "You'll break it," and "It's the only one I've got," while the informer, Selina Fong (Brigitte Lin), makes comments including "You really hurt me," "It's so small and ugly," and "Now I'm all wet." The dialogue actually refers to the mishandling of a potted cactus plant, but Selina manages to have the tape replayed during a courtroom scene, making Chan the object of derisive laughter in a situation in which the success of his investigative work requires the presumption of male authority. Her strategy disrupts both Chan's masculine self-assurance and the patriarchal institution of law itself.

Chan's interactions with women typically emphasize comedy, or even women's fighting skills, rather than romance. In this respect, Chan's films share something with U.S. action films, which generally imply the incompatibility of combat and heterosexual romance, particularly when non-white characters are involved. Hollywood action narratives often supply their heroes with love interests who disappear during fight sequences, watch helplessly from the sidelines, or are captured by villains. Women's exscription from combat scenarios clears space for homosocial dominance or bonding rituals. Action films narratively delimit their sexual energies by restricting the presence of women, the conventional repository of those energies in Hollywood films. This compartmentalization helps action cinema disavow the patent eroticism of men grappling with men. Conventionally, the action hero frequently represents an asexual type. In the heterosexual imaginary, where normative masculinity is construed as natural, male heterosexuality need not be foregrounded; it merely exists, awaiting a woman to conjure it forth. In Hollywood's terms, Asian male sexuality does not exist at all, since major studios do not yet view Asian couples as commercially viable, and Western cultural taboos still delegitimize a white woman's attraction to an Asian man. Chan's U.S. films correspondingly depict him as a sexless loner, and even in his Hong Kong productions, tender relations between the sexes receive drastically less emphasis than stunts and fight sequences (*Twin Dragons*, which showcases Chan's blundering romances, is a notable exception). In comparison, U.S. action films foreground male autonomy but often append a female romantic interest to their male heroes as tacit proof of the men's heterosexuality.

U.S. action films overwhelmingly grant women protagonists active roles only when male heroes are absent, but women participate in action sequences in many of Chan's films. Challenging U.S. action films' rigid gender polarity, Chan's fights alongside and against women both reorient his characters' masculinities and validate displays of female power. In his battles against women, he tends to perform sheepishly, attempting to distance himself from socially inappropriate male–female interactions. When he displays overtly chivalrous behavior in *Fantasy Mission Force* and *Armour of God*, his female opponents take the opportunity to inflict unreciprocated pain on him. Idealized masculinity, across Western and most Asian cultures, defers to women in situations involving physical force. Respecting taboos about harming women, the gallant male hero appears ill-equipped to cope with manifestations of female strength. Chan's skirmishes with women proceed mostly in a comic vein, but they also suggest that his version of masculinity leaves room for an accessible subtext of female power. In numerous Chan films, as in scores of Hong Kong films since the 1960s, women appear in primary combat roles. Chan's *Supercop* costar, Michelle Yeoh (credited in this film and some others as Michelle Khan), not only plays a central role in numerous fight sequences, she also performs some of the film's most breathtaking stunts, including a motorcycle jump onto a moving train.

Comic Violence and Narrative

Chan's films often reveal their comic dimension in the midst of violent or otherwise hazardous action sequences. In a 1991 interview, Chan suggested that audience tastes motivate his films' movement toward spectacles of unusual action and away from more conventional fight sequences:

> Kung fu belongs to the past. In Hong Kong, we don't talk about "kung fu" movies anymore but about "action" movies. Films are getting faster and we don't care too much about fights anymore. What people want are stunts. [. . .] I'm always trying to imagine funny and dangerous stunts.[22]

Despite their escalating reliance on spectacular stunts rather than fight sequences, Chan's Hong Kong films always include many hand-to-hand combat scenes. The deliberately comic violence of Chan's films generally runs counter to Hollywood films' graphic violence. Hollywood action violence often provokes laughter through its flagrancy or outrageousness, even when it does not appear in a comedic context. The antirealist spectacles of most Hollywood action films promote reception of screen violence as representation, not as symptom of social violence. Chan's films produce a somewhat different effect—they break down taboos about violence by showing it as a natural extension of physical comedy. The young Buster Keaton's vaudeville moniker, "the human punching bag," suggests the comic dimension of physical violence, as do the routines of vaudeville-style performers such as Laurel and Hardy and the Three Stooges. Peter Kramer, in an essay on Keaton, notes the performative skills necessary to conceive humor from violence:

> To transform acts of willful maliciousness and intense pain into comedy, performers had to signal clearly that their actions were make-believe, and constituted highly accomplished athletic routines. The actions' excess, their fantastic exaggeration, as well as performers' self-conscious address of the

audience, were the most obvious indicators of their professional and ritualistic nature.[23]

Chan's comic excesses lend the stunts and fight sequences in his films an appeal different from the purely sensational and spectacular displays of violence typical of contemporary U.S. action films. In contrast to the destructive spectacle of U.S. action-film violence, Chan's films represent physical combat as an opportunity for comic innovation, and Chan's inventive acrobatic displays supply viewers with pleasures long unavailable in U.S. action films.

To a great extent, the structure of Chan's films transforms their narratives' overarching social concerns—political instability and imperial oppression in *Drunken Master 2*, corruption and revolutionary activity in *Project A, Part 2*—into farcical components of a comic storyline. Regarding a series of silent slapstick films, Donald Crafton argues that through their physical comedy, the films indicate that "the seeming hegemony of narrative in the classical cinema is being assaulted by the militant forces of spectacle."[24] In Chan's films as well, plot elements often function principally to deliver viewers from one discrete episode of visual spectacle to another. As Tom Gunning makes clear in a response to Crafton, slapstick gags work both as spectacle and as elements of narrative.[25] Many of Chan's exploits emphasize comic spectacle over narrative cohesion. During fights or chases, for example, he often moves from one place to another in a roundabout fashion, highlighting the visual excitement of his motions rather than their utility. In a memorable scene from *Rumble in the Bronx*, Chan tracks a street gang to its lair, where conflict soon erupts. After attacking gang members with pool cues and furniture items, he moves the fight to a room filled with refrigerators and pinball machines. He uses the games and appliances as weapons and shields, and the viewer, rather than pondering the fight's outcome or its relevance to the story, simply attends to the novelty of the display. Following the battle, Chan's character makes a brief speech—saying to the gang, "You are the scum of the earth. Why lower yourselves?"—and his foes shortly become his allies. Though the scene emphasizes comic spectacle, it also further establishes Chan's abilities and advances the films' action.

Slapstick plots transform displays of violence and suffering into elements of physical comedy. Early in *Supercop*, for example, Chan is persuaded to spar with an army drill instructor. The scene helps to establish Chan's character but otherwise serves no essential narrative function. Like many fights in Chan's films, the match occurs solely to test the participants' combat skills. The action's sportive and carnivalesque elements diminish the viewer's sense of narrative drama while leaving sensation intact. The scene includes comic body language from both men, antic cheers from the onlookers, and a cartoonish denouement that leaves Chan's character hanging from a tree branch. Gunning suggests that such an emphasis on gags—or in Chan's case, on extravagant comic stunts—subverts the logic of narrative by transforming gags or stunts *into* narrative. Gags or stunts, "through their integration with narrative, their adoption of narrative's form of logical anticipation," combine narrative progress and absurdist excess.[26] To borrow Crafton's "pie and chase" terminology, the chases in Chan's films are also pies.

Male and Female Masquerade

Chan's Hong Kong films include serious or sentimental interludes that compete with the ironic demeanor his characters adopt when enmeshed in incredible action scenarios. The films' occasionally sentimental elements generally elicit camp responses among Western audiences. U.S. audiences found unintended humor, for example, in *Rumble in the Bronx*'s relationship between Chan and a boy in a wheelchair. While Chan brings a measure of earnestness to nearly all his roles, his characters simultaneously acknowledge the absurdity of their surroundings with self-reflexive deflations of convention. To this end, his films incorporate a considerable amount of masquerade. When he assumes the conventional persona of the male action hero, Chan undermines the fantasy that such a figure could actually inhabit social reality. In their excessively comic behavior, Chan's characters usually do not contribute to discourses of cinematic realism. The international adventurer he portrays in *Armour of God* and its sequel, for example, draws directly on Hollywood's Indiana Jones character. In Chan's variation on the role, he not only displays the comic fear and vulnerability of the original, he also pauses to toss pieces of candy into his mouth during chaotic chases and fights. Though Chan rarely engages in the sardonic repartee characteristic of Hollywood action heroes, his quizzical facial expressions signify a refusal to accept the film world's fantastic trappings as entirely serious, even when his life is apparently—or, in many stunt sequences, literally—at stake.

In *Drunken Master 2*, Chan masquerades as the brash young fighter, Wong Fei-hung, he played in the original film, made over fifteen years earlier.[27] At age forty, merely assuming the role of a young adult constitutes masquerade of a sort. Moreover, the character provides a notable departure from the contemporary characters who populate his films of the late 1980s and 1990s. *Drunken Master 2* gives Chan his first historical role since 1987's *Project A, Part 2* and revisits the kung fu genre that he had suggested held no further allure for audiences. He uses the role to display a broad range of comic facial expressions and body movements. In this film, Wong Fei-hung favors the "drunken boxing" style of combat, which relies upon lumbering and apparently disoriented motion, a posture that combines rigidity and slackness, and blows that appear flailing or clumsily delivered. Drunken boxing takes its name not only from the drunken appearance of those who exercise it, but also from the story's premise that consuming alcohol aids the fighter, making him more limber and anesthetizing him from pain. This conceit adds a key comic element to Chan's performance, allowing him to employ a range of contorted postures and dopey, stupefied, and bemused facial expressions. In the narrative, Wong Fei-hung's drunken boxing allows him to overcome many practitioners of conventional kung fu, which appears a considerably more masculine combat style by comparison.

Chan's films present many contestatory images of masculinity, particularly in the context of the action genre. In the first *Drunken Master* (1978), Wong Fei-hung's final victory over a macho opponent depends upon his mastery of the exaggeratedly feminine "Miss Ho" style of combat. Wong gains the upper hand with a series of exaggeratedly feminine moves, and at one point knocks down his foe by swinging his buttocks at him. In *Once a Cop* (1993, also known as *Project S*), Chan plays a cameo role in which he performs a comic stunt sequence in full female drag, complete with heels. *Drunken Master 2* also offers unusually gendered images in its fight sequences. During one sequence, Chan's Wong Fei-hung, wearing a loose, white robe (his costume for much of the film) and carrying a paper fan, squares off against a frenetic opponent clad in a leather vest and cap who fights with a heavy iron chain. The juxtaposition of the two suggests an exaggerated performance of both gender roles, with Chan's character appearing as the graceful, feminine fighter while his foe parodies familiar signifiers of aggressive masculinity. In another scene, the teahouse melee noted earlier, Chan strips to the waist at the urging of his mentor, who then sprays him with tea (to make him slippery and more elusive). Here, Chan, bare-chested and glistening, comically appropriates Bruce Lee's bodily codes as a preface to a farfetched spectacle of tumbling male bodies. Finally, the film's last battle pits Chan against a suit-clad kickboxer, John (Ken Lo), who fights mostly while standing firmly on one leg and using the other to kick with mechanical precision. Despite the athletic prowess evident in this style, John's one-legged fighting appears at odds with a masculine ideal that includes groundedness and stability. Borrowing performative codes typically deployed by women and gay men, the comic styles of Chan and his opponents in these many cases create new images of active masculinity.

Comic Masochism

Chan's actions throughout *Drunken Master 2* blend apparently incompatible body configurations. These mixtures complicate codes of action-film masculinity by adopting the narrative strategies and gender dynamics of comedy. In subjecting his body to masochistic treatment, Chan transforms the serious province of male suffering into an arena for comedy, and thus for renegotiation of the terms of masculine violence. He moves the violence of action films toward the hyperbole of comedy and transforms the traditional hero's ready-for-action body into a humorous or burlesque body. Paul Smith proposes a model for the burlesque body in his study of Clint Eastwood: "This comic body is a bundle of symptoms that is cast into the obverse diegetical situation to that of the 'erotogenic' masochism of the action movies—cast, that is, into a frame where the pleasure of contortion, complication, self-changing, and even burlesque is possible."[28] In Chan's films, the comic body manifests his characters' power as well as their limitations: the gift of nearly superhuman athletic prowess and the hindrances of modest body size and social position. Early in *Drunken Master 2*, Wong Fei-hung receives a savage and undefended beating from his kickboxing adversary, who is the son of a prominent Chinese general and the film's avatar of unscrupulous authority. Wong successfully transforms his body, through the mode of drunken boxing, into a comic body to subdue the aristocratic villain at the film's conclusion.

The beating Chan endures represents a rite of suffering characteristic of action films. As Smith suggests, "action movie narratives [. . .] tend to represent for the viewer a kind of masochistic trial of masculinity and its body" (173). Proof of masculine power lies in the male body's ability to withstand pain. The active body, then, becomes the body not only capable of action, but capable of withstanding the rigors of physical action as well. Kaja Silverman regards male masochism as a challenge to patriarchal order: "The male masochist magnifies the losses and divisions upon which culture is based, refusing to be sutured or recompensed. In short, he radiates a negativity inimical to the social order."[29] As Smith points out, though, the social order reinscribes the masochistic tendency into its own narratives: "[P]opular culture narratives in effect enclose and contain male masochism" (165). Masochism becomes an emblem of male identity rather than its opposition. Chan's films successfully retrieve masochistic suffering as a pretext for comedy, permitting laughter at the conventions that demand suffering rather than presenting those conventions as evidence of male power. The burlesque body allows masochism to regain subversive autonomy.

The burlesque body lies at the intersection of comedy and masochism. The body acted upon signifies masochism, as does the noncomedic treatment of the beaten or suffering body. As Kirkham and Thumim observe, "the 'perfect' body also implies its obverse, the mutilated or decayed body."[30] Similarly, Paul Willemen describes the American western's presentation of the male body through scenes of the male "existing" in narrative space and scenes that display "the male mutilated [. . .] and restored through violent brutality."[31] The retributive notion of regeneration through violence operates only intermittently in Chan's films. The notion of vengeance tends to contradict comic motifs and to signify an all-encompassing male power that Chan's characters do not possess. He often suffers punishment at the hands of characters who subsequently cease to be narratively relevant as adversaries. One scene in *Rumble in the Bronx*, which appears between comic fight sequences, shows the street gang pelting Chan, in slow motion, with shards of broken bottles. Later, Chan does not exact revenge in kind, but subdues the gang in the comic episode at their hideout. Similarly, when Chan's characters injure themselves through falls or collisions—which occur in *Project A* and *Supercop*, among other films—they must accept their suffering without complaint. Chan's mishaps render the masculine impulse for revenge obsolete.

The burlesque body provides visual amusement and an equivocal social critique. In the narrative logic of *Drunken Master 2*, drunken boxing denotes a historical tradition of combat as well as a scorned form of physical expression. As in many of Chan's films, Wong Fei-hung here validates traditional forms of authority while challenging corruptive strains of bureaucracy or capitalism. Here again, Smith's argument informs Chan's films: "The burlesque functions within such double expressions of class ressentiment and solidarity as an element of ironic self-deprecation that is modulated into self-celebration, and as such can be seen as a crucial element in the carnivalesque" (180). *Drunken Master 2* celebrates Wong Fei-hung's participation in the carnivalesque kung-fu subculture even as it depicts the consequences, both humiliating and physically painful, of unsuccessful negotiation of the dominant culture's terms. Between spectacular victories in combat, Wong suffers beatings at the hands of his father, the kickboxing aristocrat, and a gang of British consular police. The institutions of paternity, capitalism, and law all disavow kung fu as a means of expression or an assertion of physical autonomy.

The formulation of the burlesque body, which Smith revisits following Jean Louis Schefer's conception of the burlesque in reference to the comedians Stan Laurel and Oliver Hardy, prescribes physical reaction rather than action. Schefer contends that the burlesque body "neither carries nor guides the action: it absorbs it, and is the catastrophic and unbound place to which action returns."[32] Thus the conception of the inert male hero comes full circle: though Chan's films define his persona through perpetual movement, suggesting a dynamic model of masculine ability, the actor's motions are predicated upon escape from danger. As noted previously, viewers accustomed to Western action-film conventions may infer that Hollywood's male heroes stand motionless because of their imperviousness to harm. Chan's comic body language belies such constructions of masculinity. He moves comically but usually defeats opponents in the process, and so constant movement is revealed as a practical combat and survival strategy. At one point in the climactic fight in *Drunken Master 2*, Wong plants his feet firmly on the ground while his opponent, John, strikes at him repeatedly. His blows fail to connect, because Chan's upper body becomes rubbery, seeming to move independently of his stationary legs. Chan's serpentine movements produce a humorous effect, compounded by John's abundance of wasted effort. The scene displays the comic body's potential for control through defensive maneuvers.

Male Hysteria and Madness

The burlesque body can also appear through displacement. In Chan's interactions with other characters, the burlesque body often resituates itself in another character, apparently as a manifestation of the other's hysteria. Such displacement liberates the heroic protagonist from hysterical symptoms, locating him in a more conventionally masculine role as he responds to the predicament of his burlesque companion. For example, in *Drunken Master 2*, in the showdown with the Ax Gang, a shot of Wong's mentor trying to remove an ax from his back undercuts the tension created by the simultaneous depiction of Chan's character in serious combat. In many of his films, Chan temporarily plays the serious-fighter role while his opponents receive comic treatment through displays of hysterical cowardice or exaggerated masculinity. In *Twin Dragons*, the easy victory of Chan's character Boomer over a burly biker causes his foe later to prostrate himself before Boomer and proclaim Boomer his master. Occasionally, a partner becomes the comic foil to Chan's relative straight man. *Twin Dragons* pairs Chan's working-class Boomer with a reckless, outspoken dwarf, Tyson (Teddy Robin), who is repeatedly captured, threatened, or otherwise victimized. The tensions surrounding Chan's character are displaced onto Tyson, who exhibits hysterical symptoms throughout the film: he is boastful and abrasive, he is a failure at romance, and others scoff at his clumsy attempts to manifest male power. As Smith argues, "the hysterical body casts a light on the powerlessness that the heroic body lives with [and] on the powerlessness that such a body lives *within*" (178, emphasis his). Though Tyson displays no physical power, his brash statements, such as the hollow threats he makes to a gang of criminals, motivate Boomer to perform dangerous activities he would not otherwise undertake. In this case, displaced hysteria returns to its original source.

Rejecting the stoicism of previous action heroes, Chan's good-natured comedy humanizes his screen characters, in turn promoting audience engagement with them and the situations in which they perform. U.S. action-films' templates of hypermasculinity presume an emotional gap between performer and viewer. Even in romantic or family-based comedies, comic elements often distance viewers from situations that might elicit empathetic responses, such as scenes of domesticity or interpersonal relations. Chan's use of comedy, however, encourages empathetic responses to action-film scenarios. His version of male agency resists U.S. action films' conservative articulation of physical suffering. Through emphasis on the overriding farcical nature of action sequences or of entire narratives, comedy makes his characters' pain more bearable to viewers. Episodes showing Chan being beaten or humiliated are always countered by his ensuing comic triumphs. A more substantive "don't try this at home" disclaimer closes most of his films released since the mid-1980s. In these films, collected outtakes show Chan and his fellow performers filming stunts and fight sequences gone awry, giving viewers a sometimes disquieting reinterpretation of scenes that may appear cartoonish or fantastic in the regular flow of narrative. Notably, his Hong Kong film outtakes typically locate the sequences in physical reality (as we see that actors can and do suffer physical injury), while those of his Hollywood films promote the pleasure of filmmaking (with Chan and his supporting players misreading dialogue, to their and production crews' apparent delight).

The characteristic outtakes that appear alongside the closing credits in Chan's films contribute significantly to his star persona. The extranarrative material supplies visual proof of Chan's risk-taking in the service of realism, efforts he proudly asserts in ancillary media. Years before becoming a marketable star in U.S. films, Chan told an interviewer:

> I never use special effects or editing and camera effects in my movies. When you see me doing something on the screen, I really do it. It's my trademark, my own style. I love American movies, but I wouldn't like to work in the American way.[33]

In another interview, Chan commented on stunt players' wariness of his direction: "Everybody knows Jackie Chan is crazy."[34] Outtakes depicting other cast members grimacing in real pain or toweling off blood corroborate this view, locating his self-professed craziness in a wider experiential context. An implicit economy is established: Chan's madness imperils his coworkers but serves the film production, which then grants pleasure to viewers.

Chan's offhand comment hints also at the larger social context in which his films appear. Though his displays of androgynous physical mastery call into question conventional formulations of male identity, the attribution of madness contains his subversion, situating his conduct well beyond normative masculine behavior. Chan displays an excess of activity. Through his inevitable accidents during the performance of stunts, his behavior connotes an inability to police the reasonable boundaries of human aspiration. The evidence of Chan's hysteria is inscribed across his scarred and maimed body.[35] Patriarchal order may thus recuperate his abilities as a madman's folly. As Smith observes, one form of "hysterical residue" apparent in some action films "is an unresolved or uncontained representation of the body of the male as it exceeds the narrative process" (167). Chan's ability to overreach the screen, to perform beyond the requirements of a conventional narrative, has become his trademark. This activity occurs outside traditional social orders, particularly the order that Hollywood action films impose. Chan's persona does not adhere to dominant cinematic models of male identity—especially the models prevalent in the action genre—thus marking him as an aberration. His mass appeal, however, reaffirms the resonance of his unconventional persona.

The modification of Chan's image in the West since the 1990s represents U.S. studios' attempts to align his persona more closely with Hollywood conventions of active masculinity. As noted previously, films such as *Supercop* and *Jackie Chan's First Strike* cast him, at least superficially, in the model of the globe-trotting, James Bond–style adventurer. These films contain Chan's unconventional masculinity within a more familiar model of action-film manhood. *Rush Hour*, by contrast, emphasizes Chan's underdog status and his foreignness, which the film presents as inherently exotic. The film constructs its narrative around Chan's estrangement from the surrounding culture, a narrative strategy not utilized in his Hong Kong films. *Rush Hour* conflates Chan's masculine and racial attributes into an indistinct cluster of traits that signify his foreignness. The visibility of Chan's films in the West does represent a progressive development in Hollywood representations of active masculinity and of Asians, albeit one motivated by profits rather than by any notion of multiculturalism or social good. The steady flow of Hong Kong actors, directors, choreographers, and cinematographers to Hollywood after 1997 promised expanded opportunities at least at the level of film production, with further shifts in patterns of representation and narrative appearing imminent as well. However, most of these transplanted filmworkers remain active principally in second- or third-tier U.S. productions without Asian cast members.

In the early years of the twenty-first century, only Chan and Jet Li remain bankable stars in U.S. films. Li has found a small niche in mid-budget action films such as *Unleashed* (2005), *Cradle 2 the Grave* (2003), and *The One* (2001), while studio attempts to market Chan to younger audiences in films such as *Around the World in 80 Days* (2004), *The Medallion* (2003), and *The Tuxedo* have been resounding box-office failures. To date, the U.S. industry has swiftly absorbed Hong Kong production talent, but sympathetic—or any—treatments of Chinese characters remain in short supply. Chan's multivalent masculinity has not yet bred successors, but his very success indicates U.S. and global audiences' interest in diverse formations of action heroism.

Conclusion: The Future of Active Masculinity

As action cinema enters its second century—or third, if we rightly include the one-shot 1890s films that showcased the wholesale spectacle of physical motion—it has already begun to take on new forms and to reconfigure its existing structures. Yet some contemporary films do not seem to have registered these developments at all. An extended fire-engine chase sequence in *Terminator 3: Rise of the Machines* (2003) appears pleasurably retrograded, with its innumerable car crashes and flying storefront glass. Meanwhile, the Denzel Washington vehicle and box-office success *Man on Fire* (2004) foregrounds south-of-the-border vigilante justice that recalls self-consciously ugly post-Vietnam films such as *Rolling Thunder* (1977) and many subsequent revenge dramas (though the newer film employs a highly contemporary, frenetic visual style and editing). Finally, the expensive comic-book adaptations *League of Extraordinary Gentlemen* (2003) and *Fantastic Four* (2005) resemble a host of 1980s films in their relatively flat lighting design, their mostly workmanlike cutting, and their rosters of unfamiliar faces (in the former, in support of the durable Sean Connery).

Yet alongside these familiar narrative scenarios and formal patterns, at least three distinct trends can be discerned. First, blockbuster action films crafted for family audiences have emerged, with violence, language, and sexuality softened to PG-13 levels, and with broad thematics surrounding individual and national heroism. Second, sexy action heroines have proliferated, in films marketed to young women as well as the genre's loyal base of adolescent and postadolescent males. Third, a number of action films (including some in the above two categories) have explicitly responded to the 9/11 attacks. We might add to these trends the continuing globalization of the action cinema, both in the growth of international audiences for U.S. film and the emergence of genre films in action modes from many national cinemas.

With a few exceptions—including prominent vigilante films such *Man on Fire*, *The Punisher* (2004), and the *Kill Bill* series—the R-rated action film is an increasingly rare commodity in U.S. multiplexes.[1] Replacing it are action blockbusters promoted for viewers across age ranges, not just the traditionally lucrative 18–34 age demographic but also preteens, parents, and avid filmgoers entering middle age. Nearly all of the successful Stallone and Schwarzenegger films of the 1980s and 1990s carried R ratings for their extensive violence, profanity, and occasional female nudity. Contemporary films often deliver viewers the impression of an adult world but scrupulously withhold the sights and sounds of that world. *XXX*, for example, despite its adult-video title, pointedly strips its oversexed female supporting characters down to their underwear but no further. Likewise, its lawbreaking protagonist, Xander Cage—so extreme that his name begins with an X—conveniently avoids censorable euphemisms. Similarly, the steel-hard supercops of *S.W.A.T.* (2003) eschew the "fuck you" and "suck my dick" litanies of other movie cops, and a brief scene of a woman flashing her breasts is only half-gratuitous, filming her from behind (the film substitutes a different offense, egregious product placement, with characters reciting the names of the many soft drinks and fast-food chains the film carefully photographs). In a manner recalling the heyday of the Production Code, the adult world is made safe for all viewers' eyes and ears. Other films merge youthful and adult worlds. *Spider-Man* and *Spider-Man 2* foreground family responsibilities and their protagonist's romance-versus-work conflict in ways that might appeal to children, teenagers, and adults alike. The disaster film *The Day after Tomorrow* includes not only the overacting-politician characters of mature thrillers but also a young couple plucked from a teen romance, and uses a father–son narrative (and lest we forget, a global disaster) to link the two plots.

With their frequent recourse to fantastic worlds and consequent sidestepping of social questions, contemporary PG–13 action films model gender in multiple ways. Many films show a proclivity for exclusively male, mythologized, historical settings—the World War II milieu of *U-571* (2000) and *Pearl Harbor* (2001), or the British Empire at sea in *Master and Commander: The Far Side of the World* (2003)—that depict archaic male heroics with renewed vigor. Other films, such as the comic-book adaptation *X-Men* and its sequel *X2: X-Men United* (2003), present cartoonish, adolescent-friendly fantasies whose wildly improbable scenarios and unstable models of gender identity to some extent thwart evaluation against a particular social reality, even that of the contemporary viewer. (A rainbow coalition of genetic mutants, the X-Men—who really are X-people since their numbers include women and children—are racially, sexually, and physically othered.) Such fantastic premises can facilitate progressive ends by evading the burdens of realist representation. At the same time, the *X-Men* series foregrounds identities so fantastic and multifaceted that representations of women and of diverse ethnicities lose clarity and power. Instead, the films' narratives foreground the marginal status of an aggressive, taciturn, white character, Wolverine (Hugh Jackman). Paradoxically, Wolverine's aggression and taciturnity make him a figure of viewer identification rather than aligning him with the tired, conservative tradition the films and their cast of superpowered teens otherwise disrupt. Many other cartoonish action narratives unabashedly embrace their lack of social context and narrative depth. *The Scorpion King* (2002) showcases a supporting character from the *Mummy* franchise, a character played by ex-wrestling star The Rock, and is set in an imagined, ancient pseudo-Babylonia. Released a few months later, *XXX* self-consciously tweaks the James Bond spy mythology, offering instead action catering to early-adolescent extreme-sports sensibilities (the film's stunt sequences include motorcycling and snowboarding, with hints of skateboarding, surfing, and parasailing as well). Only *Spider-Man*, with its combination of dueling superpowers and a contemporary teen-angst narrative, gestures toward social relevance, thematizing sexual development, adolescent grief, and the minefields of parent–child relationships (and on a different level, combining corporate villainy and military technology in its antagonist character, the Green Goblin). All these films, though, showcase physically powerful male heroes, renegotiating but continuing patriarchal tradition.

Linked to the juvenilization of action cinema is the genre's showcasing of female action figures. *Charlie's Angels* and *Lara Croft: Tomb Raider* (2001) feature women protagonists who combine martial-arts prowess, facility with weapons, and conventional female sexual attractiveness. The films successfully attracted young male and female viewers (enough to produce sequels for both films), hinting at untapped narrative veins as well as new audiences for action cinema. Notably, the makers of both films found such veins in untraditional sources, the former film turning to a long-defunct television series and the latter to a popular personal-computer adventure game with an active but voiceless protagonist. Television and video games provide multiple sources and outlets for women heroes, a consequence partly of the former medium's longtime receptiveness to women-centered programs and the latter's abrogation of existing social hierarchies, including those of gender. The two *Resident Evil* films, locating Milla Jovovich amid action-horror perils, derive from the popular video game. Meanwhile, television's *Alias* (2001–) constructs Jennifer Garner as a sexy, martial-arts proficient spy; the program's relative popularity led Garner to a supporting role in *Daredevil* (2003) and the lead in its sequel *Elektra* (2005). Intertextual film references provide the basis for the female-centered *Kill Bill: Vol. 1* and *Kill Bill: Vol. 2*, which grant their nameless heroine substantial agency but also subject her to repeated 1970s-style beatings and add a decorative helping of motherhood to fix her within existing categories of femininity (meanwhile, nearly all other female characters in the films are mutilated, killed, or both). Outside U.S. cinema, the Chinese/Hong Kong martial-arts fantasies *Crouching Tiger, Hidden Dragon* and *Hero* also locate women in primary active roles, resulting in international successes that drew young viewers as well as older art-house crowds, the latter usually not a substantial segment of the action cinema's viewership. Hollywood action films overall continue to show their flexibility principally by locating women characters among otherwise all-male groups. *S.W.A.T.* and the hugely successful *Pirates of the Caribbean: The Curse of the Black Pearl* (2003), among others, offer this marginal concession to feminism, a concession already made in 1980s films such as *Aliens* (1986).

A third notable development in action cinema is Hollywood responses to the catastrophic 9/11 events. The terrorist attacks on New York and Washington, and subsequent U.S. military actions in Afghanistan and Iraq, threatened to alter significantly the landscape of media representation of active, militant masculinity and femininity. Concerns about cultural verisimilitude in fiction film led some film producers to predict the decline of "frivolous, exploitative action films" that might recall actual terrorist attacks.[2] In addition, images of uniformed soldiers in combat, on patrol, or merely situated in unfamiliar landscapes gained renewed primacy on U.S. television, first in the U.S. military campaign against the Taliban and al-Qaeda in Afghanistan, and then in the U.S.-led invasion of Iraq begun in March 2003, an operation trailed by hundreds of news correspondents and cameras.

Despite the U.S. military's saturation of television images, fiction films with military subjects have remained in short supply during the initial war in Iraq, and amid the subsequent military occupation and counterinsurgent warfare. Some films address other wars: *Tears of the Sun* situates a combat narrative in a climate akin to the U.S. military's 1993 Somalia intervention, and *The Hunted* (2003) adorns a stock chase narrative with a flashback of its antagonist's violent experiences in the former Yugoslavia. Both performed unimpressively in theatrical release, as did other post-9/11 war films. In the months following 9/11, many major news organs collected anecdotal evidence of U.S. studios' interest in helping the war effort by producing films that would depict the military in the most positive light. In one interview, director Rod Lurie asserted: "I am certain right now that the country and its citizens are very much in favor of watching soldiers being portrayed in the most patriotic way possible."[3] (Notably, Lurie himself has not directed a film showcasing soldiers in action.) Still, a surge in production of ultrapatriotic films has not occurred. In 2004,

Michael Moore's antiwar documentary *Fahrenheit 9/11* generated box-office receipts greater than any of the previous years' fiction films dealing with war. Arguably, the great popularity of the vigilante films *Man on Fire, The Punisher,* and *Kill Bill 1* and *2* is the clearest symptom of U.S. viewers' predispositions in the wake of 9/11.

Expectations that post-9/11 Hollywood films would aim for new relevancy or would use avowed cinematic realism to attract viewers (on the order of *Saving Private Ryan*'s graphic combat sequences, filmed with handheld cameras) have not been fulfilled. Hollywood studios have responded differently, or not at all, to the changing role of the United States in global affairs. The most successful U.S. film appearing during the winter of late 2002 and early 2003, when the threat of international war loomed large, was the adolescent fantasy *The Lord of the Rings: The Fellowship of the Ring* (2002), which featured abundant combat among warring armies but no specific parallels to contemporary international relations (notably, it was filmed well in advance of 9/11). Among recent action-centered fiction films, figurations of gender that explicitly promote the conservative traditions of soldiering remain marginal to Hollywood's overall output. Even those contemporary films using military personnel as subjects locate their characters in highly ambivalent positions with regard to popular morality and international law. *Tears of the Sun* asks viewers to endorse an officer's unauthorized aggression, which is undertaken for humanitarian ends, and *The Hunted* suggests that elite soldiers may become serial killers when the sanction of war no longer exists. Neither approach is remarkably contemporary, and more significantly, neither appears attuned to shifting public attitudes about war and the military.[4] In Hollywood cinema, a rhetoric of omission has prevailed.

U.S. studios' relentless courtship of teen viewers, the industry's least discriminating patrons as well as those most likely to engage in the repeat viewings that maximize blockbuster films' grosses, appears to work against putatively realist, serious military narratives. For every success such as *Saving Private Ryan* or the widely seen if generally disdained *Pearl Harbor,* a big-budget failure such as *Windtalkers* stalls a possible resurgence of war films. Some action narratives do capitalize on the climate of renewed awareness of the military and economic role of the United States in international affairs. Marketing and publicity for the film version of Mark Bowden's nonfiction best-seller *Black Hawk Down* sought to exploit interest in global military ventures, with director Ridley Scott and others asserting the film's realism, as if to position it as a text through which viewers might gain valuable experience of the adversaries of the United States in Africa or the Middle East. (The film premiered only a few weeks after the U.S. army entered Afghanistan. With a heavy publicity campaign and a handful of Academy Award nominations, the film performed well, if not spectacularly, at the U.S. box office.[5])

Audiences have not responded strongly to serious films foregrounding military figures. Military men have instead featured prominently in thoroughly fantastic, adolescent-oriented films. Near-parodic military figures appear in many contemporary films, including *X-Men* and *X2* (in the latter, a rogue military scientist is the film's chief non-superpowered villain), the summer 2003 release *The Hulk* (in which the raging monster is the object of military leaders' special enmity and destroys an array of military hardware), and *Reign of Fire*. In this last film, released in summer 2002, hordes of dragons take control of the planet, and a ragtag band of Britishers mounts a marginal resistance. Almost inexplicably, help arrives in the form of a team of U.S. soldiers with tanks and helicopters. Given its postapocalyptic English setting—along with generic iconography linking it to the science-fiction film and the fantasy film—the film somewhat surprisingly fetishizes U.S. military hardware, with both camera positions and the British characters' reaction shots signaling a reverent view of the vehicles and weapons. Overall, though, the film visually and narratively disavows any close connections to the U.S. military in historical reality. Matthew McConaughey plays the military men's leader, Van Zan, as a swaggering caricature, and the presence of fire-breathing dragons explicitly indicates the film's antirealist tone. Van Zan apparently sacrifices himself well before the film's climax to kill a key dragon (the film withholds the moment of his or the monster's death), so although the military presence is instrumental in rejuvenating the British group's morale, the U.S. characters are not responsible for the humans' ultimate triumph over their mythical adversaries. While the soldiers' presence is remarkable in a humans-versus-dragons film set in near-future England, *Reign of Fire* finally shows no particular veneration of the U.S. military.

To complement the survey of generic trends just outlined, I wish to offer two brief case studies, looking at two quite different late-1990s films that display the issues at play and at stake in the contemporary action cinema. These films—the Hollywood production *The Matrix* and the German film *Run Lola Run* (1998)—were released during the same period in the United States but diverge widely in their representations of gendered activity. *The Matrix* relies on the premise of the contemporary capitalist world as an enervating simulation, and coupled with its foregrounding of women and African American characters, the film carries progressive pleasures. The film simultaneously appropriates liberal rhetoric and style signifiers to produce emphatically conservative appeals (such as the many gun battles that account for its R rating). In a different inflection of generic discourses, *Run Lola Run* represents active, nonsexualized femininity and critiques the violent strategies of conflict resolution conventionally undertaken by men. The two films vary greatly in their generic situation, modes of address, formal properties, and reception. Nevertheless, each illuminates gendered activity in compelling ways.

The action/sci-fi film *The Matrix* earned over $170 million in U.S. receipts in 1999, making it the fifth-highest grossing film of the year. The significance of the film lies not only in its popularity but also in its savvy reconfiguration of highly conventional images of male violence. Popular and critical discourse surrounding *The Matrix* focuses on vaguely defined hipness and originality. These extratextual discourses partly efface the film's fidelity to venerable action-hero conventions—the presence of a young, white male hero; a dearth of female roles; a vision of a singular, world-saving intruder-redeemer figure; and a penchant for spectacular gunplay. After the film received four Academy Awards, hyperbolic statements of its cultural impact abounded. In his report on the March 2000 Oscar ceremony, *The New York Times*'s Rick Lyman dubbed the film "too hip for the room," despite its mass appeal and its corporate maker, the Warner Brother studio. In the same article, the film's producer, action-film veteran Joel Silver, remarks: "I felt that *The Matrix* was just a very smart action movie, if that's not an oxymoron. [. . .] It was about more than explosions and fistfights; it really raises the bar on these kind of movies."[6] These somewhat self-serving comments lend credence to an understanding of the film as narratively original, philosophically sophisticated, and ultimately countercultural. However, a close analysis of the film's gender- and race-bound representations of violent action, along with its overall figuration of heroic masculinity, reveals more conventional appeals as well. The film repackages preexisting models of male activity, violence, and control, locating these characteristics within a generic dystopian-future scenario. Like many action films, *The Matrix* crafts a fantastic world according to an adolescent worldview: here the adult, corporate world is a nefarious simulation, while the "real" world features a motley crew of revolutionaries with superhero-style names, a world-conquering race of monster aliens, and the awe generated by introductory philosophy. Clearly this conceit holds broad appeal for adults as well as adolescents.

The Matrix spawned a range of similar films—two sequels, *The Matrix Reloaded* and *The Matrix Revolutions*, appeared in 2003, and other action films such as *Charlie's Angels*, *The One*, *Equilibrium* (2003), and *Constantine* (2005) borrow from its visual and narrative style—and attracted an enormous popular fan base. The film, particularly in its countercultural positioning of conventional male violence, bears significance for the action genre and the larger culture. It follows the exploits of a computer hacker, Neo (Keanu Reeves, a part-Asian actor whitewashed in nearly all his film roles), who learns that he is the only hope for humanity, nearly all of which has been unwittingly enslaved by a malevolent alien race. A small group of rebels, led by the prophesizing Morpheus (Laurence Fishburne), rescues Neo from his enslavement and prepares him for his new role as savior, a role he executes through numerous violent encounters in the film's virtual-reality realm, known as "the matrix." Morpheus speaks in Zen-like language and comports himself with almost narcotic calmness, and the film swiftly transforms him from a powerful leader into a secondary figure, Neo's mentor and advocate. To perform his role, Neo learns both a form of martial arts—borrowing explicitly the poses and fighting style of Bruce Lee's films—and a two-handed facility with firearms that recalls the films of Hong Kong director John Woo and their many imitators. As Neo hones his superlative abilities, the film adorns him with a full-length, black-leather trenchcoat, signifying both luxury and rebellious or "alternative" masculinity. The trenchcoat not only replicates the sartorial style of blaxploitation heroes such as Richard Roundtree in *Shaft* (1971) but also Clint Eastwood's attire in 1960s Italian westerns and the costumes of 1990s westerns such as *Unforgiven* and *Tombstone* (1993). The film's portmanteau style thus derives from Asian, African American, and even Italian sources. This global admixture presages the similar corralling of diverse action iconography in the *Kill Bill* films, which also finally showcase white action figures.

Despite the film's insistence on the spiritual, cerebral nature of "the matrix," most of its action sequences involve firearms, privileging a conservative ideology of lethal masculinity. In one notable sequence, Neo's ability to control the virtual-reality environment allows him to produce an apparently infinite array of (digitally generated) machine guns, an act he punctuates with a conventional, monosyllabic, action-hero tagline: "We need guns. Lots of guns." This image of fantastic plenitude is specifically tethered to white male agency, and to technologies of violence. In addition, it constructs the acquisition of assault rifles as a utopian consumer activity (which in many respects it is—people buy guns to satisfy desires for power, personal autonomy, and often visceral pleasure). The scene's empty, white background specifically references the clean, bright environments of much television advertising, and indeed, the infinite-guns scene in *The Matrix* was borrowed not long after for an automobile broker's television ads (just as its rotating camera array was soon used in commercials for the Gap clothing chain and other products). The hazy definition of the religious or philosophical system of "the matrix," which is often indistinguishable from the *Star Wars* series' Joseph Campbell-influenced notion of "the force," enables the film to distort thoroughly the tangible implications and social consequences of violent weaponry (as well as the pacific tendencies of Eastern religions). The film positions its computer-generated image of racks of guns racing past the protagonist as somehow alternative to conditions of social reality, when in fact such an image suggests an exaggerated promotional campaign for the National Rifle Association. Indeed, at least one prominent member of the film's special-effects team later worked on a U.S. Army virtual-reality training simulation, suggesting the confraternity between the film's spectacular, fantasy violence and the ideology of realist violence promulgated in military training.[7]

The construction of violence as redemptive, regenerative, or otherwise oppositional to prevailing social ideologies has many precedents in mainstream U.S. cinema, from *Scarface* (1932) to *Death Wish* to *Pulp Fiction*. Violence takes on a different cast in the world of *The Matrix*, a world defined as simulation. In more conventional action films such as *True Lies*—in which Arnold Schwarzenegger's character leads armed troops, pilots a military fighter jet, and fires the plane's air-to-air missiles— viewers recognize the protagonist's connection to an explicitly prosocial, conservative ideology. Screen violence, when linked to conservative institutions (e.g., the police and military) or to explicitly destructive, socially antagonistic groups (criminals, terrorists) encourages viewers to contextualize such violence within a social reality: violence is shown as the product of groups or institutions with specific agendas of social discipline, political protest, or material gain. However, when reconfigured in *The Matrix* as a tool used unhesitatingly by a liberal-minded rebel hero, spectacular violence paradoxically supports a conservative project of normalizing male aggression and extending it into previously nonviolent arenas (e.g., Buddhist spirituality). *Fight Club*, released a few months after *The Matrix*, offers a parallel worldview: in both, alienated, handsome, materially comfortable men cast off the artificial trappings of their postmodern worlds, and come to greater self-knowledge, through barely regulated physical violence. Both films literally beat sense into their male subjects.

The Matrix defines its disembodied, virtual-reality environment as a proving ground for traditional, white male mastery, thereby denying agency to its few female characters. Ironically, the film's production necessitated the frequent stasis of its male lead. For repeated action sequences, Reeves assumed static poses while a series of still cameras produced rotating images of his body.[8] Hence the film's cameras produced the illusion of movement for a static figure against a virtual backdrop. In some respects, this positioning grants access to women as well—*The Matrix* and *The Matrix Reloaded* both begin with women-in-action sequences—but ultimately it is men around whom the film literally circles. The first film locates women in two substantial supporting roles: the Oracle (Gloria Foster), a stereotypical African American earth mother—almost a mammy figure—with psychic abilities; and the active Trinity (Carrie-Anne Moss).

(A third female character, Switch [Belinda McCrory], is quickly dispatched.) The film initially showcases Trinity's fighting prowess: in the opening sequence, she demonstrates her strength by rescuing Neo from his virtual-reality prison. Once Neo's abilities are manifest, however, the film redefines Trinity's character as insufficiently skilled to overcome the film's powerful male villains and relegates her to a largely decorative and romantic role. Like the black mentor Morpheus, Trinity cedes authority to the white male protagonist, whom the film characterizes as the rightful, prophesied agent of deliverance. The film thus offers a familiar narrative trajectory in which women and blacks willingly relinquish their power so that young, white men can act autonomously, to everyone's benefit.

Like *The Matrix*, *Run Lola Run* foregrounds the spectacle of motion and action, but with far different implications for its male and female characters. The film, released in Germany in 1998 as *Lola rennt* and in the United States in 1999, locates a female protagonist at the center of its action narrative and in doing so investigates the consequences of male action and inaction. A huge hit in Germany, where it spawned a popular women's hairstyle (the dyed, fire-engine red style of the film's heroine), *Run Lola Run* achieved substantial recognition and profits in the United States as well.[9] Like *The Matrix*, *Run Lola Run* calls attention to the constructedness of the cinematic world, presenting three similar but distinct versions of the same storyline and including intermittent sequences of cartoon animation. The German film, however, uses its different "realities" not as a template for male mastery but as a space for working through the problems of female representation and agency in the action genre. *Run Lola Run* tracks its heroine's movements through urban Berlin, following her actual movement through physical space (though fragmenting them repeatedly through rapid edits, jump cuts, and violations of the 180° axis of action; and occasionally filming her in slow motion). Eschewing spectacular violence and the sexual threats to women characters that constitute part of the action film's familiar syntax, *Run Lola Run* demonstrates the malleability of action-based narratives, reworking models for female and male representation. Like so many Hollywood action films, *Run Lola Run* is emphatically a film of masculinity in crisis, but the film demonstrates that the reassertion of a traditional, inflexible masculinity does not resolve this crisis. Instead, women must intervene into the spheres once managed, or mismanaged, by men.

Visually and narratively, the film applies techniques not groundbreaking in themselves, but uncharacteristic of the largely linear, illusionistic action cinema. The film tracks the frantic attempts of Lola (Franka Potente) to muster a large sum of money (100,000 deutsche marks, or about $55,000) in a twenty-minute span to prevent the likely death of her hapless boyfriend, Manni (Moritz Bleibtreu), following a mishandled payoff in a car-smuggling operation. The film repeats its central events three times, with slight variations leading to drastically different conclusions: at the end of the first version, Lola is killed by the police; in the second, Manni is run over by an ambulance; and in the final version, the lovers survive and make a tidy profit. After each of the first two versions, an intimate, red-tinted interlude appears, and the story returns to the beginning of Lola's "run" (her moped stolen, she spends much of the film dashing along city streets). In addition to this temporal disjunction, the film periodically displays series of still-photo flash-forward sequences illustrating the lives of minor characters—a woman Lola passes on the street, for instance, is shown kidnapping a child in one version, and becoming a religious zealot who distributes leaflets on the street in another. Each episode also begins with a short, animated sequence of Lola running out of her apartment building. Further violating principles of visual continuity, *Run Lola Run* alternates between film and digital-video images, with scenes not featuring Lola and Manni shot on video and the rest shot with 35 mm film.[10] Such discontinuities and departures from visual realism attest both to the film's gamelike, music-video–influenced nature and to its willingness to experiment with action-genre conventions to test their utility for representation of women protagonists.

The film's unconventional style provides a vehicle for its focus on women's experience. The narrative pointedly finds its heroine first in her bedroom in the family apartment, a bedroom that includes a row of naked Barbie-like dolls. Following the phone conversation with Manni in which she learns of his plight, the standing Lola deliberates nervously as the camera circles her. Here female stasis in domestic space accompanies thought, which precipitates action. Once she chooses a course of action, she leaves domestic space behind; the film returns there only for the beginning of the next two stories. In each case, the narrative proper begins at the moment Lola casts off domesticity, a decision emphasized by the camera's subsequent circling of Lola's immobile, benumbed mother as Lola departs (though it does so in binary fashion, the film at least acknowledges other femininities that Lola denies). In each scenario, Lola seeks the aid of her wealthy bank-executive father, without success: he rejects her appeals in the first two versions, and in the third, she fails to meet with him. The film thus demonstrates the unreliability of patriarchal and paternal authority, and Lola's ultimate refusal of it. Lola's apparently sensible choice to turn first to her father for help in resolving her personal dilemma proves fruitless, as his self-interest overcomes any notion of family responsibility. Finally, Lola must act autonomously, and she succeeds by visiting a casino and winning against astronomical odds. In this setting—in which male patrons wear tuxedos and the few women wear gowns, in contrast to Lola's punk-inflected tank top, checkered pants, and military-style boots—Lola asserts her presence by emitting a deafening scream, signaling her unwillingness to abide the decorum of her father's straitlaced, moneyed world. Her vocal outburst, which repudiates prevailing, Western notions of female propriety, punctuates (or causes) her gambling victory: she ceases screaming when the roulette ball falls into a desired slot. Additionally, her scream shatters glass in the room (as does a scream she unleashes earlier, in her father's office), granting her destructive power through aggressive but nonviolent means. (With regard to violence, in the film's first episode, Lola does acquire a gun, which she uses to help Manni rob a supermarket, and in the second episode, she robs her father's bank at gunpoint, but in neither case do her actions lead to a successful resolution.) In contrast to U.S. action films in which women characters enter the phallic, masculine world of firearms—films such as *Blue Steel* (1990), *Point of No Return* (1993), and *The Long Kiss Goodnight*—*Run Lola Run* presents its heroine's activity and agency through her vocal power, her visual centrality, and her displays of athletic exertion.

Run Lola Run indicates the action genre's largely untapped potential for depiction of physically active, psychologically strong women characters. U.S. films that feature women protagonists routinely subject these figures to sexual violence. Female action heroes periodically engage in violent action after being stripped to their undergarments, and they almost always must fend off a group of sexual predators or a single, rapine villain. (*Charlie's Angels* and other PG-13 female action films rein in these impulses somewhat, relying on implicit rather than explicit rape threats and creating characters who seem to prefer spending time in their underwear; *Charlie's Angels* combines the worlds of action, comedy, and girls' sleepover party.) *Run Lola Run* proves that neither treatment is requisite within the generic framework of the action film. In another striking departure from U.S. action films, the film does not eroticize Lola's character: the frequent running sequences foreground her body's physical exertion, not its sexual characteristics; and even in the bedroom interludes that connect the three episodes, Lola is not objectified by the camera but framed from the shoulders up, visually equivalent to Manni.

The film also works through tensions surrounding male/female power relations. Lola's activity initially requires Manni's stasis—she instructs him to wait by a phone booth (in which the film photographs him, with the booth's intersecting bars visually entrapping him) rather than perform a foolhardy robbery. In the story's first version, Manni becomes impatient and proceeds to rob the store, setting in motion the events that lead to Lola's death. The film thus shows male unwillingness to accept an inactive role, and the fatal consequences to women of this obstinacy (notably, Lola is shot by a nervous, young policeman, hinting at men's capacity for mismanagement of the weapons they conventionally master). In its final episode, Manni himself becomes active as well, chasing and catching the homeless man who has taken the money Manni had lost earlier. The film thus accommodates active roles for both partners, rejecting the frequent dictate in action narratives that one character's activity demands a male or female partner's relative passivity. Ultimately, Manni uneasily relinquishes his gun to the homeless man, who the film suggests (from the wily look in his eyes when he receives the weapon) might use it to redress his own economic inequality. The film acknowledges the potential violence of this exchange (i.e., the possibility that the homeless man might shoot Manni upon receiving the weapon) through Manni's caution in handing over the gun. Viewers already subjected to characters' untimely deaths may fear for the male hero's safety, but the film rewards him for his willingness to abandon this tool of violent masculinity, as he finally reunites with Lola in the next, concluding scene.

Although *Run Lola Run* demonstrates a new range of agency for women protagonists, the film's challenge to cultural assumptions surrounding men's and women's access to spheres of physical activity is partly limited by its generic situation and its structural emphasis on heterosexual romance. Transcending its narrated familial crises and the deaths of its protagonists, the film ends in a utopian space, far removed from social reality (with Lola and Manni free from conflict, their relationship secure, and flush with spending money). Lola's gambling success occurs wholly within the realm of cinematic fantasy, as does a brief sequence in which she angelically saves the life of a heart-attack victim by holding his hand. One might view such utopian elements as essential to the transmission of a progressive ideology, given the long-standing disenfranchisement of women, people of color, and the working class within realist discourses such as journalism, social science, the law, and even literary schools such as realism and naturalism. In terms of social reality, for example, the couple's criminal status (as smugglers or armed robbers) might raise moral objections among some viewers. According to the terms of the action genre, such transgressions often position characters positively at the margins of social behavior. Even in this marginal position, the film does not grant its heroine complete autonomy, as Lola's activity is predicated on her allegiance to her boyfriend. Taking account of its fantasy, lawlessness, and heteronormativity, though, the film creates a space for visually arresting female activity, an antidote to the U.S. action genre's conventional, largely conservative images of male aggression. It is perhaps fitting that the action genre— historically and generically a key site of exaggerated, conflicted, and shifting representations of manhood—should so successfully interrogate active masculinity in a film featuring a female hero and a largely static male protagonist, and that this text should come from outside the U.S. film industry.

Changes in the action genre's global situation, and its models of gender identity, continue to occur at a rapid rate, often through the influence of films produced outside Hollywood. Just as the Hong Kong model constructed by Jackie Chan provides a progressive alternative to U.S. cinema's conventions of male activity, *Run Lola Run*'s departure from action-film conventions originates far from Hollywood. *Run Lola Run*, like Chan's films, participates in a generic and cross-cultural dialogue with U.S. action films. This dialogue is partly a consequence of the dominance of U.S. films in the global film industry. U.S. films, particularly action films, command a disproportionate share of global film audiences, even in countries such as Hong Kong that have substantial domestic film industries. Many cultural commentators, both in the United States and abroad, view such economic and cultural influences as troubling signs of the homogenization—or more precisely, the Americanization—of national and regional cultures, industries, and art forms. However, the action film's generic framework, which U.S. films have been most instrumental in shaping, also provides a narrative and formal structure that films from other national cinemas can mobilize in culturally specific, often progressive ways. International films rearticulate paradigms of heroic, adversarial, or even revolutionary masculinity (and periodically, femininity as well) and critique prevailing cultural mythologies surrounding gender and violence in particular. Moreover, the global legibility of action cinema crucially improves non-U.S. film's chances of international distribution. Widely distributed films in the action genre or applying its codes include Jamaica's *Third World Cop* (1998); Brazil's *City of God* (2002); India's *Bandit Queen* (1994); Thailand's *Ong-Bak: The Thai Warrior* (2003); South Korea's *Shiri* and *Nowhere to Hide* (both 1999); and from Japan, the ultraviolent *Battle Royale* (2000) and *Battle Royale 2* (2003), the 1980s and 1990s yakuza dramas from actor-director Takeshi Kitano (including *Fireworks* [aka *Hana-bi*, 1997] and *Sonatine* [1993]), and director Takashi Miike's streamlined, frenetic action-exploitation films (including *City of Lost Souls* [2000] and the *Dead or Alive* trilogy [1999–2002]). While the domestic film industries of many countries undoubtedly have suffered commercially because of inroads made by U.S. films, filmmakers outside the United States have nevertheless proved themselves adept at modifying local production practices and narrative styles to cope with Hollywood's challenges, often resulting in genre-invigorating fare such as *Run Lola Run*.

Media outside the United States have also appropriated the signifiers of active masculinity in thoroughly unpredictable ways, merging social reality and mass-produced artifice for explicitly political ends. Many commentators have noted the disturbing but politically expedient use of media technologies by radical Islamic groups, who use videotapes (training videos, footage of suicide bombings, and other forms) to recruit new members, to communicate instructions among terrorist cells, to broadcast propaganda messages through regional and international news media, and as evidence of kidnappings and brutal killings. Yet amid this overwhelmingly grim use of videotape, television, and digital media, one event has occurred that weds global media, the U.S. military, and consumable icons of active masculinity in a surreally comic way. In late January 2005, a website known for posting statements from Arab militants featured a communiqué from the al Mujahedeen Brigade, a group that had claimed responsibility in 2004 for a pair of civilian kidnappings. In the 2005 statement, the group claimed it had captured a U.S. soldier, John Adam, and posted a photo of a bound soldier with a machine gun pointed at his head. As Western news outlets soon reported, the captured soldier was in reality a foot-high action figure, "Special Ops Cody," produced for sale at U.S. military bases in Kuwait. "The figure appeared stiff and expressionless," reported The Associated Press.[11] Moreover, the group was threatening the toy soldier with his own tiny, plastic gun. Some headlines surrounding the incident showed sober, journalistic restraint: the New York Times headlined its account "U.S. Military Says No Soldier Missing in Iraq," while MSNBC's website carried the story as "Doubts Cast on Claim U.S. Soldier Kidnapped."[12] This figure—mute, emotionless, rigid, in a tight spot—was of course virtually indistinguishable from the archetypal protagonist of American action cinema. Only CNN's website could state the plain facts: "So-Called U.S. Hostage Appears to Be Toy."[13] Yet again, the images of active masculinity, and the apparent threats to that masculinity, continue to inspire media spectacle, careful analysis, and sometimes, relieving comedy.

Notes

Introduction: Popular Representations of Active Masculinity since the Late 1960s

1. Faludi, *Stiffed*, 13.
2. See Cohan, *Masked Men*.
3. See Dyer, *Stars*, 59–61. Dyer notes McQueen as an example of the rebel antihero but does not pursue the issue of male rebellion in depth.
4. Dyer observes that "the heavy emphasis on youth in the [rebel] type carries with it the notion of the 'passing phase,' the 'inevitable,' 'natural' rebellion [. . .] Youth is the ideal material term on which to displace social discontent, since young people always get older (and 'grow up')" (*Stars*, 60).
5. McQueen and Heston appeared in films such as *The Towering Inferno* (1974) and *Two-Minute Warning* (1976), respectively. Marvin appeared in a number of idiosyncratic roles throughout the 1970s, then finally appeared in mature authority-figure roles late in his career, in films such as *Gorky Park* (1983).
6. Mellen, *Big Bad Wolves*, 294.
7. See Smith, *Clint Eastwood*.
8. Clancy's novels often receive the label of "techno-thriller," a category used some years earlier to describe works such as Michael Crichton's *The Andromeda Strain* (1969), a thriller fortified with descriptions of medicine and biology, drawing on the author's medical background.
9. In naming this phenomenon in the 1950s, Whyte's *The Organization Man* presents a critique of the corporate sphere's group mentality and the effects of such a mentality on other aspects of U.S. education and domestic life. In Clancy's novels, though, the organization man is the solution instead of the problem.
10. See Heartfield, "There is No Masculinity Crisis" (*Genders* 35 [2002]; <www.genders.org/g35/g35_heartfield.html>, accessed June 3, 2004).
11. Holmlund, "Masculinity as Multiple Masquerade," 224.

1 Armchair Thrills and the New Adventurer

1. Christopher Probst, "Screen Gems," *American Cinematographer* 83.6 (June 2002), 82, 84.

2. Green, *The Adventurous Male*, 32.

3. Nichols, *Representing Reality: Issues and Concepts in Documentary* (Bloomington: Indiana UP, 1990), ix–x (italics his).

4. Kaplan, *The Social Construction of American Realism* (Chicago: U of Chicago P, 1988), 7.

5. Green observes that "the novel-form was difficult for Stevenson (and for Kipling) because it was realistic—by virtue of what the great realistic writers had made of it—because of its claim to be *responsible*. It claims to tell the whole truth, especially about personal relations between adults and about life in a real city or real village. [. . .] In beginning *Treasure Island*, Stevenson had escaped the constraints that a mixed audience and mature themes put on a novel" (*The Adventurous Male*, 203–204, emphasis his).

6. For example, in an interview about his work on the blockbuster comic-book adaptation *Spider-Man*, cinematographer Don Burgess asserts, "*Spider-Man* isn't a stylized, Tim Burton kind of movie. [. . .] Our approach is much more reality-based, a kind of heightened reality" (Jay Holben, "Spider's Strategem," *American Cinematographer* 83.6 [June 2002], 35). Keep in mind that he refers to a film about a superhero who produces a ropelike webbing from his wrists and whose adversary travels on an antigravity glider and carries small bombs that can vaporize people instantaneously.

7. Judith Kegan Gardiner, "Introduction," in *Masculinity Studies and Feminist Theory: New Directions*, ed. Gardiner (New York: Columbia UP, 2002), 10.

8. See Peter Marks, "The Ad Campaign: Gore as Mountain Conqueror," *New York Times* February 27, 2000: sec. 1, 19.

9. Among other literature on the gendering of sensation, see Jane Tompkins, *Sensational Designs: The Cultural Work of American Fiction 1790–1860s* (New York: Oxford UP, 1985).

10. As of 2001, in the United States, "more women journalists work in magazines (37%) than in any other media, only 10% work in newspapers" (International Federation of Journalists [prepared by Bettina Peters], "Equality and Quality: Setting Standards for Women in Journalism; IFJ Survey on the Status of Women Journalists," Brussels, June 2001; <www.ifj.org>, accessed March 19, 2002). Consequently, men overwhelmingly perform the traditional news-gathering functions associated with newspapers. Though the writers discussed in this section, Krakauer and Junger, also work for magazines, their sponsoring publications employ predominantly male writers. For example, while the editorial board of *Outside* (*Into Thin Air* and *The Perfect Storm* began as *Outside* features) included women in half of its top editorial positions as of April 2002, its seventeen contributing editors were all men, as were thirty-one of its thirty-six correspondents (<www.outsidemag.com/magazine/ommast.html>, accessed April 4, 2002).

11. A small number of women, including Gail Sheehy and Joan Didion, have secured entry into the New Journalism canon, though with emphasis on traditionally male spheres, including crime, politics, and Vietnam-era radicalism.

12. According to the book, Pittman, the wife of MTV cofounder and later AOL Time Warner Chief Operating Officer Bob Pittman, brings an exceptionally

large amount of equipment and "adhere[s] as closely as possible to the proprieties of high society" on the mountain (Krakauer, *Into Thin Air*, 154). She is repeatedly characterized as weak, ill-prepared, and requiring excessive aid from more experienced climbers.

13. Margalit Fox, "2020 Foresight," *New York Times Book Review* January 2, 2000: 23. The "single M&M" references the ethos of asceticism that underwrites such accounts. For instance, in Krakauer's earlier *Into the Wild* (New York: Villard, 1996) an outdoorsman goes nearly empty-handed into the Alaskan wilderness, carrying only a bag of rice, and does not return.
14. See Martin Dugard, *Knockdown: The Harrowing True Account of a Yacht Race Turned Deadly* (New York: Pocket Books, 1999).
15. Neale, "Masculinity as Spectacle," 19.
16. *Everest*, still playing at some IMAX theatres nearly two years after its initial release, earned US$74.5 million in theatres (<www.variety.com>, accessed February 7, 2000).
17. Jamie Malanowski, " 'Black Hawk Down': War, without Any Answers," *New York Times* December 16, 2001: sec. 2, 1.

2   "I Married Rambo": Action, Spectacle, and Melodrama

1. Challenging critical definitions of melodrama as a particular genre, Linda Williams's 1998 article "Melodrama Revised" argues for melodrama as "the foundation of the classical Hollywood movie" and the model for all U.S. popular cinema (42). I discuss the implications of Williams's position later in this chapter.
2. Indeed, Susan Jeffords's central argument in *Hard Bodies* is that 1980s action films extend into cinema the ideological project of the so-called Reagan revolution, suggesting that the genre is at least as reactionary as its critics contend.
3. For example, *True Lies*, to assert male mastery of firearms, includes a comic sequence demonstrating its female protagonist's inability to fire a gun properly.
4. See Fiske, *Understanding Popular Culture*, 134–137.
5. The film's combination of action and melodrama was successful in drawing viewers both in the United States and abroad. Budgeted at $100 million, it earned $146 million in its U.S. theatrical run and another $218 million internationally (<us.imdb.com/Business?0111503>, accessed April 21, 2000).
6. Rather than presenting sexual tension or emotional conflict *as* spectacle, though, action films substitute episodes of spectacular violence at moments in which different genres (e.g., the romantic comedy or sexual suspense thriller) would present sexually or emotionally charged character interactions.
7. See Steve Neale, *Genre and Hollywood* (London: Routledge, 2000), Chapter 2, in particular 31–35.
8. A healthy dose of skepticism is still in order when dealing with violent films whose makers claim to deplore violence. Such films clearly participate in

cultural fascination with and fantasies about violence. The good intentions of most filmmakers and viewers aside, clearly a segment of the filmgoing population responds to cinematic violence in socially antagonistic ways.

9. Robin Wood, "Ideology, Genre, Auteur," in *Film Theory and Criticism,* 4th Edition, ed. Gerald Mast, Marshall Cohen, and Leo Braudy (New York: Oxford UP, 1992), 478.

10. Tasker, *Spectacular Bodies,* 89.

11. Jeffords, "Can Masculinity Be Terminated?," 245.

12. Jeffords, "Can Masculinity Be Terminated?," 256.

13. For example, Snipes paired with Woody Harrelson in *The Money Train* (1995) and with Kris Kristofferson in *Blade* and its sequels; Smith joined with the much older Tommy Lee Jones in *Men in Black* and with Gene Hackman in *Enemy of the State* (1998); and before his films with Chan, Tucker appeared alongside Charlie Sheen in *Money Talks* (1997).

14. Fuchs, "The Buddy Politic," 195.

15. See Holmlund, "Masculinity as Multiple Masquerade" for analysis of this phrase.

16. Collins, "Television and Postmodernism," 335.

17. In John Ellis's formulation, fetishism "represents the opposite tendency to that of voyeurism. [. . .] Fetishistic looking implies the direct acknowledgement and participation of the object viewed. [. . .] The fetishistic look has much to do with display and the spectacular" (Ellis, *Visible Fictions,* 47). In action films, fetishistic looking involves engaging the viewer in male rituals of camaraderie, suspicion, or antagonism.

18. Neale, "Masculinity as Spectacle," 17.

19. For more on the film's visual effects, see Stephen Pizello, "*True Lies* Tests Cinema's Limits" (*American Cinematographer* 75.9 [September 1994]: 38ff.); and Stephen Prince, "True Lies: Perceptual Realism, Digital Images, and Film Theory" (*Film Quarterly* 49.3 [Spring 1996]: 37–48).

20. For an exhaustive, compelling analysis of the function and reception of special effects, see Michele Pierson, *Special Effects: Still in Search of Wonder* (New York: Columbia UP, 2002).

21. Here Williams follows the example of Steve Neale. See Neale, "Melo Talk: On the Meaning and Use of the Term 'Melodrama' in the American Trade Press," *Velvet Light Trap* 32 (Fall 1993): 66–89.

22. Williams's overall project is not to dismiss critical analysis of the melodrama as a genre, but to call for recognition of "the typicality, rather than the exceptionality, of film melodrama" (82).

23. Gledhill, "Rethinking Genre," 227.

24. Doane, *The Desire to Desire,* 95.

25. Willis, "Disputed Territories," 274.

26. Elsaesser, "Tales of Sound and Fury," 44.

27. Christine Gledhill observes that "the neo-Marxist perspective [of film criticism] looked to stylistic 'excess' and narrative disjunction for their 'expo-sure' of contradictions between a mainstream film's aesthetic and ideological

programmes" ("The Melodramatic Field," 6). Gledhill's work complicates this view, but still admits the significance of formal excess in melodrama.

28. Nowell-Smith, "Minnelli and Melodrama," 74.

29. On the gendering of popular culture, see Huyssen, "Mass Culture as Woman."

30. Julia Hallam and Margaret Marshment, *Realism and Popular Cinema* (Manchester, UK: Manchester UP, 2000), 70. The concept of "real-isation," they note, "is a useful way of thinking about the relationship between melodrama and contemporary action cinema. Gaps are created in the chain of character-centered causality, foregrounding artistic motivation; this can take the form of spectacular action sequences that characterize films such as *True Lies* and *Cliffhanger*" (70–71).

31. See Holmlund, "Masculinity as Multiple Masquerade."

32. Modleski, "Time and Desire in the Woman's Film," 542.

33. Of course, not all viewers regard action-film conventions as ironic or artificial representations of masculinity. As Chris Holmlund cautions, "it would be a mistake to underestimate how much and how often spectators, and performers too, see masquerade as reinforcing hegemonic power relations" ("Masculinity as Multiple Masquerade," 224).

34. Some exceptions exist; the cramped locations of the submarine-thriller subgenre, for example, mobilize viewer interest precisely because of the inherent restrictions such settings place on male mobility.

35. Chuck Kleinhans makes a similar point in his work on action film: "[T]he action formula often uses public space as a site for masculine adventure, but it is always crucially paired with domestic space. Often at significant moments the two worlds intersect, as when the villain enters familial space or personal matters are enacted in public spaces" (Kleinhans, "Class in Action," 245).

36. Schneider, "With Violence If Necessary," 4.

37. In addition to articulating the notion of "home," this line of dialogue is also a staple line of 1950s television's *I Love Lucy*, with the film thus acknowledging its debt to screwball-comedy narratives.

38. In both films, such connections are narratively impossible. The Terminator is mechanical rather than human, and *The Last Action Hero*'s Jack Slater is a fictional character within the film's "real" world.

39. See Brooks, "The Melodramatic Imagination," 61.

40. Claudia Springer, "Comprehension and Crisis: Reporter Films and the Third World," in *Unspeakable Images: Ethnicity and the American Cinema*, ed. Lester Friedman (Urbana: U of Illinois P, 1991), 169.

41. During the first sequence that shows him in his domestic role, for example, he spills hot coffee on his hand while awkwardly chasing after his daughter.

42. Shohat and Stam, *Unthinking Eurocentrism*, 148.

43. Dyer, "Entertainment and Utopia," 278.

44. The film does not grant her a specific ethnicity, but the Hawaiian-born Carrere is of mixed Chinese, Filipino, and Spanish ancestry (Internet Movie Database, <www.imdb.com>, accessed July 15, 2002).

45. *The Rock*, for example, humanizes its villain (Ed Harris) through his visits to his late wife's grave. The film thus links him to a marital ideal without having to include a living wife in the film.
46. For a useful assessment of the varied popular responses to *Titanic* in different countries, see Alan Riding et al., "Why *Titanic* Conquered the World: Reports from Britain to Beijing," *New York Times* April 26, 1998; <www.nytimes.com/yr/mo/day/artleisure/film-titanic-world.html>, accessed April 30, 1998.
47. With *Pearl Harbor*, Disney tried to repeat *Titanic*'s formula by producing its own action/romance epic with a successful action film director (Michael Bay). Hugely expensive and a critical disaster, *Pearl Harbor* nonetheless drew large audiences and profited its producers.

3   Omega Men: Late 1960s and Early 1970s Action Heroes

1. Thomas Schatz, for example, refers in his 1981 work to "the New Hollywood of the 1960s and '70s" (Schatz, *Hollywood Genres*, 147). Yet in a later essay entitled "The New Hollywood," Schatz redefines the term to refer to the blockbuster era of *Jaws* and its descendants, observing that "this post-1975 era best warrants the term 'the New Hollywood' " (*Film Theory Goes to the Movies*, ed. Jim Collins, Hilary Radner, and Ava Preacher Collins [London: Routledge, 1993], 9). Other works of film criticism use "New Hollywood" to designate either the period before or after the rise of the blockbuster, though works appearing since the 1990s have tended to favor the post-1975 definition. Consequently, "Art Hollywood" seems to me to be a flexible enough term to refer to the practices of film production and reception during the Vietnam era and following the 1966 dismantling of the MPAA's Production Code, but preceding the production of calculated blockbusters such as *Jaws*, *King Kong* (1976), and *Star Wars*.
2. For filmmakers' accounts from the period, see Biskind, *Easy Riders, Raging Bulls* and Madsen, *The New Hollywood*.
3. See Wyatt, *High Concept*, 72–73.
4. See Thomas Frank, *The Conquest of Cool: Business Culture, Counterculture, and the Rise of Hip Consumerism* (Chicago: U of Chicago P, 1997).
5. Quoted in Sharon Waxman, "Hollywood's He-Men Are Bumped by Sensitive Guys," *New York Times* July 1, 2004; <www.nytimes.com/2004/07/01/movies/01MEN.html>, accessed July 1, 2004. Notably, McQueen did not fight in a war, though he did serve in the Marines between 1947 and 1950 (Ephriam Katz, *The Film Encyclopedia*, 4th Edition [New York: HarperResource, 2001], 879). Of the other male stars this chapter studies, Charlton Heston served in the Air Force during World War II (Katz, *The Film Encyclopedia*, 625), and Lee Marvin served in the Marines but as Katz notes, was "[i]nvalidated out of WW II service" (911).
6. Eastwood resurrected the Callahan character for *The Dead Pool* (1988), though this film did not achieve the financial success or the ensuing cultural visibility of its predecessors.

7. Such contradictions occur frequently in representations of idealized masculinity. In the western genre, for example, protagonists often operate in both modes, as violent, vengeful outlaws who nonetheless abide by a prosocial moral code.

8. See Roszak, *The Making of a Counter Culture* (New York: Anchor Books, 1969).

9. On this point, see Jack Shadoian, *Dreams and Dead Ends: The American Gangster/Crime Film* (Cambridge, MA: MIT Press, 1977), 308–325.

10. Willis, *High Contrast*, 31.

11. Frank Krutnik, *In a Lonely Street: Film Noir, Genre, Masculinity* (London: Routledge, 1991), 242.

12. While *Point Blank*'s female characters do not explicitly embody feminism, the film's two prominent women display agency in ways akin to 1960s feminist ideology: Chris resists male authority (Walker's and the Organization's), and Lynn, though the film defines her character almost exclusively in relation to her male lovers, uses male violence to her advantage, promoting conflict between the two men who compete for her affections.

13. Herb A. Lightman, "Director John Boorman Talks about His Work," *American Cinematographer* 56.3 (March 1975), 284.

14. See Neale, *Genre and Hollywood*, 9–29.

15. Other male stars of the period similarly cultivated images of male athleticism and risk-taking. Clint Eastwood performed mountain-climbing scenes with George Kennedy for *The Eiger Sanction* (1975) and performed a leap onto a moving bus for *Dirty Harry*. Paul Newman, like McQueen, spent time as a professional automobile racer.

16. The name "the Family" links the group to Charles Manson's "Family" of the same period and to the popular images of murderous, Satanic hippies that Manson's 1969 crimes spawned. In an act of narrative sleight-of-hand, the film grafts the murderous, criminal associations of the all-white Manson family onto the image of the politically active Black Panther Party. *Dirty Harry* similarly articulates fears of a deadly counterculture, modeling its long-haired psychopath "Scorpio" after the real-life "Zodiac killer" of the San Francisco Bay area.

4 Airport Fiction: The Men of Mass-Market Literature

1. *Apocalypse Now* (1979) is a notable exception, though even this film departs from war-film conventions by showing relatively little armed conflict, and highlighting psychological breakdown instead.

2. For a discussion of these three authors, see Ryan, "The Genesis of the Techno-Thriller," 24–40.

3. Daisy Maryles, "The Cardinal of the Lists," *Publishers Weekly* July 13, 1998, 52. Maryles provides other relevant figures for comparison: from 1994 on, his publisher, MCA's Putnam Berkley Group, produced initial hardcover print runs of two million copies for each new Clancy novel, and Clancy's greatest success, *The Hunt for Red October*, sold nearly nine million copies in its North American paperback edition alone. Overall, Maryles states, "Combined

hardcover/paperback U.S. sales for all of the Clancy titles, including the *Op-Center* and nonfiction books, total more than 80 million."

4. Daisy Maryles, "Clancy's Latest Victory," *Publishers Weekly* August 17, 1998, 20.

5. According to *Publishers Weekly*, Cussler's overall output, because he began writing novels nearly twenty years before Clancy, rivals the more prominent author's: "[he] now has 70 million books in print in 40 languages, sold in some 105 countries" (Daisy Maryles, "Behind the Bestsellers: Wrecks Rex," *Publishers Weekly* August 11, 1997, 240).

6. The NEA's 2004 "Reading at Risk" survey finds a measurable decline in reading of literature among all Americans between 1982 and 2002. Bruce Weber writes: "The steepest declines of any demographic group are among the youngest adults. In 1982, 59.8 percent of 18-to-24-year-olds read literature; by 2002 that figure had dropped to 42.8 percent. In the 25-to-34 age group, the percentage of literary readers dropped to 47.7 from 62.1 over the same period" (Weber, "Fewer Noses Stuck in Books in America, Survey Finds," *New York Times* July 8, 2004; <www.nytimes.com/2004/07/08/books/08READ.html>, accessed July 9, 2004).

7. French, "Radical Feminist Tom Clancy Deserves to Be Taken Seriously," 34.

8. Clancy's *Patriot Games* does devote considerable attention to its protagonist's private life and domestic space, transforming it into the site of heroism and danger. In this novel, villains' intrusion into private space makes that space public, necessitating male action.

9. Michael Lewis, "The Artist in the Gray Flannel Pajamas," *New York Times Magazine* March 5, 2000: 45ff.

10. Gibson's "Redeeming Vietnam" (79–202) devotes attention to Clancy's construction of military units as family hierarchies. Delgado's "Technico-Military Thrills" (125–152) argues for Jack Ryan's significance as the humanizing agent of surveillance technology and notes Clancy's interest in processes of male mastery.

11. See Chapter 29 of *Executive Orders*, esp. 599–604, for the clandestine meeting of the conspiracy-minded liberal Vice President Kealty and unnamed reporters from major newspapers (papers connoted as liberal-aligned: the *New York Times*, the *Washington Post*, the *Boston Globe*, and the *San Francisco Examiner*).

12. Jeffords, "The Patriot System, or Managerial Heroism," 552 (italics in original).

13. Notably, Clancy includes women among all gatherings of reporters in *Patriot Games*, whereas groups of police or intelligence agents are all male.

14. Hixson, " 'Red Storm Rising,' " 609.

15. Clancy's multiple White House meetings with Presidents Reagan and Bush were well reported. See, for example, Walter Shapiro, "Of Arms and the Man: Tom Clancy, the Military's Minstrel, Longs to Live the Life He Writes About," *Time* August 21, 1989: 66ff. Shapiro's article, like others, also notes Clancy's speculations about running for a Congressional seat or other political office. In addition, many readers are familiar with the author's one-quarter ownership of the Baltimore Orioles baseball team and his failed 1998 attempt to buy the

NFL's Minnesota Vikings (see Jeff Zaleski, "The Hunt for Tom Clancy," *Publishers Weekly* July 13, 1998: 43ff.).

16. One profile of Clancy calls attention to his exaggerated display of deadly weaponry in his secluded, well-appointed home. Given a tour of a closet arsenal and basement firing range, Jeffrey Goldberg observes that the novelist "keeps his guns where most men keep their socks" and "keeps a shooting range where most people keep their washers and dryers." Later, criticizing the interviewer's target-shooting form, the novelist boasts of his contacts, telling Goldberg: " 'You weren't trained by the best instructors in the F.B.I. like I was' " (Goldberg, "Playing with Firearms," *New York Times Magazine* June 13, 1999, 24).

17. Shapiro, "Of Arms and the Man," 68.

18. Zaleski, "The Hunt for Tom Clancy," 43.

19. See Scott Shuger, "Paperback Fighter," *Washington Monthly* November 1989: 10ff.

20. The author photos for *Dragon* and other novels show Cussler posing next to classic cars in his collection, a collection Dirk Pitt has as well.

21. See Judy Quinn, "Clancy's Deals Top $100 Million," *Publishers Weekly* August 25, 1997: 12. Quinn notes of the book series that its publication contract "calls for six adult novels and eighteen young-adult novels."

22. See "New Clive Cussler Series Targets Teenage Boys" (author's name not given), *Publishers Weekly* September 14, 1998: 29. The series, the article states, abridges some of Cussler's 1990s novels and edits their "adult content" for younger readers.

23. Lewis Burke Frumkes, "A Conversation with . . . Clive Cussler," *The Writer* September 1996, 16.

24. While most of these films were written specifically for the screen, *The General's Daughter* adapts Nelson DeMille's 1992 novel of the same name.

5 Restaging Heroic Masculinity: Jackie Chan and the Hong Kong Action Film

1. On this subject, see David Desser, "The Martial Arts Film in the 1990s," in *Film Genre 2000: New Critical Essays*, ed. Wheeler Winston Dixon (Albany: State U of New York P, 2000).

2. On Seagal's films, see Kleinhans, "Class in Action"; and Aaron Anderson, "Violent Dances in Martial Arts Films," *Jump Cut* 44 (Fall 2001); <www.ejumpcut.org/aarona>, accessed February 20, 2002. Tasker's *Spectacular Bodies* periodically interrogates Van Damme's films.

3. The normative views of the United States and the West on gender identity are by no means identical. I use "Western" here and elsewhere to distinguish the culturally specific—i.e., East Asian, and more precisely, Hong Kong Chinese—aspects of Chan's male persona from those elements that correspond to cinematic and social conventions apparent in the democratic, capitalist nations of the West, particularly in North America and to a lesser extent in Great Britain and elsewhere in northern and western Europe.

4. Steve Neale and Frank Krutnik, *Popular Film and Television Comedy* (London: Routledge, 1990), 18.

5. Until 1997, Hong Kong films far outgrossed their foreign competition (principally from Hollywood) at the Hong Kong box office. The ready availability of new Hong Kong films on pirated VCDs, U.S. films' increasing penetration of the Hong Kong film market, and the 1997 transition to Chinese rule severely hurt the country's domestic film industry. See Neil Strauss, "Hong Kong Film: Exit the Dragon?," *New York Times* August 2, 1998: sec. 2, 1ff.

6. See <www.variety.com/top100.asp>, accessed February 22, 1999. *Rush Hour*, with more than $136 million in U.S. receipts in 1998, narrowly outperformed the far-costlier *Godzilla* and earned slightly more than another action-comedy with a mixed-race cast, *Lethal Weapon 4* (which grossed just over $130 million in the United States in 1998).

7. *Rumble in the Bronx*, budgeted at US$7.5 million, earned over $33 million in the United States as of August 1996 (<us.imdb.com/Business?0113326>, accessed April 21, 2000). In comparison, *Supercop* grossed just over $16 million in its 1996 U.S. re-release, a strong return given the minimal marketing, editing, and soundtrack expenses incurred by its U.S. distributor, Dimension Films (<us.imdb.com/Business?0104558>, accessed April 21, 2000).

8. Most of Chan's U.S. re-releases appear with many scenes deleted, particularly dialogue and exposition but also elements of fight sequences. The Asian version of *Rumble in the Bronx* reportedly grants a much larger role to its female lead, including fight sequences, and the U.S. release of *Jackie Chan's First Strike* runs approximately twenty-five minutes shorter than its subtitled original. About the latter, see Ian D. Garlick, "First Strike Cuts," <www.primenet.com/~tonylane/fst.htm>, accessed October 19, 1998.

9. In one scene, the film's FBI leaders send fellow agents into a warehouse that explodes, but the aftermath of this event does not appear. Later, at the film's conclusion, the FBI men admit their mistakes to Tucker's character, who then brusquely denies their offer of an FBI position. The agents appear in only a brief reaction shot that ends the dialogue.

10. Studios have specifically marketed Chan's films and other martial-arts themed productions to African American viewers. Taking cues from the huge 1990s success of U.S. rap stars the Wu-Tang Clan and their many spinoffs, which construct a pop mythology combining Afrocentric ideology with kung fu iconography, the U.S. versions of *Rumble in the Bronx*, *Supercop*, and *Rush Hour* all featured contemporary hip-hop soundtracks. Similarly, the racial combination of Chan and Tucker in *Rush Hour* recalls Lee's pairing in *Enter the Dragon* with black kung fu star Jim Kelly (who later headlined in the kung fu/blaxploitation films *Black Belt Jones* [1974] and *Three the Hard Way* [1974]).

11. Mulvey, "Visual Pleasure and Narrative Cinema," 34.

12. De Lauretis, *Alice Doesn't* (Bloomington: Indiana UP, 1984), 139.

13. Chinese-trained film-fight choreographer Craig Reid describes a familiar situation in action films: "Say you have a man fighting seven attackers inside a large house. An American stunt coordinator [. . .] will have the hero stand in one room and let himself get surrounded. Each opponent will attack [. . .] one

at a time [...] Many of the attackers will let themselves get hit four or five times in a row without trying to move away, while the other attackers watch their buddy get pummeled. This is typical of Chuck Norris's films" (Reid, "Fighting Without Fighting," 31).

14. Kirkham and Thumim, *You Tarzan*, 12.
15. Reid, "Fighting without Fighting," 34–35.
16. During some sequences in *Rumble in the Bronx*, Chan appears in a black muscle-T, offering a visual referent to the ritual garb of Western action stars. More typically, displays of his body appear for comic effect. In one scene in *Jackie Chan's First Strike*, villains strip Chan's character of his clothing, and he appears naked in a long shot from behind. In another scene in the film, he appears in a pair of novelty briefs. Both scenes depict him as vulnerable and embarrassed.
17. Mast, *The Comic Mind*, 24.
18. Gunning, "Crazy Machines in the Garden of Forking Paths: Mischief Gags and the Origins of American Film Comedy," in *Classical Hollywood Comedy*, ed. Kristine Brunovska Karnick and Henry Jenkins (London: Routledge, 1995), 99.
19. Bakhtin, *Rabelais and His World*, 318.
20. See Bakhtin, *Rabelais and His World*, 330.
21. Yau, "Border Crossing," 181.
22. Caroline Vie, "Caroline Vie talks with Jackie Chan," from *MAMA* 23 (Fall 1991), a French fanzine (n. pag.; served online through "Project A: The Unofficial Jackie Chan Web Site," <weber.u.washington.edu/~magritte/chan.html>, accessed December 1, 1995.).
23. Kramer, "The Making of a Comic Star: Buster Keaton and *The Saphead*," in *Classical Hollywood Comedy*, 200.
24. Crafton, "Pie and Chase: Gag, Spectacle and Narrative in Slapstick Comedy," in *Classical Hollywood Comedy*, 117.
25. See Gunning, "Response to 'Pie and Chase'," in *Classical Hollywood Comedy*.
26. Gunning, "Response to 'Pie and Chase,'" 121.
27. Wong Fei-hung (or Huang Feihong) was a real Cantonese martial artist, mythologized in dozens of films since the late 1940s. For more on this figure and his portrayals in film, see Bordwell, *Planet Hong Kong*, esp. 204–209.
28. Smith, *Clint Eastwood*, 173–174.
29. Silverman, "Masochism and Male Subjectivity," 53.
30. Kirkham and Thumim, *You Tarzan*, 14.
31. Willemen, "Anthony Mann: Looking at the Male," *Framework* Nos. 15/16/17 (Summer 1981), 16.
32. Schefer, *L'homme ordinaire du cinéma* (Paris: Cahiers du Cinéma, 1980), 73; quoted in translation in Smith, *Clint Eastwood*, 174.
33. Vie (online; n. pag.).
34. Fredric Dannen, "Hong Kong Babylon," *New Yorker* August 7, 1995, 33–34.
35. Stories of Chan's mishaps are legion. They include a scene in *Rumble in the Bronx* in which Chan breaks his ankle while leaping from a pier onto a hovercraft, a fall during the filming of *Armor of God* that left the actor with a small

hole in his skull, and an incident in which Chan, for a scene in *Police Story*, slid
down a pole strung with live electrical cables, burning his hands.

Conclusion: The Future of Active Masculinity

1. Major R-rated action films of recent years include *Terminator 3* (even the
   blockbuster *Terminator 2*, with its child coprotagonist, was rated R), *Kill Bill:
   Vol. 1* and *Vol. 2*, the *Matrix* trilogy, the historical epics *Gladiator* (2000) and
   Troy (2004), and the action-horror *Resident Evil* series (these last virtually the
   only R-rated films in recent years showcasing action heroines). Most other
   major-studio action and adventure films received PG-13 ratings.
2. Independent producer David Ladd, quoted in John Leland and Peter
   Marks, "New Look for Entertainment in a Terror-Conscious World," *New York
   Times* September 24, 2001; <www.nytimes.com/arts/24POP.html>, accessed
   September 24, 2001.
3. Quoted in Rick Lyman, "This Season Fewer Soldiers March Onscreen,"
   New York Times October 16, 2001; <www.nytimes.com/movies/16FILM.
   html>, accessed October 16, 2001.
4. A perhaps more significant, if much less visible, development has been the U.S.
   military's recruitment from the film industry for work on military-training
   simulations. See, for example, Hugh Hart, "Bringing Hollywood Pizzazz to
   Military Training," *New York Times* November 15, 2001; <www.nytimes.
   com/movies/15ARTS.html>, accessed November 16, 2001. Claudia Springer's
   2004 Society for Cinema and Media Studies conference paper, "Hollywood
   Returns to War: The Pentagon's New Media Mission," addresses this development
   as well.
5. *Black Hawk Down*, budgeted at $95 million, earned $108.6 million in its
   U.S. theatrical release; <us.imdb.com/Business?0265086>, accessed June 30,
   2003.
6. Quoted in Rick Lyman, "At the Movies: More and More of *The Matrix*,"
   New York Times March 31, 2000: B22. Silver and another Warner Brothers
   executive also call the film "groundbreaking" and "totally unique," respectively.
7. In 2001, the University of Southern California's Institute for Creative
   Technologies began developing the "Mission Rehearsal Exercise" for the
   U.S. Army, with contributors including Paul Debevec, attributed with
   the design of *The Matrix*'s so-called bullet time effect. See Hart, "Bringing
   Hollywood Pizzazz to Military Training."
8. For more on the visual effects of *The Matrix*, see Christopher Probst,
   "Welcome to the Machine," *American Cinematographer* April 1999: 32ff.; and
   Ron Magid, "Techno Babel," same issue: 46ff.
9. According to publicity surrounding the film's U.S. release, it was Germany's
   second most-popular film in 1998. In the United States, the film, budgeted
   at about $2 million and distributed by Sony Pictures Classics, earned over
   $7.2 million in box-office receipts, making it a substantial success for a foreign
   film (<us.imdb.com/Business?0130827>, accessed April 19, 2000).

10. The film's director, Tom Tykwer, notes this feature in his "Director's Statement" on the film's promotional website (<www.spe.sony.com/classics/ runlolarun/statement/statement_text.html>, accessed April 19, 2000). Tykwer describes the video images as "a synthetic, artificial world." He continues: "The film image is true, and the others are untrue, as it were. So when Lola runs through a video image, it becomes film." Tykwer's statement is only partly true: Lola appears in a number of sequences shot in digital video, including her interactions with her father in his bank office, and some scenes appear in film even without Lola present. Still, to some extent Lola's presence literally transforms the image of the world around her.

11. The Associated Press, "U.S. Military Says No Soldier Missing in Iraq," *New York Times* February 1, 2005; <www.nytimes.com/aponline/international/ AP-Iraq-Soldier.html>, accessed February 2, 2005.

12. NBC News and news services, "Doubts Cast on Claim U.S. Soldier Kidnapped," *MSNBC.com* February 1, 2005; <www.msnbc.msn.com/id/ 6894934/>, accessed February 2, 2005.

13. "So-called U.S. Hostage Appears to Be Toy," *CNN.com* February 1, 2005; <www.cnn.com/2005/WORLD/meast/02/01/iraq.hostage/index.html>, accessed February 2, 2005.

Select Bibliography

Bakhtin, Mikhail. *Rabelais and His World*. Trans. Helene Iswolsky. Bloomington: Indiana UP, 1984.

Bennett, Tony and Janet Woollacott. *Bond and Beyond: The Political Career of a Popular Hero*. London: Macmillan, 1987.

Biskind, Peter. *Easy Riders, Raging Bulls*. New York: Simon & Schuster, 1998.

Bordwell, David. *Planet Hong Kong: Popular Cinema and the Art of Entertainment*. Cambridge, MA: Harvard UP, 2000.

Bowden, Mark. *Black Hawk Down: A True Story of Modern War*. New York: Atlantic Monthly Press, 1999.

Brooks, Peter. "The Melodramatic Imagination." *Imitations of Life: A Reader on Film & Television Melodrama*. Ed. Marcia Landy. Detroit: Wayne State UP, 1991. 50–67.

Butler, Judith. *Gender Trouble: Feminism and the Subversion of Identity*. London: Routledge, 1990.

Chan, Jackie, and Jeff Yang. *I Am Jackie Chan: My Life in Action*. New York: Ballantine Books, 1998.

Clancy, Tom. *Clear and Present Danger*. New York: G.P. Putnam's Sons, 1989.

———. *Debt of Honor*. New York: G.P. Putnam's Sons, 1994.

———. *Executive Orders*. New York: Berkeley Books, 1997.

———. *Patriot Games*. New York: Berkeley Books, 1988.

———. *Rainbow Six*. New York: G.P. Putnam's Sons, 1998.

———. *Red Storm Rising*. New York: G.P. Putnam's Sons, 1986.

———. *The Hunt for Red October*. New York: Berkeley Books, 1985.

———. *The Sum of All Fears*. New York: Berkeley Books, 1992.

———. *The Teeth of the Tiger*. New York: G.P. Putnam's Sons, 2003.

———. *Without Remorse*. New York: G.P. Putnam's Sons, 1993.

Cohan, Steven. *Masked Men: Masculinity and the Movies in the Fifties*. Bloomington: Indiana UP, 1997.

Collins, Jim. "Television and Postmodernism." *Channels of Discourse, Reassembled*. Ed. Robert C. Allen. Chapel Hill: U of North Carolina P, 1993. 327–353.

Cussler, Clive. *Atlantis Found*. New York: Simon & Schuster, 1999.

———. *Deep Six*. New York: Pocket Books, 1985.

———. *Dragon*. New York: Pocket Books, 1991.

———. *Inca Gold*. New York: Simon & Schuster, 1994.

———. *Raise the Titanic*. New York: Simon & Schuster, 1976.

Cussler, Clive. *Sahara*. New York: Pocket Books, 1993.

———. *Treasure*. New York: Pocket Books, 1988.

———. *Trojan Odyssey*. New York: G.P. Putnam's Sons, 2003.

———. *Valhalla Rising*. New York: G.P. Putnam's Sons, 2001.

De Lauretis, Teresa. *Alice Doesn't: Feminism, Semiotics, Cinema*. Bloomington: Indiana UP, 1984.

Delgado, Celeste Fraser. "Technico-Military Thrills and the Technology of Terror: Tom Clancy and the Commission on the Disappeared." *Cultural Critique* 32 (Winter 1995–1996): 125–152.

Doane, Mary Ann. *The Desire to Desire: The Woman's Film of the 1940s*. Bloomington: Indiana UP, 1987.

Doyle, Arthur Conan. *The Lost World*. Ed. Ian Duncan. Oxford: Oxford UP, 1998.

Dyer, Richard. "Entertainment and Utopia." *The Cultural Studies Reader*. Ed. Simon During. London: Routledge, 1993. 271–283.

———. *Stars*. London: BFI, 1979.

———. *White*. London: Routledge, 1997.

Ellis, John. *Visible Fictions*. London: Routledge, 1982.

Elsaesser, Thomas. "Tales of Sound and Fury: Observations on the Family Melodrama." *Home Is Where the Heart Is: Studies in Melodrama and the Woman's Film*. Ed. Christine Gledhill. London: BFI, 1987. 43–69.

Faludi, Susan. *Stiffed: The Betrayal of the American Man*. New York: William Morrow and Company, 1999.

Fiske, John. *Understanding Popular Culture*. Boston: Unwin Hyman, 1989.

French, Sean. "Radical Feminist Tom Clancy Deserves to Be Taken Seriously." *New Statesman & Society* 2 September 1994: 34.

Fuchs, Cynthia J. "The Buddy Politic." *Screening the Male: Exploring Masculinities in Hollywood Cinema*. Ed. Steven Cohan and Ina Rae Hark. London: Routledge, 1993. 194–210.

Gibson, J. William. "Redeeming Vietnam: Techno-Thriller Novels of the 1980s." *Cultural Critique* 19 (Fall 1991): 179–202.

Gledhill, Christine. "The Melodramatic Field: An Investigation." *Home Is Where the Heart Is: Studies in Melodrama and the Woman's Film*. Ed. Christine Gledhill. London: BFI, 1987. 5–39.

———. "Rethinking Genre." *Reinventing Film Studies*. Ed. Christine Gledhill and Linda Williams. London: Arnold, 2000. 221–243.

Green, Martin. *The Adventurous Male: Chapters in the History of the White Male Mind*. University Park, PA: Penn State UP, 1993.

Hixson, Walter L. " 'Red Storm Rising': Tom Clancy Novels and the Cult of National Security." *Diplomatic History* 17.4 (Fall 1993): 599–613.

Holmlund, Chris. "Masculinity as Multiple Masquerade: The 'Mature' Stallone and the Stallone Clone." *Screening the Male: Exploring Masculinities in Hollywood Cinema*. Ed. Steven Cohan and Ina Rae Hark. London: Routledge, 1993. 213–229.

Huyssen, Andreas. "Mass Culture as Woman: Modernism's Other." *After the Great Divide: Modernism, Mass Culture, Postmodernism*. Ed. Tania Modleski. Bloomington: Indiana UP, 1986. 188–207.

Jeffords, Susan. "Can Masculinity Be Terminated?" *Screening the Male: Exploring Masculinities in Hollywood Cinema*. Ed. Steven Cohan and Ina Rae Hark. London: Routledge, 1993. 245–262.

———. *Hard Bodies: Hollywood Masculinity in the Reagan Era*. New Brunswick: Rutgers UP, 1994.

———. "The Patriot System, or Managerial Heroism." *Cultures of United States Imperialism*. Ed. Amy Kaplan and Donald E. Pease. Durham: Duke UP, 1993. 535–556.

Junger, Sebastian. *The Perfect Storm: A True Story of Men Against the Sea*. New York: W.W. Norton & Co., 1997.

Kirkham, Pat and Janet Thumim, eds. *Me Jane: Masculinity, Movies and Women*. New York: St. Martin's Press, 1995.

———. *You Tarzan: Movies, Masculinity and Men*. New York: St. Martin's Press, 1993.

Kleinhans, Chuck. "Class in Action." *The Hidden Foundation: Cinema and the Question of Class*. Ed. David E. James and Rick Berg. Minneapolis: U of Minnesota P, 1996. 245–263.

Krakauer, Jon. *Into Thin Air: A Personal Account of the Mount Everest Disaster*. New York: Anchor Books/Doubleday, 1997.

Lehman, Peter. *Running Scared: Masculinity and the Representation of the Male Body*. Philadelphia: Temple UP, 1993.

Madsen, Axel. *The New Hollywood*. New York: Thomas Y. Crowell Company, 1975.

Mast, Gerald. *The Comic Mind: Comedy and the Movies*. 2nd Edition. Chicago: U of Chicago P, 1979.

Mellen, Joan. *Big Bad Wolves: Masculinity in the American Film*. New York: Pantheon Books, 1977.

Modleski, Tania. "Time and Desire in the Woman's Film." *Film Theory and Criticism*. 4th Edition. Ed. Gerald Mast, Marshall Cohen, and Leo Braudy. New York: Oxford UP, 1992. 536–548.

Mulvey, Laura. "Visual Pleasure and Narrative Cinema." *Issues in Feminist Film Criticism*. Ed. Patricia Erens. Bloomington: Indiana UP, 1990. 28–40.

Neale, Steve. "Masculinity as Spectacle: Reflections on Men and Mainstream Cinema." *Screening the Male: Exploring Masculinities in Hollywood Cinema*. Ed. Steven Cohan and Ina Rae Hark. London: Routledge, 1993. 9–20.

Nowell-Smith, Geoffrey. "Minnelli and Melodrama." *Home Is Where the Heart Is: Studies in Melodrama and the Woman's Film*. Ed. Christine Gledhill. London: BFI, 1987. 70–74.

Osgerby, Bill. *Playboys in Paradise: Masculinity, Youth and Leisure Style in Modern America*. New York: Berg, 2001.

Pfeil, Fred. *White Guys: Studies in Postmodern Domination and Difference*. New York: Verso, 1995.

Reid, Craig D. "Fighting without Fighting: Film Action Fight Choreography." *Film Quarterly* 47.2 (Winter 1993–1994): 30–35.

Ryan, William F. "The Genesis of the Techno-Thriller." *Virginia Quarterly Review* 69.1 (Winter 1993): 24–40.

Schatz, Thomas. *Hollywood Genres: Formulas, Filmmaking, and the Studio System*. New York: McGraw-Hill, 1981.

Schatz, Thomas. "The New Hollywood." *Film Theory Goes to the Movies*. Ed. Jim Collins, Hilary Radner, and Ava Preacher Collins. London: Routledge, 1993. 8–36.

Schneider, Karen. "With Violence if Necessary: Rearticulating the Family in the Contemporary Action-Thriller." *Journal of Popular Film & Television* 27.1 (Spring 1999): 3–11.

Sedgwick, Eve Kosofsky. *Between Men: English Literature and Male Homosocial Desire*. New York: Columbia UP, 1985.

Shohat, Ella and Robert Stam. *Unthinking Eurocentrism: Multiculturalism and the Media*. London: Routledge, 1994.

Silverman, Kaja. "Masochism and Male Subjectivity." *Male Trouble*. Ed. Constance Penley and Sharon Willis. Minneapolis: U of Minnesota P, 1993. 33–64.

Slotkin, Richard. *Gunfighter Nation: The Myth of the Frontier in Twentieth-Century America*. New York: HarperCollins, 1992.

Smith, Paul. *Clint Eastwood: A Cultural Production*. Minneapolis: U of Minnesota P, 1993.

Springer, Claudia. "Comprehension and Crisis: Reporter Films and the Third World." *Unspeakable Images: Ethnicity and the American Cinema*. Ed. Lester Friedman. Urbana: U of Illinois P, 1991. 167–189.

Studlar, Gaylyn. *In the Realm of Pleasure: Von Sternberg, Dietrich, and the Masochistic Aesthetic*. Urbana: U of Illinois P, 1988.

Tasker, Yvonne, Ed. *Action and Adventure Cinema*. London: Routledge, 2004.

———. "Dumb Movies for Dumb People: Masculinity, the Body, and the Voice in Contemporary Action Cinema." *Screening the Male: Exploring Masculinities in Hollywood Cinema*. Ed. Steven Cohan and Ina Rae Hark. London: Routledge, 1993. 230–244.

———. *Spectacular Bodies: Gender, Genre, and the Action Cinema*. London: Routledge, 1993.

Teo, Stephen. *Hong Kong Cinema: The Extra Dimensions*. London: BFI, 1997.

Whyte, William H. Jr. *The Organization Man*. New York: Simon and Schuster, 1956.

Willemen, Paul. "Anthony Mann: Looking at the Male." *Framework* 15/16/17 (Summer 1981): 16.

Williams, Linda. "Melodrama Revised." *Refiguring American Film Genres*. Ed. Nick Browne. Berkeley: U of California P, 1998. 42–88.

Williams, Tony. "Space, Place, and Spectacle: The Crisis Cinema of John Woo." *Cinema Journal* 36:2 (Winter 1997): 67–84.

Willis, Sharon. "Disputed Territories: Masculinity and Social Space." *Male Trouble*. Ed. Constance Penley and Sharon Willis. Minneapolis: U of Minnesota P, 1993. 263–281.

———. *High Contrast: Race and Gender in Contemporary Hollywood Film*. Durham: Duke UP, 1997.

Wyatt, Justin. *High Concept: Movies and Marketing in Hollywood*. Austin: U of Texas P, 1994.

Yau, Esther. "Border Crossing: Mainland China's Presence in Hong Kong Cinema." *New Chinese Cinemas: Forms, Identities, Politics*. Ed. Nick Browne, Paul Pickowicz, Vivian Sobchack, and Esther Yau. Cambridge, England: Cambridge UP, 1994. 180–201.

Index

Printed in the United Kingdom
by Lightning Source UK Ltd.
130845UK00001B/136-147/A